SEX SENSE AND NONSENSE

FELICITY GREEN ON THE '60s FASHION SCENE

FELICITY GREEN
WITH SINTY STEMP

Art Directed by Stephen Reid

ACC EDITIONS

“

There’s more to life than just fashion...

”

“Mirror moments were made of this: cuddling up to my favourite film star, Roger Moore at the Cannes Film Festival”

"Me – in the days when fashion and Fleet Street were fun!"

CONTENTS

6 ***Foreword*** *by Barbara Hulanicki*

8 ***Why Style Works Better than Fashion*** *Felicity Green explains why she has always preferred style to fashion – and still does*

12 ***Me and the Mirror*** *At last my dream job – joining the Mirror just before the '60s started to Swing and I was able to introduce a new look and a new tone of voice*

16 ***Mirror People*** *What took the Mirror readership sky-high in the Swinging '60s? The editors, the writers, the photographers whose talents raised the Mirror to those 5 million-plus daily sales*

22 ***Back Views Only!*** *Mirror cartoonist Moira Hodell illustrates the high spots of my Mirror round-the-world travels*

24 ***The Mirror Pages: Fun Plus Fashion '60s Style*** *The Mirror highlights the Swinging '60s – a words-and-pictures guide to the '60s Youthquake style revolution that swept the world*
The Image Makers *The Big Names that made both style and fashion news in the decade that changed everything:* ***John French*** *page 48,* ***Jill Kennington and John Cowan*** *page 58,* ***Vidal Sassoon*** *page 90,* ***Jean Shrimpton*** *page 108,* ***Twiggy*** *page 132,* ***Mary Quant*** *page 136,* ***Justin de Villeneuve*** *page 148,* ***Terry O'Neill*** *page 152,* ***Barbara Hulanicki*** *page 160,* ***Jeff Banks*** *page 164,* ***Bailey*** *page 176*

180 ***Women in a Man's World*** *Fleet Street in the '60s was a bastion of male chauvinism. It took courage, talent, determination – and humour – for women to break down a barrier or two*

184 ***View from the Top*** *The men at the top – and, of course, they were all men up there – give their views on what made the Mirror a world-beater in the Swinging '60s*

186 ***Mirror Memories are Made of This***

188 ***Acknowledgements***

189 ***Photographic Credits***

190 ***Index***

FOREWORD

BARBARA HULANICKI takes us back to 1964 when the '60s were in full swing. London was the centre of the fashion revolution. Daily Mirror fashion editor Felicity Green wanted a mail-order dress for her readers – and the Biba business exploded

Felicity Green and Barbara Hulanicki in 2014 – still trendy after all these years. Photograph by Terry O'Neill

My life as a freelance fashion illustrator started in the 1950s. After graduating at Brighton University I got a job in a London studio, first making coffee and then working up to drawing the latest fashions. Very soon I was working with fashion editors, advertising agencies, magazines and newspapers. I was very lucky to have known some of the most famous editors of the '60s.

The person who made a strong impression on me right from our first meeting was the famous Felicity Green of the mighty *Daily Mirror* – one of Fleet Street's most powerful fashion and woman's editors at that time. If it weren't for Felicity and our gingham frock, my life would have been quite different. I would have been the wife of a Mad Men advertising executive as that was where the career of my husband, Fitz was definitely heading.

I had been working quite a long time with Felicity doing fashion illustrations for her trailblazing style pages. But then came that different request. It was spring 1964. Felicity was working on a feature about four career girls and she wanted me to be one of them, and that's how it all started.

At the time, Fitz and I were dabbling in designing and selling mail-order dolly dresses and we were both exhausted! We each had our day jobs, he in advertising and me in fashion illustration. In the evenings, in our basements, we packed those dolly dresses – we were selling 200-300 pieces of each style and not making any profit and we were just about to give up. And then came The Call.

Shaking in my Biba boots, I arranged to meet Miss Green – who wasn't nearly as frightening as I'd imagined. Would I please design and make up a summer dress specially for the *Mirror* readers? I certainly would – and suggested something ultra-simple in pink gingham cotton. Miss Green said there would be a coupon on the page and the dress had to cost the readers no more than 25 shillings and it ought to have some rather "interesting" feature. We discussed this vital point and decided on a cut-out bit at the back, plus a matching kerchief like Brigitte Bardot had worn in Saint Tropez that summer. (And when Audrey Hepburn wore one it swept the world.)

Miss Green – now Felicity – and Fitz all held our breath. We hoped for 3,000. Then Fitz and I saw the massive editorial in the *Daily Mirror* pages – a big, beautiful, sexy picture of model Paulene Stone in our gingham shift dress and headscarf. The effect was humongous! The first time Fitz and I went to collect all those postal orders and cheques from our post office box in Oxford Street, Fitz's face reflected the profit of five shillings we made on each dress! Each day Fitz lugged a sack of mail from that one editorial – so many sacks they fitted into our Sunbeam Alpine car only with the top down – more than 17,000 orders in all!

That dress emptied England of every bit of pink gingham cotton and Fitz spent his time on the phone frantically tracking down all available sources from every corner of the country!

We learned a lot that summer and we never looked back. And that's how Biba was born.

Throughout the years, Felicity has become a precious friend consistently supporting Fitz and me in all our endeavours as our Biba shops grew bigger and bigger, and we moved from shops to mail order, from make-up to interiors. But all of this is fashion history: the story of how a simple, two-side-seam pink gingham dress with its matching headscarf made '60s fashion history. That pink gingham dress is now Biba legend. Thank you Felicity! ■

WHY STYLE WORKS BETTER THAN FASHION

FELICITY GREEN, former fashion, woman's and associate editor of the Daily Mirror, takes a highly personal – and somewhat controversial – view of how the two forces of contemporary design continue to wage a war of opposites!

At home in my '60s flat in London's Baker Street, wearing a '60s outfit – black top, cream short skirt, black tights and black boots – just as stylish today in 2014. (see page 187)

This is a picture of me in 1965 and it sums up very nicely my whole philosophy of fashion. The outfit in question – designed by me, and made for me by Mabel, the dressmaker who lived next door to my father's Walk-Rite Shoe Shop in Reede Road, Dagenham, Essex – is one I would wear today, roughly fifty years later. I was size ten then, and I am size twelve now, but that apart the skirt is the right length, the boots are the right height and only the lack of sleeves requires attention – older arms can't cope with such exposure. The moral of all this is that when this picture was taken I had already scaled the first heights of my career in fashion. I had become Associate Editor, Woman's Editor and Fashion Editor of the *Daily Mirror*, the world's top-selling newspaper, reaching the now preposterous level of more than five million copies a day.

Those three 'simultaneous' job titles worried me. I was intensely proud of being an associate editor and woman's editor on such a prestigious national newspaper – but fashion editor? For me then – and it remains for me now – fashion is something to be followed at a very firm and respectful distance. Get too close and you get burned. How many of us fell for the charms of the puffball skirt and finished up all too soon with a trip to the nearest Oxfam shop? Of course there certainly *is* a place for frivolity in the fashion world. My philosophy: just don't spend a fortune on that latest look.

Do I dismiss fashion altogether? No, of course not. But I was never in love with fashion as were many of my fellow fashion journalists. Style has always been first on my list of meaningful fashion terms. Style is a constant and another helpful phrase for the same thing is simplicity versus novelty. Style takes a bit of practice to get right, but it's definitely worth the effort. Fashion is a short-term love affair. Style is a long-term romance that will be there as long as you are!

I realise my minimal style started extremely early. I think I was practising minimalism long before it even existed as a style. I had never revelled in the frilly party frock world of children's wear. Everything I wore was simple and, I hope, stylish. Like my outfit over the page – with its neutral colour scheme, my signature palette ever since – caramel wool coat trimmed in dark chocolate brown and, of course, the hat to match. I now know I inherited my minimalist style from my mother. A Jewish immigrant who came to London aged three, she lived with her family in the Jewish 'village' of Whitechapel in London's East End. Where my mother got her sense of style from God only knows, but then she did come from a very religious family!

When I look at my mother's 1924 wedding pictures, I am bowled over by her obvious sense of style. She designed her own wedding dress and it was made by the local dressmaker in flesh-coloured georgette trimmed with pearls and rhinestones and had a headdress to match. This photograph gives me a true vision of style to treasure all my life.

For me, style and the cinema are synonymous. A film fan from the age of four, when each Thursday my father shut his Walk-Rite Shoe Shop in Dagenham and off we went to the pictures, I was well and truly hooked on the cinema. My first favourite stylish star was Norma Shearer and my heart was broken when, at the age of six, a violent attack of whooping cough caused me to whoop all over my five-hundred picture scrapbook of Miss Shearer. It had to be burnt and I conducted a film star pyre, weeping away. Much later came Audrey Hepburn when I became less starstruck, but was totally style-struck. Opposite the irresistible Gregory Peck in *Roman Holiday*, Audrey Hepburn was a revelation. I recognised Style when I saw it and throughout her career Miss Hepburn, dressed by Givenchy, lived and breathed Style. Then came *Breakfast at Tiffany's* and Givenchy created that black-nothing of a gown with no interruption from neck to hem. Audrey Hepburn's chic style and minimalism made a worldwide impact and postcards of this image still sweep the Western world – I have ten!

OSCAR
WILDE

"My minimal style started extremely early. I was practising minimalism long before it existed as a style"

But for me the high point of her style magnetism was reached when she appeared in a huge charity concert in London in the early '60s. All the starry cast vied with each other to make a fashion statement. And then came Miss Hepburn and the difference was delightful – minimal make-up, minimal jewellery, just that long black slink of a dress and my heart was hers forever.

Phyllis Digby Morton, wife of couturier Digby Morton, was my No.1 journalist mentor and the word mentor wasn't bandied around much in those days. Phyllis edited *Woman and Beauty*, a rule-breaking, pocket-sized pre-'60s magazine that was way ahead of the game. When other women's magazines were teaching readers how to knit an egg cosy for Easter, *Woman and Beauty* wrote about virginity, frigidity, infidelity – and style! *Woman and Beauty* changed my life; as did Phyllis Digby Morton. I wrote her an emotional letter saying do please give me a job. So she wrote and said come and see me. So I did and after ten minutes she invited me to come and stand by her desk. She then gave me the first brilliant piece of advice in my grown-up life: "Felicity, hold your stomach in!" And I have been trying to do so ever since.

My daily duties: light the fire, make the tea and walk the dog, Frankie, an overweight dachshund who hated me even more than he hated walking. Time passed as I looked and learned and in six months PDM must have seen a glimmer of editorial talent as she made me assistant to the fashion editor, Ruth Sheradski, whose very presence taught me the importance of style. She combined severe, traditional tailoring with touches of dressmaker madness: crazy hats and alarming colour combinations.

I loved working with these two brilliant women and my career as a Fashion Editor was born. PDM not only taught me the rules and rites of fashion journalism, she took me from Dagenham to Mayfair – not

literally as I still travelled to work via eighteen stops on the District Line.

Phyllis worked closely with the art director to produce minimalist pages illustrated with stylish drawings by Francis Marshall, one of the most famous fashion artists of that time. I went to fashion shows, I read all the other women's magazines and revelled in the stylish superiority of the *W&B* pages. And when it came to practising the art of style, PDM was a chameleon. During the day, simple Digby Morton suits. But at night in the upper echelons of London society, she embraced glamour with enthusiasm and success. What a university of learning was *W&B* and then came the day I became a practising fashion journalist. I had an idea: Buns for Easter, all about hairstyles. Write it said Phyllis. So I did and there it was, my first byline.

One other memorable *W&B* moment, I had given myself a Toni home perm. Phyllis loved the effect. A week later she invited me to dinner with her and Digby in their glamorous Mayfair flat. Other guests she told me would be Harold Wilson, President of the Board of Trade (later to become Prime Minister) and his wife, Mary and would I please give Mary a Toni home perm? Good grief! But I hadn't yet learned to say no to PDM. And so it happened. After dinner, Mrs Wilson and I retreated to the bathroom and the perming ceremony began. All I remember of this harrowing experience was opening the Toni box to find this message inside the lid: IN CASE OF EMERGENCY PLEASE CALL KINGSTON 7777. The perm was perfect and Mary wrote a poem to thank me.

PDM, my mentor, was a wonderful, generous, remarkable woman who had many detractors and was frequently described as a "bitch". I never saw it. To me PDM was generous, kind, glamorous and beautiful. I owe my start in journalistic life entirely to her. So thank you, PDM, Mentor No.1. ■

The four faces of style – me in my minimalistic childhood; my mother's wedding dress and bridesmaids' outfits, all designed by the style-conscious bride; minimalist goddess Audrey Hepburn; Phyllis Digby Morton, by night a star on the London social scene and by day a pioneering journalist

ME AND THE MIRROR

My life in Fleet Street was full of excitement and surprises. I never knew who I might be interviewing next – politicians, film stars, the latest pop stars, fashion designers. Wow! I was thrilled to be working for the Daily Mirror

So there I was enjoying being a grown-up fashion editor on *Woman and Beauty* when I got a Very Important Call from the Very Important Hugh Cudlipp, editorial director of the Mirror Group, who would like to see me. A date was made and the meeting was brief. "Good morning. What do you think of the *Woman's Sunday Mirror*, our new newspaper for women?" I said I thought it was awful. "I do, too," he said looking at his watch. It was lunchtime. "Right. How soon can you start? How about two weeks' time? You can be the women's editor." I thought quickly and refused the title – a women's editor of a women's newspaper, no thank you. I would, however, be associate editor. Cudlipp, in even more of a hurry, agreed.

This title, plus the roles of woman's editor and fashion editor, were mine through all my editorial *Mirror* years – on the *Sunday Pictorial,* which became the *Sunday Mirror,* and then the *Daily Mirror*. And then, in 1973, I became a director: the first woman on the board of a national newspaper. But that's another story.

Joining the *Daily Mirror* in 1960 catapulted me to the upper echelons of national newspapers and I was truly a woman in a man's world. I was not so much nervous as wary. What would all these senior male journalists make of this female intruder? The fact I had been employed by Hugh Cudlipp must have had an impact on any animosity, since I didn't feel any. (I was wrong!) My first oops came on my first day. 11am. News Conference in the Editor's office. Lots of chatter. I made my way to the only empty seat – nice, big comfy armchair. Stony silence. "It's the lawyer's chair" whispered the man beside me, shoving up to make room.

I was definitely now that Woman in a Man's World and I immediately encountered some questionable questions. The Editor: Trousers in the office? Please Felicity, you really shouldn't wear trousers. Suppose you had to interview the Queen? Me: Are you seriously suggesting I shouldn't wear trousers in case I get a call to meet the Queen? Forget it! So he did. But this question in the '60s from a brilliant editor? I ask you !

Another issue I had to face: Fleet Street was awash with liquor and I wasn't going to join in. I didn't like the local pubs – too noisy and I didn't like getting my change from my round in beer-sodden coins. In fact my appearances became so rare that the reaction from my colleagues was something like: Felicity's here, it must be someone's birthday.

And then soon, very soon, I got into my stride and immediately put into action my plan to make the so-called women's pages appeal to all five million readers – even to the sports fanatics. I wanted every page to appeal to both sexes – always scintillating and sometimes sexy, but never ever vulgar. To help me observe this delicate boundary I called on the talent

Proud, excited and dedicated – Associate Editor and Woman's Editor of the multi-million Daily Mirror! What a job! No wonder I'm happy

Daily
Mirror
Meeting
in
Progress.

"I chatted amiably with Prime Minister Harold Wilson, but didn't mention I had permed his wife's hair"

of the most famous photographers of the time and their remarkable, classy pictures. List of honour: first and foremost, the late lamented John French, the lighting genius who brought black and white fashion images to previously grey newsprint. Then came the '60s stars: David Bailey, Terry Donovan, John Cowan, Brian Duffy, Lewis Morley, John Adriaan and, of course, Terry O'Neill. The pages were striking, saucy and stylish – that word again – and who was it who said one picture is worth a thousand words? Whoever it was, she was right.

Bringing visual excitement to the *Mirror* pages became almost a doddle when the '60s explosion arrived. All those magical names – which journalist could fail to shine? There was the inimitable Mary Quant, the sheer style genius of Barbara Hulanicki, and, of course, the irresistible Twiggy. There was Kiki Byrne, Foale and Tuffin, Jean Muir, John Bates, and Ossie Clark. I sailed happily through all this excitement, confident and proud of the *Mirror*'s rising circulation. In 1967 the *Mirror* circulation reached 5,282,137 copies a day, the highest newspaper circulation in the world – except for the Soviet newspaper *Pravda!* Everyone was having a good time.

My role expanded and became more exciting with each new involvement. The world of politics? Yes, of course – a voice at every party political conference and a member of the *Mirror* team at all party conferences. When instructed to make a call from the political editor's hotel bedroom, I found a pale blue frilly nightie under his pillow and I discovered everyone knew whose it was except me. His secretary's, of course! I chatted amiably with Prime Minister Harold Wilson (but didn't mention I had permed his wife's hair). I got on famously with Barbara Castle, who, like me, had been made in Dagenham – and agreed women politicians were undervalued. Though a staunch Labourite, she squared up to the unions, no mean feat,

and was criticised for forcing motorists to wear the compulsory car seatbelts and also introduced the breathalyser. At all the political conferences, we gravitated towards each other and I found her completely relaxed, friendly, feminine and fascinating with no political axes to grind with this *Mirror* journalist. We talked so long, frequently non-politically, that we had to be prised apart. She was needed elsewhere to talk serious politics with the increasingly impatient all-male *Mirror* political bigwigs.

There were other similarities between Mrs Castle and me. Like me, she was small, feisty and a woman in a man's world.

Didn't we do well!

And then there was that exciting Royal visit. Our chairman, Edward Pickering was a Real Royalist and we were all taught how to address Her Majesty and under NO circumstances were we ever to start a conversation. Of course not! After some five minutes of chat we were all lined up to be presented. I was at the end of the line and was told that immediately I had been presented someone would come and take Her Majesty away. Except they didn't. After an agonising wait – for both of us – I took the polite initiative. "This is your fourth newspaper today, Ma'am – you must be quite tired." The Queen looked me in the eye and spoke very slowly, "No," she said. Just that,followed by the longest, loudest silence. Eventually – probably no more than seconds later – Her Majesty was swept away and I was presented to the Duke of Edinburgh and took him to meet the photographers.

Total success: he loved them, they loved him – jokes all round. But he particularly enjoyed talking to them about what he called "Those gorgeous girly pin-ups". "Do they let you choose all those pretty girls?" he asked me. "No, Sir, they don't, but they should because women are better than men at nearly everything!" "*You,*" he said "are telling *me*!" ■

Moving in high circles from politics to royalty, Prime Minister Harold Wilson and Minister for Transport Barbara Castle at a Labour Party conference. The Queen and the Duke of Edinburgh visit the Daily Mirror

MIRROR PEOPLE

The Daily Mirror was always a words-and-pictures paper and it took a wide and varied range of journalistic talents to take it up, up and away to the unsurpassed '60s circulation of 5 million-plus copies every day

Long before her famous Dear Marje column was born, she and I together represented the voice of women for the Mirror. I was Fashion and Marje was Features

Marje Proops, forever just Proops, famous *Daily Mirror* columnist and agony aunt had been beloved by the multi-million readers for six years when I came on board as associate editor. How would these two powerful women get along with each other? Immediate office atmosphere – light fuse and retire! Except there was no fire. From the start Marje and I respected each other, admired each other, without any difficulties along the way, and until she died in 1996 Marje and I loved each other and Marje always referred to me as "my little friend."

Now no-one could ever call Marje beautiful – certainly not Marje – but her sex appeal was potent across any crowded room. Her tales to me about her latest lovers held me not only spellbound, but deeply impressed. But what impressed me most of all was watching Marje write those millions of words, always in longhand and almost without a moment's hesitation. It was pure journalistic genius and created a relationship with the *Mirror* readers unequalled before, then or since. One reader telephoned Marje during one of our office-to-office calls. "Sorry," said Marje, "have to go. There's a very upset reader on the phone. Her husband is having sex in the kitchen with their dog."

Marje was much more than a columnist. She was a cross between an icon and a film star. Wherever she went she was recognised and the demand for autographs was immediate and impressive. She was sensational on television and her skill in communicating with one other person or a hall full of a hundred-plus fans reflected her journalistic genius.

In the office, Marje was genial and friendly to everyone, but anyone who tried to cross her immediately knew the error of their ways. Marje was as tough as they come, but only the slow-witted could fail to spot the danger signals that no smile could disguise. They certainly don't make 'em like Marje any more.

Fleet Street at this time was full of Big Characters. Turn the page and you'll see a photograph of me with two powerful *Mirror* men – the Editor and the Gossip Columnist. The man in the middle is Lee Howard, editor of the *Daily Mirror* from 1961 to 1971. A leader of men – and women – every member of his staff wanted to do well for him. If they made a real cock-up, not a word of criticism ensued. But they knew it and they suffered. They had failed him! Lee had been my editor at the *Sunday Mirror* and he took me with him to the *Daily Mirror*. And he gave me probably the best piece of journalistic advice ever. "Felicity, you'll now find yourself senior to many male *Mirror* journalists who are more experienced and older than you. Anytime you have to give them a bollocking, make sure they leave your presence with their balls intact." I did my best. His second piece of advice was almost as valuable, " Felicity, learn to write in a fucking straight line!"

Lee weighed a lot and ate very little. Lee was king among the hard drinkers – two bottles of scotch a day. But under Lee Howard's aegis, the *Mirror* was soaring and all of us journos on the *Mirror* soared with him. He was a talented writer, a talented visualiser and he made encouragement an art. Lee was my Mentor No.2 and I owe him more than I could ever repay. On the right, Rex North, the leading gossip columnist of his time. In those days the gossip he reported was uniformly friendly. No scandals, no nasty revelations. The celebrities Rex wrote about loved him and he loved them. He could surely RIP.

But it was Hugh Cudlipp the internationally famous Fleet Street journalist who took the *Daily Mirror* up to the spectacular circulation of more than five million copies a day. This is about Hugh Cudlipp, the man whom I got to know so well during my twenty-one years with the Mirror Group, and he was my Mentor No.3. Hugh joined the *Daily Mirror* as features editor

How I enjoyed being a woman in a man's world! My dream of being a successful journalist on a national newspaper had become a reality. Me with Daily Mirror Editor Lee Howard and Columnist Rex North. Opposite, Editorial Director Hugh Cudlipp who steered the Mirror to unparalleled success

in 1935 and later became Editor-in-Chief, then Mirror Group Editorial Director and then Chairman.

Hugh was warm-hearted, sentimental, generous and kind. He could also be cruel and vicious. He would issue spontaneous invitations to lunch – seven or eight of us – pick a victim (thankfully, never me) and do a spectacular demolition job over the Steak Diane. He would then send a bottle of scotch to say sorry in the afternoon. Hugh loathed what he called "cripples" – anyone with a slight limp – and those he called "beardies" – anyone with a neat bit of fuzz around their chin. Hugh was also the journalistic genius who in two minutes with a pencil and some layout pages could take the top story on the day's news schedule and create a headline that jumped off the front page.

Hugh was not only a journalistic genius – he was also a lot of fun, and my *Mirror* days reflected that side of this remarkable, unpredictable man. Mind you, he wasn't infallible. At one daily news conference he asked the following question, "What are these Debutante Balls I keep reading about?" I explained. "Occasions where a rich mother arranges a ball so her daughter can meet – and marry – a rich man." Hugh thought for about two seconds and spoke: "The *Mirror* will have its own ball." And so it happened; about five hundred people were invited to a ball in the Albert Hall to celebrate the paper's record five million circulation: the cabaret, Lulu and The Beatles. Hugh was enthusiastic about music, but not this kind. When the cabaret was over, the proud promotions manager brought The Beatles in to the royal box to meet Mr Cudlipp. Hugh's shoulders rose up to his ears – always a bad sign. Polite introductions were exchanged and The Beatles left. Hugh sent for the promotions manager and delivered the following memorable message: "Don't ever let me see anything about those fuckers in the *Mirror* ever again!"

On the *Mirror* I had a pretty free rein. Hugh paid

"I don't understand what you're doing, but I trust you. So I'm giving you the front and back pages"

me the compliment of not interfering in any way with my pages – and the one who tried, failed. One day, the chairman of the Mirror Group, Cecil King, accosted me on the back stairwell. "When are you going to stop putting those dreadful mini-skirts in the *Mirror*?" "Only when they stop being fashionable, Mr King," I said. "In that case I'll fire you," said Mr King. I reported this threat to Hugh. "Forget it," he said, so I did.

One day, Hugh paid me the following compliment: "I don't understand what you're doing, but I trust you. So I've decided to give you the front and back pages of the *Mirror* to tell our readers what the Swinging '60s are all about." It was 1964. And there they are in this book on pages 92-93, two memorable pages with a bite out at the bottom left corner in order to make room for a late-night murder!

When the *Mirror*'s new *Sun* newspaper – previously the Labour Party's *Herald* – failed to fulfil its promise, it was bought by Australian Rupert Murdoch for one pound. Rupert wanted to talk to me about a job. I told Hugh. "I'm not leaving the *Mirror,* but I'm curious about this man." Hugh glowered. Then smiled "Okay, you can go provided you take my Rolls and my driver will park right outside Rupert's flat in Portman Square. And when you leave you make sure Rupert sees you – he knows my car!"

One Friday afternoon after I'd been on the paper for thirteen years I got a call from Hugh. Please be in his office at 9.30am on Monday. The pessimist in me feared The Worst. In fact it was The Best. Hugh had decided to make me a director on the main *Mirror* board. And thus Hugh became the first man in Fleet Street to make such a dramatic appointment – and I became the first woman on the main board of a national newspaper. So, of course, I loved Hugh then and I love my memories of him now.

Hugh Cudlipp, a feminist?

Well, just a little bit.

Two honorary members of my Daily Mirror Emotional Support Team – first my beloved husband Geoffrey and then our brilliant poodle Polly, a popular office visitor and another bitch in that virtually all-male world!

Before Hugh elevated me to the peerage – moving from the *Sunday Mirror* to the *Daily* – I had been giving a lot of thought to what I felt was lacking in the women's pages in all the national newspapers. Due to too many male features editors, I thought. All these pages at this evolving time were lagging behind the way the UK profile was beginning to change. It surely wasn't a revolution, but women began slowly to demand or at least call for a voice. Equality, we felt, was just around the corner. (Hmm?)

But perhaps the most important – even turbulent – change of all was that the oncoming youth generation was beginning to take over the world. I felt this was so important that the *Mirror* had to be the first national newspaper to recognise such a social earthquake. Before our very eyes the age profile of our readers dropped down a whole generation, with interests to match: music, dance, film and fashion. I certainly can't claim my ideas were completely clear and I certainly wouldn't claim I had any golden rules – they were more like pale Green rules, which were beginning to sprout, but slowly.

These were my first practical moves: to make the fashion pages less about the usual stuff and more about people and what they might like to dare to wear. Or, if not, why not. I decided that what was needed was CONVERSATION. LET'S TALK. Let's make fashion fun. Yes, fashion was an important industry, but let's deal with it in a light-hearted way. So, in came the Conversational Headlines and, since no-one objected, I figured I must be doing something right. Example: "Where's it all leading, this mania for sexy clothes?" (see page 118).

Next big move: the importance of PICTURES. I invited the most talented – even the most famous – photographers to move out of the glossy magazine world and take some of their exciting images to liven up the national newspaper pages. I'm confident

you'll notice some of these wonderful pictures, which were largely lacking until the *Mirror* moved in.

Another *Mirror* must: I encouraged the talented *Mirror* staff photographers – more used to photographing news in general and sweaty sportsmen in particular – to take an interest in what the *Mirror* readers in general were wearing and, in particular, the new exciting generation of mini-skirted dolly birds. Strangely enough, there was no opposition and the talented *Mirror* photographers produced some wonderful fashion – people pictures that pleased the readers – of both sexes. PS Lots of them in this book.

Finally, my most determined idea of all concerned the proportion of male readers to female, which was roughly 50/50. It had to be possible to produce pages that appealed equally to both sexes. Why not? So I chose sexy sub-editor Christopher Ward to be the *Mirror*'s first fashion editor for men; I punished him by sending him off to Paris in a space helmet and cosmonaut kit by Pierre Cardin and I'm not sure he ever forgave me (see pages 144-145). These new style pages had to reflect the social revolution taking place in our midst. Yes, a proportion of the fashion pictures were sexy, but they had to appeal to me as well as all the chaps in the office. The pictures in this book – plus that soaring *Mirror* circulation will, I hope, prove we must have been doing something right.

PS Though not strictly *Mirror* People, above are two special members of my support team. My husband Geoffrey Hill without whom I wouldn't have been able to sustain such a demanding career. When Geoffrey retired from his cigar importing company – he hated cigars – he decided he'd had enough of work and dedicated himself to looking after me. Lucky me! And then there was Polly the Poodle, beloved by Geoffrey and me. Polly was a frequent visitor to the *Mirror* – specially after she'd had a haircut and wanted to show off her latest style. Polly was a real *Mirror* girl. ■

BACK VIEWS ONLY!

Thanks to cartoonist Moira Hodell, I join the ranks of favourite *Mirror* cartoon characters – the famous Jane, the first sexy pin-up on newsprint (see page 40) and then the infamous Andy Capp, the original male chauvinist pig and Florrie, his downtrodden missus.

Moira's perky cartoons provided an accurate, if faceless, version of the Felicity Green personality: short (only five feet one inch), sharp (only when required) and coping with strange places from Fleet Street to the far west of the USA, from New York and Hollywood to Texas and Las Vegas.

When I was despatched to foreign parts, it was decided I too should be cartooned and artist Moira Hodell and I agreed it should be my back view that would immortalise me. Without hesitation, Moira and I initially chose to dress my signature back view figure in my favourite '60s style: black T-shirt, cream skirt and black boots – fashionable then, fashionable now. God bless style. ■

DIRECTOR

NEW YORK
TEXAS

FELICITY
GREEN
BYE-BYE
LUNCH

THE MIRROR PAGES FUN PLUS FASHION '60s STYLE

The Italian Fashion Shows

IT'S FUN . . IT'S FASHION

So cute —these bikini 'covers'

Florence, Sunday

SIX hundred of the world's top fashion buyers saw the famous knitwear house of Mirsa present twelve outfits in the Pitti Palace here today.

Twelve models, showing in groups of three, wore tops and slacks, coats, suits and two-pieces, all in brilliant green, red and white jersey.

This spectacular scene was just one of the many bright ideas in the sportswear and boutique collections.

It doesn't matter a hoot that you can't identify the occasion when a girl would wear some of these outfits. They're the sort of fun Italian boutiques thrive on.

Among other highlights were:

KNEE-LENGTH TUNICS, oriental in inspiration, to wear with tapered pants. Made of brilliantly-patterned silk, the tunics were slit to the waist at both sides.

Smocks

In the same mood were knee-length silk smocks and heavy-knit tunics—long enough to be worn alone but all shown with pants.

NOVELTY SILK SHIRTS lined with light-weight flannel were a cosy idea for the winter.

So were **FOOTBALLERS' STRIPED SCARVES,** trimmed with pom-poms, that drape round the shoulders of sleeveless dresses and knot at the back.

Scarves and mufflers are a feature of the collections. So are brilliantly-coloured, spiralling stripes, and swirling, knitted fringe capes to wear with pants.

Colours seem brighter than ever — emerald, scarlet, purple and flashes of orange.

Gimmicks

Woollen stockings in these colours are often worn with very short knitted skirts or tunics.

Gimmicks include check slack suits with matching Apache caps and plain, knee-length knitted coats.

● Panic-stricken buyers fled from the palace when smoke billowed around them during the show. They came back after firemen put out a blaze—in the air-conditioning plant.

Top Italian designer Scarabocchio gives beachwear a glamorous new look with his bikini "cover-ups"—a printed cotton apron (right) that fastens at the back with a bow, and a frilled "sandwich board" in black and white print.

A new slant on Paris? Well, yes and no. This is Paris in 1961 showing its new looks for the following spring and we can see that nothing much has happened in the French fashion world. The clothes are elegant and dignified, and the Big Names have been Big Names for quite some time. Secrecy was all-important and publicity was an unknown art. No pictures of the new collections were allowed for one month, so Paris style was a Big Secret until the international manufacturers could produce their copies. The clothes were classy, but short on excitement and there wasn't even a whiff of the upcoming fashion explosion lurking on the London scene – the Youthquake was yet to happen.

First loo

A NEW S

THIS season'
pictures o
They make r

★ *DRAMA and the slant—the most talked-about and dramatic outfit shown in Paris. This reversible cape-cum-coat has only one sleeve. The other side finishes in a swashbuckling cape which is thrown over the shoulder. The hat is in chinchilla. Nina Ricci.*

A real
copy

SHOWN here, one of
very few outfits yo
be able to buy wh
admits to being a real D
copy.

This coat, sketched
Paris for the Mirror by
fashion artist Falk, w
bought by Wallis Sho
and copies will be on s
next week in black worst
at 25 guineas.

To use the name Di
Wallis Shops have to
produce the coat line
line, seam for seam in
original fabric.

This is the law as la
down by Dior, who s
they will no longer all
manufacturers to chan
the fabric or use the wo
"inspired by" or "adapt
from."

We still think there will
a lot of "inspirations" a
"adaptations," but you'll ha
to study your fashions
recognise them without
label.

the fashions for 1962

ANT ON PARIS

.ICITY GREEN

ashions, as you can see from the e, are a vintage crop.

it's good news at that—for two ain reasons:

Women become more womanly as clothes move in closer to the figure.

Everything—buttons, bows and collars—has taken on a sideways ant. Even belts—back for the first me in ages—tie or buckle at the side.

Revealing

Gone, at least for a while, is the ugly mour that hemlines would drop to ver a pair of shapely calves.

They stay, prettily and becomingly vealed, just below a knee-level skirt.

Look closely at the pictures on this page to find ways to give a 1962 fillip to a 1961 outfit:

The new clothes have a sideways look about them. Next important point—S-H-A-P-E has come back

- ☆ **Wear** a huge stole, preferably to match, round the shoulders of a suit
- ☆ **Remove** the "dummy" line of buttons on a double-breasted suit.
- ☆ **Wear** a midriff-wide leather belt round a woollen dress.
- ☆ **Tuck** all your hair away inside a furry helmet and wear a matching furry scarf.
- ☆ **Have** something-for-best in brown.

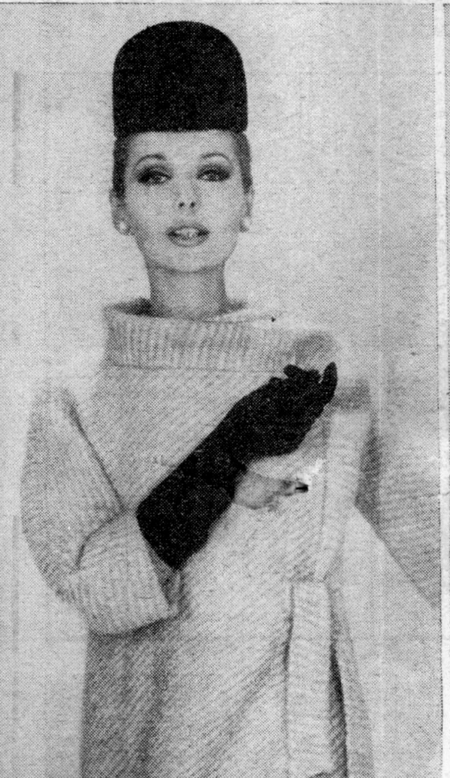

★ *NECKLINES and the slant—a blue and white diagonal tweed coat cut with subtle waist shaping, a side-fastening collar and casual waist tie. The hat is a forward-tilting cap in black velvet. By Pierre Cardin.*

★ *THE MIDRIFF and the slant—an example of the "corseted" look which is the tightest silhouette of all, fastened with side buttons above and below the waist. Dior.*

★ *SHAPE and the slant—a fitted suit with the new longer-length jacket worn over a slightly flared skirt. The gently shaped fingertip-length jacket has just the suggestion of a raised waistline. The side interest is in the throw-around matching muffler which buttons into place When the muffler is removed, the suit has a collarless neckline. The hat: A "wig" of looped woollen fringe. Suit in grey tweed by Nina Ricci.*

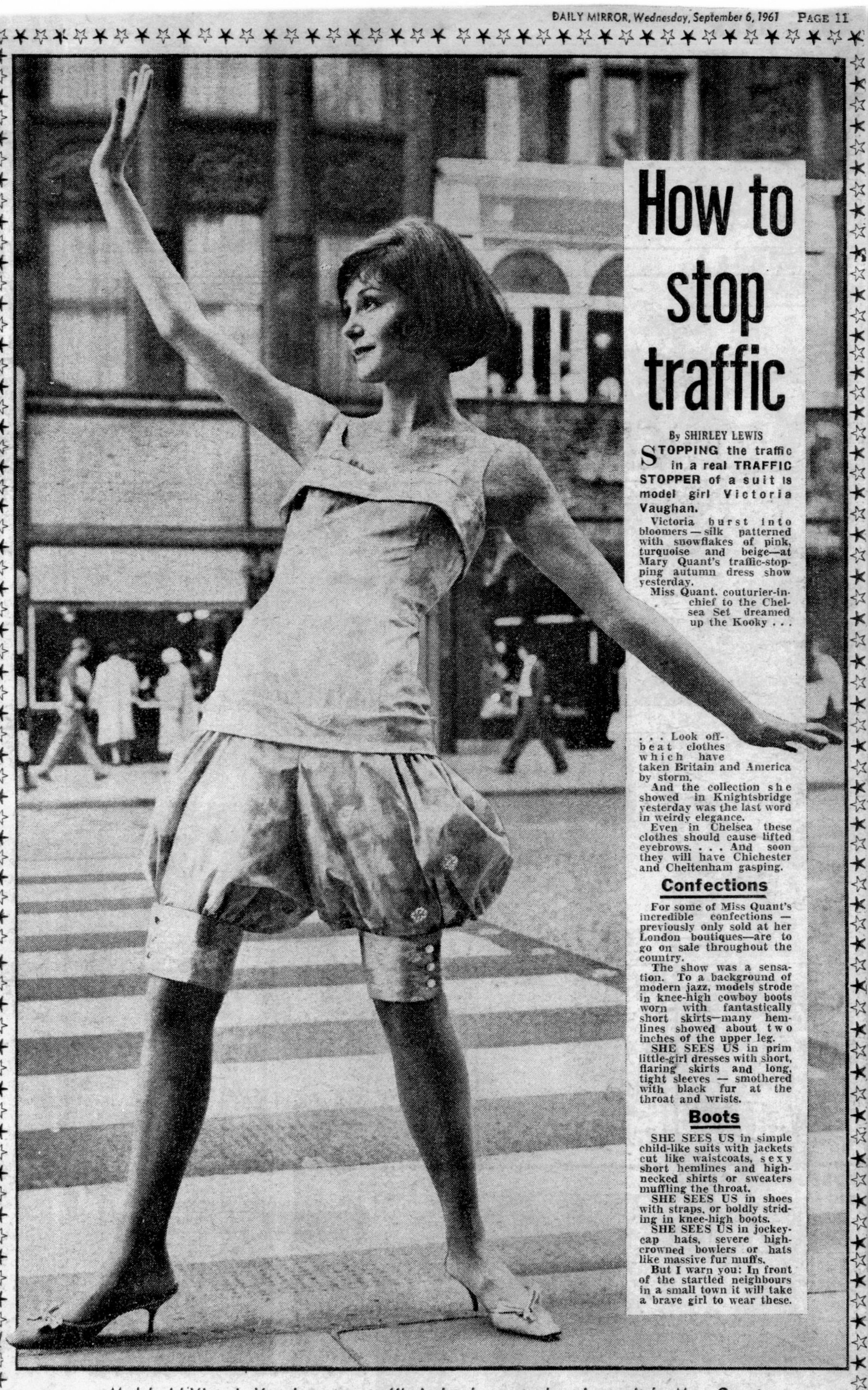

DAILY MIRROR, Wednesday, September 6, 1961 PAGE 11

How to stop traffic

By SHIRLEY LEWIS

STOPPING the traffic in a real TRAFFIC STOPPER of a suit is model girl Victoria Vaughan.

Victoria burst into bloomers — silk patterned with snowflakes of pink, turquoise and beige—at Mary Quant's traffic-stopping autumn dress show yesterday.

Miss Quant, couturier-in-chief to the Chelsea Set dreamed up the Kooky . . .

. . . Look off-beat clothes which have taken Britain and America by storm.

And the collection she showed in Knightsbridge yesterday was the last word in weirdy elegance.

Even in Chelsea these clothes should cause lifted eyebrows. . . . And soon they will have Chichester and Cheltenham gasping.

Confections

For some of Miss Quant's incredible confections — previously only sold at her London boutiques—are to go on sale throughout the country.

The show was a sensation. To a background of modern jazz, models strode in knee-high cowboy boots worn with fantastically short skirts—many hemlines showed about two inches of the upper leg.

SHE SEES US in prim little-girl dresses with short, flaring skirts and long, tight sleeves — smothered with black fur at the throat and wrists.

Boots

SHE SEES US in simple child-like suits with jackets cut like waistcoats, sexy short hemlines and high-necked shirts or sweaters muffling the throat.

SHE SEES US in shoes with straps, or boldly striding in knee-high boots.

SHE SEES US in jockey-cap hats, severe high-crowned bowlers or hats like massive fur muffs.

But I warn you: In front of the startled neighbours in a small town it will take a brave girl to wear these.

Model girl Victoria Vaughan stops traffic in London yesterday—in a suit by Mary Quant.

BEND . . Follow my leader. . . how you start Th

AND TWIST . . Now they've t weight on le

. . AND BEND He's leaning ov Twist—this

DAILY MIRROR, Friday, October 27, 1961 PAGE 17

THE TWIST!

The world's WACKIEST dance comes to Britain

DOUBLE BEND! *He bends forward. She bends back. It's a double bend that can have the onlookers bent double with laughter. But twenty-two-year-old model Natasha and Nicky Haslam, 22, find The Twist exhilarating. They are two of the few people in Britain who know how to do it.*

is called The Twist—the wackiest, gayest dance since the Charleston.

nd it looks like being Britain's latest ce craze.

lready it is catching on in London.

hese pictures of The Twist were taken Mirror Cameraman ARTHUR SIDEY the Satire Club, run by Lord Ulick ne, where he and bandleader Paul Adam made The Twist top dance.

Rock Beat

ere's how you do The Twist.

is danced to a rock beat—in twos, es or even by yourself. You do not touch partner, and hardly move your feet.

ur hips, too, keep more or less still.

how you move those shoulders and knees!

shoulders gyrate one way and your knees rotate in the opposite direction—left knee forward taking your weight as the right shoulder comes forward.

Then, putting your left shoulder forward, your whole body twists and the weight is transferred to your other foot.

Said Paul Adam: "I've watched the gyrations come and go, but watching this just fractures me. It's so energetic.

Watching it, you think it is the ugliest dance ever.

Then you try it, you get the beat and you're a fan. You should also be several inches slimmer round the waist in no time at all.

Started

The Twist started in San Francisco. Skipping New York, it turned up next in Paris, where it is the rage of every Left Bank night club.

Next place to get Twist Fever was St. Tropez, on the French Riviera, where they dance it till dawn on moonlit beaches.

The rage went from there to New York. Now—London.

And soon—your local dance.

dance The riations.

Who knew how to stop traffic on London's '60s fashion scene? Mary Quant, of course – see left with these blooming bloomers. Bare arms, bare legs, no hat, no gloves – Mary knew which way the fashion wind was blowing. She chose outdoor photography, she chose street casual rather than studio elegant. Mary's model is leaping about in London rather than posing in the Paris studio. And then came The Twist… and movement and fashion came together in a whole new exciting way – and this explosive combination started in London. The Twist, the newest dance craze, launched by singer Chubby Checker in America, snaked its way via Paris and St Tropez to London in 1961, where it was demonstrated by a youthful Nicky Haslam, then an acknowledged expert, who demonstrated the dance on television's *Six-Five Special*. And here he's doing the same for *Mirror* readers. Haslam, now a famous society interior designer and author, recalls dancing the Twist with friends: "Jean Shrimpton's long legs and David Bailey's agility in his pointed boots were the perfect instruments for this new craze, and we would dance for hours together at the Saddle Room, the smartest nightclub in London's swanky Park Lane."

DAILY MIRROR, *Thursday, December 28, 1961* PAGE 9

'61 was a vintage year. Fashions came and went —new trends buzzed around. How many of last year's good ideas did you fall for?

IN A WOMAN'S WORLD '61 was a swinging, fast-moving, pace-setting year. There was so much happening all the time it took a really "with-it" girl to keep up.

Did you keep up? To find out how with-it you were in 1961, get with our quiz below, allowing one mark for each question to which you can answer "yes."

☆ **DID YOU . . .**

BUY something with a flared skirt . . . eat chilli con carne (or any other Mexican dish) . . . holiday (or wish you could) in the Greek Islands . . . try out false eyelashes?

START the summer by shortening all your dresses . . . redecorate a room using stark white paint for woodwork and doors instead of grey or cream . . . sample a meal-in-a-glass diet . . . buy a hat, coat, jerkin or boots in a leopard spot fur?

FASHION

SAY that Chelsea's Mary Quant seemed as big an influence in fashion as Dior . . . cease to care whether Liz Taylor ever made "Cleopatra" . . . learn to dance the Twist . . . drink Vodka?

WEAR a Chanel type pin with a Chanel type suit . . . fall for Yuri Gagarin . . . wear square-toed shoes at Easter or before . . grow your hair?

WEAR something pink in the spring . . . something green in the autumn . . . buy cutlery or tableware in stainless steel . . . wear a medallion chain round your hips . . . buy a Helen Shapiro record?

AN EYE ON WOMEN

presented by FELICITY GREEN

with Peggy Briggs • Shirley Lewis • Jane Bream

A typically '61 with-it girl photographed by Roy Cuthbert

SEE "Breakfast at Tiffany's" . . consider how you'd look in a one-bare-shoulder dress . . . want a "mini" before Royalty started to use them . . . talk about the Establishment?

THINK that if you were buying a dog, you'd really prefer a pug to a poodle . . . try out and go mad about softening rinses for woollies, nappies and blankets . . . drink Dubonnet or Campari with soda or lemon . . . wish you had a rocking chair?

LIKE the look of bare midriff pants . . . at least think about central heating, or the next best thing (which is super-efficient room-by-room heat) . . . dig the Temperance Seven rhythm . . . use green eye make-up?

LATCH ON to such phrases as "that's the way the cookie crumbles" and all that jazz . . . serve your main course straight from oven to table in one of the newest heat-resistant dishes designed specially for the job . . . wear a headband?

DEVELOP (along with Bardot) a softer, sleeker, more feminine, less Beatnik look . . . wear navy with emerald green . . . wear stretch pants . . . swoon over Sammy Davis?

LEARN to shop around before buying groceries, meat and greengroceries (this is the age of supermarkets and special offers, and even small firms have them) . . . remain faithful to Adam and Cliff . . . wear a bauble on a long chain, a la Chanel? (See picture above.)

WELL, how did you make out? How many "yeses" did you get?

To anyone who scored nearly a full card (40 marks or over) and is standing by for praise we have only one word: WHOA!

You're going too far. You're not only with-it, you're out in front.

If you continue to live at this dizzy pace you'll soon be wailing "Stop the world, I want to get off."

Be a bit more selective in your acceptance of new ideas. They're not all that good, and if you're not careful you'll lose your own personality beneath a surfeit of gimmicks.

DREAM

If you scored 25 to 39—you're truly with-it, girl. You're the girl dress manufacturers dream about, hairdressers drool over and adverts are aimed at.

New ideas stimulate you to new heights of personal endeavour.

But if you scored between 36 and 39, beware of getting the with-it habit so that you're not having fun — you're just keeping up with it.

Score 10 to 24 — you're doing your best, but frankly it's not quite good enough. Don't say you don't care—what are you doing reading this quiz anyway?

Adopt a new motto for 1962: if you think a new idea is fun but not for you, re-think and do it. And don't wait until everyone else has stopped doing it.

WAKEY

Score under 10—wake up there! You've no idea what you're missing.

If you go through life with a permanent rejection slip in your hand you're the one who'll get rejected.

Learn to stop, look and listen before you shake your head . . . and remember that inside every square (we do mean you) there's a with-it girl trying to get out and have fun.

Shown in the picture on the left, three with-it ideas you might have tried. Mary Quant's with-it shirt in white crepe, turtle-necked with deep cuffs, 6½ gns. Gilt chain with pearly bauble, 1 guinea; girl-size pearl cuff-links, 17s. 6d. Both by Rosita.

'61 HEADLINES

EVERY YEAR has its Hat—and invariably it's a woman who makes The Hat of the Year. Remember Leslie Caron and her Gigi hat, Julie Andrews and her Doolittle boater, and, further back still, Eva Bartok and her cloche?

This year it was Jackie Kennedy and her pillbox. Attractively promoted by America's First Lady, this stark little shape became the most with-it hat of 1961.

Milliners vied with each other to produce variations on the Kennedy titfer. Left, see one of their bright ideas: a velvet pillbox worn atop a knitted helmet. (Both are by Jaeger, the pillbox 39s. 6d., the helmet, 1 guinea.)

Other 1961 with-it hats: Bretons with wide sloping brims, fluffy feather wig hats, outsize fur berets.

AN EYE ON WOMEN presented by FELICITY GREEN with Peggy Briggs and Shirley Lewis

THE SUBJECT: Woman and her ever-changing moods

THE OBJECT: To forecast how she'll look this year

YOU IN '62

FASHION FORECAST coming up: '62 will be the year when all the trends and gimmicks that have been kicking around for the past eighteen months will crystallise and emerge as the most important New Look since that other New Look.

It will be a young look—ultra-female rather than ultra-feminine, and owing more to Chelsea's Mary Quant and the better-groomed Bardot than to the Best-Dressed Ladies.

It will be a curvy look—the threat of the banished bosom has passed. (This more shapely you will wear lighter foundation garments, many of them made in the new non-rubber elastic yarns.)

It will be a leggy look. Skirts will stay short, and good legs will get more than their fair share of attention under the swirly, flirty skirts that are top favourite for spring.

We predict that by Easter Monday any female who cares about fashion will own . . .

. . . a semi-fitted coat with a gently flaring skirt
a princess dress with a low flare
a suit with a waist
an after-office-hours dress in a business-like fabric—i.e., grey flannel
a frilly blouse
a pair of shoes with instep straps and a rounded toe
a pair of bell-bottomed pants
a low-slung hipster skirt.

Top colours for the summer will be the fruit shades—tangerine, orange, melon, apricot, lemon, banana, raspberry—all the pinks and blues.

Top fabrics: Grey flannel and crisp weaves that look like linen or hopsack.

Bare

We predict that the new sex symbol will be your bare middle. Nine out of ten of this year's beach outfits bare the navel in no uncertain way, with low slung pants and skirts hitched from the hips below brief boleros.

Bulges are out—or should be. Try a meal-in-a-glass diet food or a long-term sensible eating plan. (There are 150-odd slimming days to Whitsun.)

It will be the year of summer dresses that are sleeveless and collarless. Just a slip of mouthwatering colour which slinks down from neck to hips and breaks out in a rush of gores or pleats at the hem.

It will be a year of more and more Chanel-type suits and all that goes with them—two-toned braiding, gilt chains, medallions, deep shirt cuffs. (You must have a pair of cuff-links of your own.)

It will be a year of longer hair-do's, sleek and smooth in front and dressed high at the back . . . of the all-in-one cosmetic (powders with built-in foundation, foundations with built-in moisturisers) . . . and of eye-shadow used as often as lipstick.

Think

The Paris fashion shows take place this month. We predict that The Master, Balenciaga, will think about giving up designing. Sad—but inevitable. At least this year there is enough new blood around to give Paris fashion a whacking great transfusion.

There is 25-year-old **Yves St. Laurent**, the babe who failed when he was forced to don the Dior mantle.

He now has a set-up of his own in Paris, and we predict that he'll not only do well but lead a whole new school of with-it fashion designing. For the young, by the young—and everyone, young or old, will want it.

Other newcomers: **Roberto Capucci**, who has arrived in Paris via a dazzlingly successful career in Florence.

Andre Courreges, an ex-Balenciaga boy, showing for the second time. (The buyers went wild about his tiny first collection—are hopeful of even bigger and better things this time.)

Two more new names: **Philippe Venet** and **Jacqueline de Sthen.**

With at least four new houses exploding into the world of Paris couture, we safely predict that there will be plenty of fashion excitement in 1962.

YOUR DRESS will slink from a collarless neckline to a low hip and break out into a swirling flare, or a rush of gores or pleats. This one, in black and white tweed, is braided in black. Price 6 gns. Wallis Shops.

Picture by JOHN ADRIAAN.

YOUR HAIR will be longer. Mayfair stylist Rose Evansky dresses hair that is six inches long on the top into a beret of soft swirls, with an eyebrow-level fringe and sleek sides brushed flat at the ears.

YOUR MIDDLE will be bare on the beach this summer. Pants and skirts for the summer hitch cowboy style on the hips below cropped and sleeveless bolero tops.

YOUR SHAPE will be moulded in lighter foundations. Above, Dorothy Perkins bra with a featherweight interlining to give firm shape. Price 12s. 11d.

FASHION IS REALLY

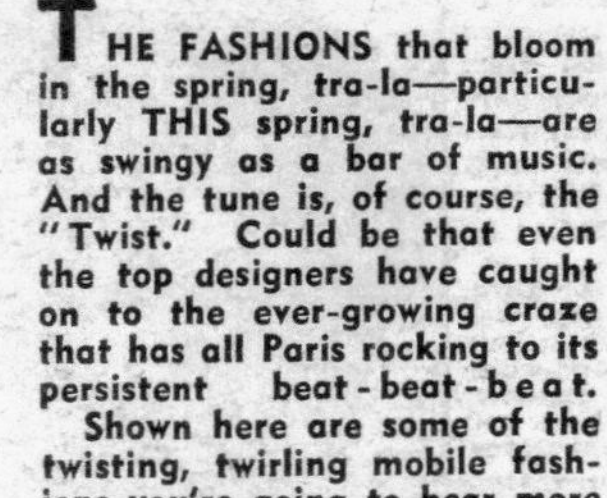

THE FASHIONS that bloom in the spring, tra-la—particularly THIS spring, tra-la—are as swingy as a bar of music. And the tune is, of course, the "Twist." Could be that even the top designers have caught on to the ever-growing craze that has all Paris rocking to its persistent beat-beat-beat.

Shown here are some of the twisting, twirling mobile fashions you're going to hear more about. British manufacturers who look to Paris for inspiration will make sure of that.

You'll hear more about the Jazz in Paris. What's the Jazz? It's the spirit of dash and daring that only Paris can create and get away with. For instance, Cardin's kerchief dresses with triangular shawls to cover a bare-backed look; Lanvin's evening skirts slit in panels to above knee level; Laroche's bare midriffs veiled with fringing.

CAREFREE

You'll hear more about the Classics in Paris. The gentle fashions that change little and live a long and healthy fashion life. Goma's suits with little girl collars and carefree pleated skirts; Balmain's printed silk blouses tucked into firmly belted skirts; St. Laurent's tunic dresses in bold black and white prints.

You'll hear more about the Pops in Paris—the fashions that everyone wants, most people can wear. Dior's seam "matchbox" skirts worn w pouched tops belted on t hipbone; Ricci's little lo jackets in tangerine colou Heim's crisp white gilets a bibs; military-looking belts.

You'll hear more ab the Trad in Paris. The evergre ideas that never fail. The fl tery printed chiffon for sumn dresses; ruffles cascad down the fronts of blouses a the backs of evening dress Chanel's straight skirts w side wrap front and ba

WITH-IT

You'll hear more about t Beat in Paris. Fashions for t with-it black-stockinge brigade—the chic ones. Dic Left Bank berets perched o one ear and kept there by w power; Crahay at Ricci's ric striped silk college mufflers long tailored suit jackets.

A slashed back on a belted purple wool dress. By Cardin.

A short, high-waisted evening dress in printed sunray pleated chiffon. By Ricci.

The brief m skirt in grey with pouched c firmly belted on bone. By

DAILY MIRROR, Tuesday, February 27, 1962 PAGE 13

line for 1962

WINGING

AN EYE ON WOMEN

resented by

elicity Green with Peggy Briggs

Two rows of buttons on a little-girl jacket and carefree pleated skirt. In clear yellow wool. By Goma.

The colour, orange . . . the fabric, linen . . . the look, a snugly-fitting bodice, small waist and twirling skirt. Fun accessories: the embroidered orange handkerchief knotted and fluttering just above the belt, the owl-like sunglasses with orange frames, and the miniature boater banded in the same colour atop the heavy fringe seen everywhere in Paris. By Ricci.

Why was fashion suddenly swinging in '62? It was all because of a dance! The Twist had started its energetic way, twisting and swinging round the world – and fashion got the message. In Paris the required silhouette was achieved with a degree of dignity – just gently flaring skirts, pleats or the swish of a high-waisted, soft, silken flare. But they all had flair. Closer to home, the scene was more energetic. Dance halls and clubs were suddenly overflowing with young Twisting experts.

DAILY MIRROR, *Thursday, March 8, 1962* PAGE 15

★ Above: Carefree dress in checked Acrilan. Susan Small, about £9. Right: Easy jersey two-piece, Holyrood, 9½ gns.

★ Echo of the new Paris craze for waists and sunray pleating in easy-care Terylene lawn. By Frederica, 7½ gns.

GO, TAKE A RUNNING JUMP!

YOU could, if you felt like it, go and take a running jump in any of the new spring clothes.

They all seem to have been designed with athletes in mind—pretty athletes, mind you, who wouldn't dream of allowing their taste for action to diminish their feminine appeal.

Never have clothes been so carefree, so easy to move around in.

AN EYE ON WOMEN
presented by Felicity Green
WITH PEGGY BRIGGS AND SHIRLEY LEWIS

SKIRT

In the shops now you can find every possible version of the happy-go-lucky pleated skirt that never hampers, never restricts, never wriggles.

It just swings and sways around your knees as you walk. Or as you run, clamber on buses, twist, skate, climb or even ride a pogo stick like the girl in the centre picture, above.

What is your favourite version of today's swingy silhouette?

Could be it's the sunray pleating that whooshes out from a tiny waistline, or the wide box pleat that slants outward to a gentle flare. It may be the all-round, flat knife pleat that, despite the slender line it gives, will twirl and twist with the best of them.

Or the love of the "with-it" ones—the kick-out pleat that's stitched down to just above the knee and then bursts into action. They're fashion in motion, all of them—as the pictures on this page illustrate—and just right for this spring's ready-to-go girls.

LEFT BANK

☆ OFF and on, the beret has always been the British girl's favourite.

This spring, Dior showed a new, pert Left Bank beret, and the mood has already Channel-hopped.

If the saucy Left Bank beret, worn at a gravity-defying tilt, frightens you, then look for an easy-to-wear version, the Basque beret, which sits on the back of the head. Kangol are selling them for 18s. 11d. in the popular citrus colours.

Accessory sense

WHAT'S new in buttons, bows and belts . . . to say nothing of plastic macs and knitting wools?

A tour around the Smallwares Fair showed that the accessory and trimmings designers are not lagging behind the current fashion crazes.

The new belts are right in line with Paris; even the new plastic macs have been glammed-up with gorgeous colours.

The big rave belts will be Paris-style, four-inch wide ones decorated with cut-out eyelets edged with gilt. Or take your pick from thin bootlace belts with gilt tassel or coin ends. Or half-inch wide leather sashes plaited with gilt chain.

The big rave bags will be basket-weave, outsize shapes in dark chocolate straw spiced with natural-coloured cotton rope handles.

RAVE

The big rave knitting wools will be the ones the Paris girls are already mad about, with all the accent on surface texture.

EXAMPLE: An extra-bulky tweed in a range of off-beat flecked shades for making sweaters and suits.

EXAMPLE: A quick-knit wool in muted colours which has a subtle golden shimmer on the surface.

False lashes made of seal fur, 15s. a pair.

BLINKING MINK

IN AMERICA even false eyelashes have been elevated into status symbols and the cost of blinking with mink works out at about £16. Here, fur lashes are proving a hit, too. But the British ones are made of seal fur and cost a more reasonable 15s. Advantage of these particular lashes—the seal fur gives fine individual tips plus the uneven depth of real lashes.

Fabrics had become user-friendly by 1962. Skirts with the kind of pleats that could be washed and NOT ironed brought freedom to the increasingly active girls who were taking to the more active spots previously in the men-only category. Suggested activities from the manufacturers of these new carefree clothes included twist, skate or even a pogo stick. Think that last one might have been suggested by a man! How lucky we are now that easy-care clothes are taken for granted and we no longer have to be grateful. Opposite page: Today, sensitive people wear fake fur. In the '60s, the insensitive ones wore the Real Thing, including the Queen, Jackie Kennedy and Elizabeth Taylor. Shame on them! PS Animal prints were big in the '60s and they're even bigger today.

All the Best People are wearing leopard, including the Queen, pictured at Sandown Park races ten days ago

. . . and Jackie Kennedy, wife of the American President, when she arrived in Italy for a State visit

. . . and Liz Taylor—who wore her coat, with a leopard hat to match, in Rome at the week-end.

The new status symbol..

By FELICITY GREEN

CHORUS girls used to dream of it; rich wives nagged their husbands for it; millionairesses went shopping in it; film stars at premieres fairly dipped in it.

MINK, the fur that every woman wanted, was definitely status symbol No. 1.

But today mink is slipping out of the top place.

Suddenly another fur is appearing in All the Best Places, worn by all the Best-known Faces.

The fur that is getting to the top is LEOPARD—the sporty, spotty skin that was once found stuffed, snarling and spread out on the drawing-room floor.

JACKIE KENNEDY, one of the world's better-dressed women, and wife of the American President, wore leopard when she arrived in Rome three weeks ago.

Dicey

LIZ TAYLOR wore leopard when she went night-clubbing in Rome this week-end. (She wore a hat to match which, fashionably speaking, is a bit dicey—but that's Liz for you. She always was an individualist.)

THE QUEEN wore leopard to watch steeplechasing at Sandown Park recently.

Comparing the three coats shown above I'd say an expert would place Mrs. Kennedy's coat first — small regular markings, ultra-chic cut, black bone buttons; the Queen's coat second—bold markings but a bit conservative in shape; and Liz's coat third.

The reason why leopard is likely to stay a status symbol—and out of reach of most of us—is that it's expensive, nowadays, due to its rarity.

A full length coat in the rarest and best skin of all, the Somali leopard, can cost up to £3,000. Cheaper ones cost much less—a few hundred pounds—but who wants a CHEAP status symbol?

THE FEATURES THAT MAKE FORTUNES * WHAT BETT

Today's Face

1928 Lady Diana Cooper

1933 Margaret Whigham

1937 Carole Lombard

1943 Veronica Lake

1952 Joan Crawford

1961 Brig Bar

by FELICITY GREEN

HER lips were like ripe cherries, her eyes like twin moonlit pools.

She was the typical beauty of the 1920's and she bears as much resemblance to the typical beauty of today as the E-type Jaguar does to the model T Ford.

For women, like cars, tend to produce a new model every year. And suddenly everyone wants the new model. (For some previous models, see the line-up of famous faces above.)

Each face shows the look of beauty that was the ideal at that time. Men sighed over it, women envied it—and tried, as is their way, to copy it.

Factory lasses were warned about catching their Veronica Lake wartime locks in the machines.

Haunting

First prototype for this year's face is seen on the right. With its haunting quality it could set a million girls reaching for their purses . . . spending even more than last year's record £80 million on new cosmetics, different hair-do's.

Men, it's well known, may implore women to stay as sweet as they are . . . don't ever change, dear.

Women, however, change as often as their fancy takes them and a chameleon has nothing on a woman with a new image in mind.

Remember the first impact of Bardot on the teenagers . . . of Monroe . . . of doe-eyed model Barbara Goalen?

Even women who have no wish to be a carbon copy of somebody else, still move relentlessly on from one look to another, casting off the old, accepting the new with hardly a backward glance.

The Duchess of Argyll, for instance—a typical beauty in 1920. A different beauty today.

THE pattern for today's face—Vintage Spring '62—is just emerging.

It's set, not by a film star, but by a model girl. Ros Watkins, a blonde, slightly fey beauty, is seen on the right, pictured by photographer John French.

Says John French of Ros's face: "It's the face of an innocent sophisticate with a charmed life suggesting that its owner knows it all yet still remains a baby."

Says Ros of Ros's face: "It's the result of sitting down and experimenting with lots of pots until I discovered **me.**

"I found I had to wipe out everything before I started . . . the face should be pale to focus attention on the eyes and mouth. . . .

Goo-ey

"I like deep lipstick to make my mouth look larger and I like it to spread all over my face and look all shiny and goo-ey."

YOU'LL agree that today's face is startlingly different from all other faces. And that in itself is desirable in a woman.

For a woman, to stay the same is to stagnate.

For a man to tell a woman: "My goodness, how you've changed," is not a statement of fact; it's a compliment.

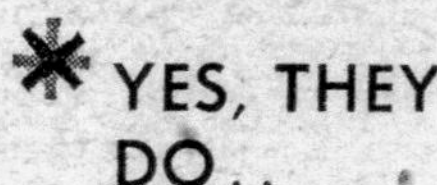

* YES, THEY DO . .

The face of Brigitte Bardot, as expressed in her films, has been a more profitable "export" for France than even the big motor companies'. (And think of all those whizzing French cars!)

WHO IS THE GIRL?

Ros Watkins, 23, married. Says her eyes are "grey-blue-green, but mainly grey." Is 5ft. 9in and reed-slim. Wears false eyelashes—"strictly for modelling only."

Faces change just as much as fashion and there's always a role model demonstrating the new look: model Ros Watkins shows the red lips and sooty eyes of the early '60s. But before cosmetics were so helpful we had to look elsewhere for our role models. First came the society beauties and then the film stars, who went from the contrived glamour of the '30s Carole Lombard to the outdoor informality of the '60s Brigitte Bardot. Today, anything goes, but the top looks in 2014 suggest sooty eyes and bright red lips are once again the Big New Look. What goes around comes around.

ME THAN **EASTER** FOR A NEW ASSESSMENT?

PICTURE BY JOHN FRENCH

Chanel herself . .

No designer anywhere, anytime did as much for style-conscious women worldwide as Gabrielle "Coco" Chanel. She was a fashion revolutionary not once but twice. First in 1920, when she advised women to give up their stays. And they did. And then in the '50s after her pre-war exit to America, she returned to Paris and decided there were too many men designing for women. What was needed was her soft, relaxed ultra-feminine tweed suits, which became a success round the world. (I had three Wallis Shops High Street copies.) All her designs were soft and casual and construction was out. Chanel died in 1971 but, under designer Karl Lagerfeld, the Chanel name remains a potent fashion force. But perhaps her greatest gift to women was Chanel No. 5 – still a favourite perfume after nearly a century.

THAT LAUNCHED A MILLION SUITS

—to say nothing of Chanel No 5

THIS is Gabrielle Chanel, born, as far as anyone knows, about seventy-nine years ago in France. ruculent, temperamental and talented, she is one of the gest names in Paris fashion today. Her influence reaches nd the world and is as strong at the £100 level as it is in bargain basement.

by **FELICITY GREEN**

wice in her life nel has led a revolu- ary movement that nged the way women ed and dressed.

was "Coco" Chanel, she is always called, persuaded women he 1920's to give up r stays, shorten r skirts and throw y their monstrous, loaded hats.

First

he felt cold one day, on a man's pullover nd the first sweater was born.

he introduced nky costume jewel-

he turned jersey, a erial used only for t's underpants, into igh fashion fabric. he created the Flapper. he invented the soft al look which was as erent from the rigid nes of her time as a strand of cooked spaghetti is from a raw one.

Chanel was the reigning queen of Paris couture until 1938 when she gave up and left for America, where she stayed until 1954. (Her name, though, was kept alive by her Chanel No. 5 perfume which, even today is the best known scent in the world.)

Rebel

Then, on her return to Paris, this extraordinary woman became a fashion rebel—a a fashion rage —for the second time in her life.

There were too many men, s said, lording it over the Paris fashion scene. ior, Balenciaga, Heim, es and the rest might ery talented and all that, but what was needed was a woman's touch.

ONCE AGAIN, she decided that fashion had become too restricting, too "corseted."

Enemies

ONCE AGAIN, she regarded boning, padding and tightly fitting clothes as her natural enemies.

ONCE AGAIN she made the loose, almost floppy-looking clothes that had been such a success twenty years earlier.

AND ONCE AGAIN women were right there, loving and wearing the Chanel Look.

They still are, and look like doing so just as long as there's a Chanel around to provide **The Look.**

The newest Chanel look

HERE is the first picture from Paris of the new Chanel suits for autumn and winter 1962-63.

They are typical of the Chanel Look—casual, wearable, "dress-makery" and comfortable.

They differ from last season's suits in only the smallest details for "Coco" Chanel is a woman who thought of a good idea back in the 20's—and it's still as good today.

This season's newnesses include deep cape collars, long jackets belted with a woollen string, coats with fur revers and a skirt with a pleat at the side-front.

Still in favour—the soft lacy-looking tweed suits shown here and bound, as always, with a contrast braid.

Phooey!

Other designers would faint with horror—and probably sue for damages—if any newspaper published pictures of their clothes so soon after the opening shows.

Chanel says "phooey" to such restrictive practices.

"I shall not stop anyone copying my designs," she announced. "On the contrary, I say to everyone, 'Come and pinch ALL my ideas if you like.'

"I am on the side of women, not the fashion houses."

Her generosity, however, does not extend to trade buyers who still have to pay upwards of £250 to buy a Chanel model.

But they know it's worth it.

And they know, too, that they are not risking their money, since Chanel—more than any other designer in Paris today—seems to have discovered the secret of what women WANT to wear. Not what male designers think they OUGHT to wear.

Copied

Such is the appeal of the Chanel Look that no woman seems to mind meeting it face-to-face on another woman. And, as Chanel is far and away the most copied designer in the world today, this is more than likely to happen.

Line for line reproductions of Chanel suits or coat-skirt-and-shirt combinations sell in the original fabrics at around £30 to £50 a time in shops all over the country.

Reasonable facsimiles can cost anything from £5 up.

If you own a suit with a cardigan jacket, or a blouse to match the suit lining, or a jacket with coin-type buttons, or a coat with contrast facing on the lapels, or a shirt with cuffs and cuff-links, then you owe something to Chanel, the designer with a million imitators.

A CHANELISM: For women there is only one science—to love and, if possible, to be loved.

In 1962 we spent £84 million on stockings and we laddered 34 million pairs. And the battle of the seamless versus the seamed began. They put their views succinctly. Sportsman Danny Blanchflower put it this way: "I can't bear stockings. Whoever heard of a leg with seams?" But almost to a man, men preferred a seam. A well-known stocking manufacturer said stockings were a sex symbol and seams "lead somewhere". Despite all this male preference, seamless stockings remained a firm feminine favourite. Until tights took over. Below, meet Jane the famous, first daily *Daily Mirror* pin-up.

BEHIND THIS PICTURE..A S
324 MILLIC

Which pair of stockings is <u>SHE</u> going to buy?

by FELICITY GREEN

A MEMBER of the Fair Sex is sitting quietly at her desk . . sink . . or dressing-table. Suddenly, she jumps six inches in the air, shrieks and clasps her ankle.

She has laddered her stocking. Yet another notch has been added to the astronomical bill for the nylons we women snag, wear and tear our way through each year.

Latest figures show that in 1961 we dented our budgets to the tune of £84,000,000, or approximately 324 million pairs.

FORECAST

The forecast for 1962 is that the stocking fatality list will be up—to around 400 million pairs.

From all this you can see that stockings, by any standard, are Big Business and fortunes are made and lost every time madam decides to change her brand of leg lure.

TAKE, for instance, the case of the seamless stocking. . . . Ten years ago they were the poor relations of the nylon family.

These knitted-in-a-tube stockings were even given a false seam up the back to simulate their fully-fashioned cousins that were knitted flat and then sewn up into their finished leg shape.

SYMBOLS

Now seamless stockings are front rank fashion on their own account and add up to two thirds of the stocking business in Britain today.

DESPITE the prejudice that leads sportsman Danny Blanchflower to say that he can't bear stockings with seams because "whoever heard of a leg with seams?" . . .

DESPITE the statement of a well-known stocking manufacturer who says that after all stockings are sex symbols and seams intriguingly "lead somewhere" . . .

DESPITE all this, seamless stockings are as much a with-it craze of today as heavy eye make-up, pale lipstick and square-toed shoes.

As girls wear stockings to attract men (yes, they do whether they admit it or not) and men notice girls' stockings (yes they do whether they admit it or not), a man's eye view of a girl's legs is an important factor in the stocking selection scene . .

You'll see what I mean by reading what the men on the right of the picture have to say.

ALSO with-it today are non-run stockings made on a lock-stitch principle that prolongs their life if not indefinitely then to a new and notable extent.

Just how long-lived these stockings are I'll be able to tell you in a week or so, when I'll have the results of a two-month wearing test now being conducted among 200 girls.

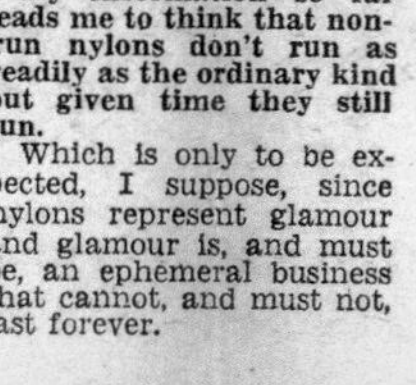

SO FAR . .

My information so far leads me to think that non-run nylons don't run as readily as the ordinary kind but given time they still run.

Which is only to be expected, I suppose, since nylons represent glamour and glamour is, and must be, an ephemeral business that cannot, and must not, last forever.

The variety
or

GERING BILL FOR £84,000,000 A YEAR,
NFURIATING LADDERS AND TWO EVER-INTRIGUING QUESTIONS

Which stockings will HE look at—and why?

Picture by John Adriaan

is infinite but the types break down into roughly six categories—seamless, seamed, dark and black. One London store sells 61 different brands and 2,400 sizes and colours.

MALCOLM MUGGERIDGE
—Author and TV Personality

I like pale, seam-free stockings very much. They look just like legs and, after all, that is surely the aim of all these very sheer stockings?

PREJUDICE: The dark patterned mesh. It's not that I don't like them, but I think they are stockings for girl friends rather than wives.

TOM HUSTLER
—the photographer

I prefer dark seamed stockings. Tremendous! Sophisticated sex appeal for the strictly female female. They're my idea of a real come-hither.

PREJUDICE: Pale, seam-free stockings. This type doesn't inspire me at all. They remind me of pale flesh and who likes pale flesh?

MICHAEL
—the dress designer

I choose dark seamed stockings for the woman who is elegant and confident. Any man would like to be seen with a woman wearing these.

PREJUDICE: I loathe all seam-free stockings. I'd rather have a crooked seam than none at all.

DONALD ZEC
—Mirror Columnist

I love black stockings with a seam. Wow! Shades of Sadie Thompson—but who's complaining?

PREJUDICE: Pale seam-free stockings. These do nothing to me or for her! I see them on a red-nosed Highland lassie prancing round in a Scottish mist echoing bird calls between cups of tepid cocoa.

Daily Mirror

FELICITY GREEN talks to women every week

Blot out her freckles, and what have you got?

JUST AN ORDINARY PRETTY GIRL

I HAVE just had a suspicion confirmed—freckles are not a drawback at all; they're a definite asset.

My source of information on this controversial subject is the much-freckled Samantha Eggar, a 22-year-old actress who will be seen in her first starring role when the new film "The Wild and The Willing" comes to the West End next week.

Sam, as she's called, has more freckles than a leopard has spots. And she doesn't mind them one single bit. Looking at the two pictures—Sam with freckles and Sam without—I think she is dead right.

Impact—and Charm

Sam-plus-freckles adds up to a face full of impact and peculiar charm. A face that strikes a chord of friendliness in women and responsiveness in men.

Sam-minus-freckles adds up, in my opinion, to a whole lot less. The **extraordinary** attractive girl becomes the **ordinary** attractive one. The personality has been flattened under a thick application of make-up.

What does Sam herself think about this?

"I've never minded having freckles," she told me. "Not even when I was at school.

"In fact, we were so innocent and unaware of ourselves and our appearance that I don't even think I knew I had them—or looked different from all the other girls."

Did she ever attempt to cover them up at night?

"Heavens, no," she said. "In fact, apart from mascara I never wear make-up at all. Anyway, men don't like it. They like to see actual skin."

Samantha — without freckles — "The personality has been flattened under thick make-up."

Fading

Why then, had she allowed herself to be turned in films into the stereotyped pretty girl with not a freckle in sight?

"The director had a problem," said Sam. "I had just come back from a holiday in Greece and I was covered all over my nose and cheekbones with these masses of freckles.

"He was afraid they'd fade a bit during the ten or twelve weeks' shooting time.

"So he thought the best thing to do was to tone them down before we started."

I said I thought it was a pity and I wondered why he hadn't decided to start shooting, freckles and all, and touch them in if they faded, rather than blot them out.

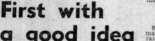

Glory

Sam said, tactfully, that maybe freckles looked like a rash or something in black and white photography.

I said maybe, but that the director who would make a picture in colour of Sam in all her freckled glory would probably be on to a very exciting new look that women might well want to imitate in the way that they imitated Bardot.

After talking to Sam I was left with the firm conviction that if you have a freckled face it is nothing to worry about.

In fact, I can even see the day when freckles are so desirable that the unfortunate, unfreckled faces will even want to buy false freckles.

First with a good idea

ANTOINE of Paris was one of the first of the big-name hairdressers of modern times.

He has now chalked up another "first."

For he has introduced into this country a handbag-size aerosol spray of hair lacquer, which can be refilled from a larger pack.

The noise it makes is a little alarming—like an angry soda-syphon—but it works smoothly and efficiently.

This refillable lacquer pack is a good idea. It has been on sale in America for years.

But it took a Frenchman to bring it over to Britain.

Available in two strengths—Salon Set Firm and Salon Set Soft. The large spray costs 10s. 6d. and the smaller handbag size, 4s. 11d

Samantha with freckles... She has more of them than a leopard has spots. And she doesn't mind one single bit.

Hollywood actress Samantha Eggar, a natural beauty, shows off her freckles and no, she didn't want to cover them under make-up when she became a film star. Freckles, she pointed out, were more like beauty spots than a blemish. And I agreed with her. In fact I predicted that those of us who didn't have them naturally would be adding fake ones. PS Twiggy tried the same effect a few years later.

DAILY MIRROR, *Tuesday, October 9, 1962* PAGE 15

TWO EXCITING NAMES IN THE MIRROR

DOSSIER ON THE FACES OF TOMORROW

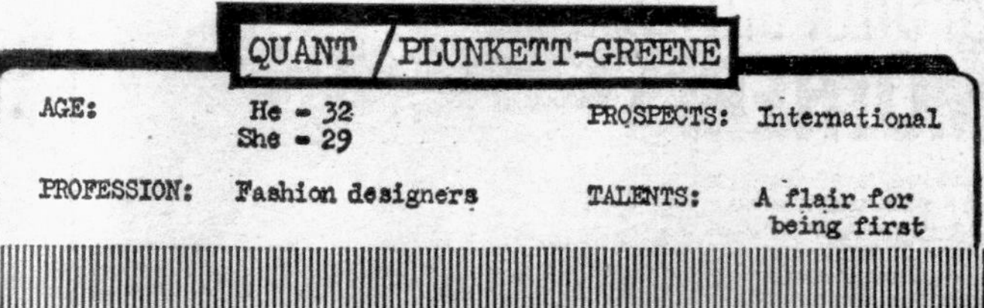

QUANT / PLUNKETT-GREENE

AGE:	He - 32 She - 29	PROSPECTS:	International
PROFESSION:	Fashion designers	TALENTS:	A flair for being first

Two with talent: Mary Quant and her husband, Alexander Plunkett-Greene, have given British fashion the biggest booster shot in years. Seen here in their Knightsbridge shop, "Bazaar," which caters for all those in search of way-out fashion.

The couple who gave a new meaning to the words 'with it'

by **FELICITY GREEN**

MARY QUANT is to fashion what Vostok Four is to air travel; what Hi-Fi is to sound.

Phrases like "way out" and "with it" might have been coined expressly to describe the chic Miss Quant and her gangling, elegant husband, Alexander Plunkett-Greene.

SHE is the daughter of a couple of Welsh schoolteachers ("My mother thinks our designs are lunatic"), HE is related to the Duke of Bedford and was a friend of Tony's.

Between them this talented twosome have given British fashion an unparalleled shot in the arm.

At the Top

Both as Chelsea in their outlook as the first Espresso coffee bar, the Plunkett-Greenes have arrived at the top of their chosen career via an art school training (both of them) a training in millinery design (her) a stint in fashion photography (him) running two restaurants (both) and a course on the flugelhorn (him).

Back in 1959 when they married, Mary couldn't buy the sort of clothes she liked.

So she made them. So they opened a shop to sell them. So they discovered all sorts of people liked the same sort of clothes.

Selling

So today they have two shops called "Bazaar" in London — one in Chelsea, one in Knightsbridge—and a wholesale business called "Mary Quant" — which sells to twenty stores all over Britain.

Bazaar clothes, it must be admitted, are not for everyone. They're for extroverts who want to be noticed. (Try being insignificant in an evening dress of black and white oilskin or black and beige horizontally striped knee-length shorts worn with long black socks.)

But Bazaar clothes sell. They sell to debs, they sell to models, they sell to girls who want to look like models and this, don't forget, includes quite a large proportion of the Young Ones today.

Meteoric

"I reckon," said Mary, "that we cater for about 5 per cent. of the women in this country." I reckoned that was quite a lot of women.

"Perhaps one day it will be 5 per cent. of the world," said Alexander happily. "That's a lot of women."

As they are now off on a trip to America to launch the Mary Quant look in a chain of 1,600 stores this is not such a farfetched idea after all.

Progress for Bazaar has been meteoric. Where was it going next?

"A couple of years ago we nearly sold out to one of the biggest wholesale firms," said Alexander. "There were all sorts of negotiations, but finally we thought we were worth double what they were prepared to pay."

"Now we're glad it didn't go through," said Mary. "We'd much rather belong to ourselves."

"If anyone else was running us," said Alexander, "we'd have to conform."

"Now we can please ourselves," said Mary.

"We don't have to add water to our designs," said Alexander.

I saw what they meant, as an undiluted Quant suit in purple wool lined with lame descended from the balcony dressing-room.

Who is the real brains behind this highly successful team?

Buffer

I'd say Alexander is the buffer between Mary's way-out talent and the necessity for operating on a sound, commercial basis.

He is also the ideas man with a nose for publicity unrivalled outside show business.

Do they ever disagree about fashion in general and the Quant look in particular?

"All the time," said Alexander.

"Who gives in?" I asked.

"I do," said Alexander. "All the time."

Miss Quant just smiled.

Mary Quant and her husband, Alexander Plunkett-Greene were two sides of the same stylish coin: uninhibited, entrepreneurial, mercurial talents. As the '60s ushered in a slew of power couples, it was Quant and Plunkett-Greene who showed a real flair for creating fashion firsts. Together they gave Chelsea its first fashion kick and put the King's Road on the style map. If Quant was called quaint, she didn't care, while her shop, Bazaar and its off-beat offerings were often called bizarre. Quant launched the Chelsea Look, the London Look, and made the Quant Look – way-out, with-it fashion – the in-thing around the world.

EXTRA!

For football starved fans

EXTRA!

For fashion conscious girls

HOW TO LOOK SMART IN THE QPR STEAM BATH..

THE fashions to be photographed had a distinctly football flavour about them. Club colours, wasp-striped jerseys, supporters' scarves.

It was nearly enough to bring tears to a football fan's eyes at a time when snow was virtually stopping play.

But, even if the actual games have been iced off, training still goes on. And that's how top model Grace Coddington came to be in the steam bath with the boys from Queen's Park Rangers.

Alec Stock, Queen's Park Rangers manager, commented: "You never know what footballers will do for a laugh. I was afraid someone was going to leap out of the bath. But the boys were great . . . perfect gentlemen."

The photographic session lasted two hours—"It took place during a serious training period," said the photographer, "and we did our best not to disrupt it"—finishing up with the steam bath shot on the right.

Coach Jimmy Andrews had no trouble getting the boys out for this session. He said: "I had my best ever turn out."

An unusual shot, to say the least.

Said the photographer: "Grace was marvellous—it takes a lot of guts for a girl to plunge into a room where there's a bathful of naked men."

Said Grace, whose cool professionalism had the boys on her side from the start: "I told them not to be nervous. I walk into bathfuls of footballers every day of my life!"

Said one of the boys: "I wonder what my wife will say about this lot!"

I know what footballers' wives and girl friends can be like. But don't worry, girls—trainer Alec Farmer was around to keep things in order.

VERDICT BY QPR ON THE FOOTBALL KICK IN FASHION: They liked it. They thought it was amusing.

MY VERDICT on QPR as fashion forecasters: They're on the ball.

FELICITY GREEN

Sporting commentary —by KEN JONES

Fashion point

The genuine thing for way-out followers of football fashions, above—jersey, scarf and socks, all in green and white—from the school uniform department of a London store. The jersey costs £2 17s. 6d.

Football note

Team talk in the dressing room . . . and model girl Grace poses while inside forward John Collins looks on. Why don't QPR make her a mascot? They were beaten 5—0 at Swindon on Saturday.

DAILY MIRROR, Monday, January 14, 1963 PAGE 13

Fashion point

How authentic can a fashion be? This jumper suit (above) in two shades of blue stripes could fool a footballer at fifty yards. Made by Wallis Shops, it costs 7½ gns.

In this sort of weather two sweaters are not only good fashion—they're good sense, too. Seen left, Grace in a black Shetland sweater edged in mustard and white worn over a mustard sweater with a polo neck. Both by John Laing, 4½ gns and 3½ gns. Tweed skirt by Gor-Ray, £3 10s.

Football note

After training, it's into the bath for the Q P R team—and to pose for the fashion picture extraordinary, above.

On the left, Sheffield Wednesday and England goalkeeper Ron Springett—who trains with Q P R—is not showing his International form. He hasn't got his eye on the ball—or the girl.

This is a typically unusual *Daily Mirror* '60s fashion picture. The clothes are certainly there, but the location is the Queen's Park Rangers football ground and their steam bath and the supporting cast, to say the least, is an unlikely one. The model, Grace Coddington – currently Creative Director of American *Vogue* – and in the steambath, the whole cast of the QPR football team. Everyone was having a good time. Fashion was fun in the '60s. I had decided that, yes, fashion is a serious business, but fashion photographs pre-'60s had mostly been static images captured in the same static manner. My aim for fashion in the *Daily Mirror* was to make it fun and make it appeal to both men and women. This one surely did the trick.

LAST EDITION ONLY

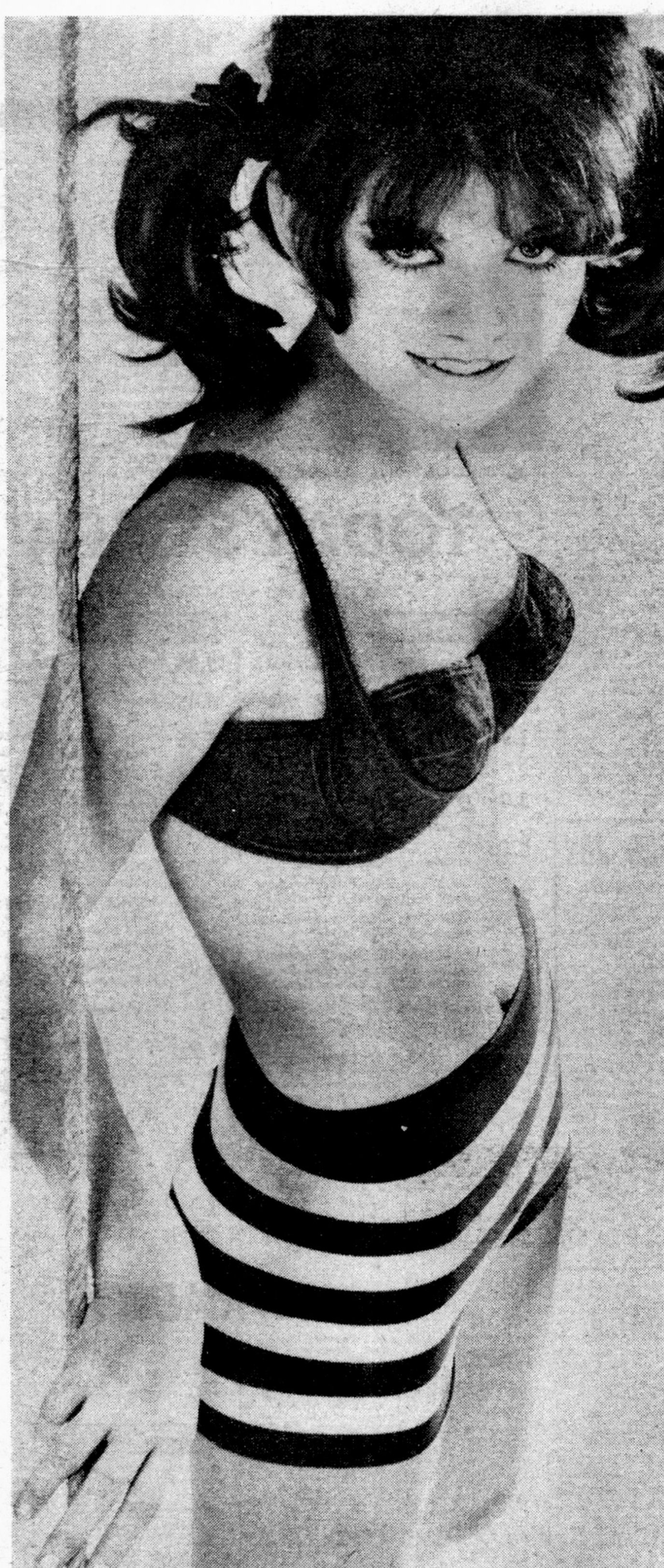

Right now, chic little Parisiennes are snapping up undies like these. The navy bra (it's the Rage colour) and the sailor-striped pantie girdle follow Dior's rounded little-girl shape.

DIOR DAY IN PARIS

THE LITTLE GIRL LOOK THAT WILL DRIVE BOYS MAD

Paris, Thursday.

TODAY is D for Dior Day in Paris and there's no doubt that Dior is still the most familiar name in the fashion world.

Today's collection by Dior's designer Marc Bohan could have been inspired by only one female—Marc's eight-year-old daughter Marie-Anne.

In common with most other women I adore young-looking clothes but I have a sneaking suspicion that the chaps who do the designing are taking us for a tiny ride.

Doll

Some of the prettiest clothes at today's show would look too young even on a twelve-year-old.

In fact, if we go on at this rate we'll all be in nappies and safety pins before we can say gripe water.

The mannequin who did the most justice to the adorable Dior Little Doll look was Muriel, a fair-haired twenty-year-old whose statistics can't be a fraction more vital than 29in. top and bottom (I just can't bring myself to call it a bust).

She looked picture-book pretty in clothes which could have stepped straight out of the school outfitting department.

She wore little high-necked navy shifts with no sleeves to hide her fragile arms.

Bright

Over these dresses she wore brightly coloured blazer jackets in school house colours like emerald, yellow or rosy red.

Her narrow top coat only needed a badge on the top pocket for everybody in the audience to shout "Up the Lower Fourth!"

All her day clothes had the new Dior sleeve which is going to be copied by a thousand on-the-ball manufacturers from Tooting to Toronto.

It looks like a cross between a puff sleeve and a leg-of-mutton with a tiny Tarzan's shoulder muscle thrown in.

The Dior hats added their twopennyworth to the schoolgirl image. Big back-of-the-head Gigi boaters, muffin berets and big brimmed Bretons.

Strap

One big Breton in white cotton even had a strap under the chin to stop those nasty boys at the school over the road from pulling it off on the way home.

Most newsworthy hat of all was a tiny Andy Capp in striped silk worn back to front on the back of the head.

I tried it on and took it off hurriedly when the salesgirl said, "That would be £30. madam."

DOES the Dior girl ever grow up? Yes, she does and after dark leads a rather interesting double life

She's either behaving like the dreamiest deb ever in layers of white organdie with frilly skirts, ribbon-tied waist and flowers in her hair.

Or else she's done up to the nines in slinky black crepe with her back bared to the waist in a way that would certainly rock the most shockproof headmistress.

Plunge

What the headmistress would say about a cerise cocktail dress that plunges in front to BELOW waist level with only a brooch between neck and navel to hold things together is impossible to imagine.

Expulsion would seem inevitable.

VERDICT ON DIOR: Little Girl Dresses to drive Little Boys Wild.

The Little Girl Look from Dior . . . Drawing by MARJORIE PROOPS.

DAILY MIRROR, Monday, February 11, 1963 PAGE 11

With summer in mind

FASHION PREVIEW by FELICITY GREEN

THIS is the Bazaar Look for the beaches in 1963.

Like all the previous Bazaar Looks that have burst on us in the past five years, it's way-out, with-it, kookie, zany, beat, and all the other adjectives that have been used to describe the clothes designed by the talented young Mary Quant.

And, like all the previous Bazaar Looks, it will influence our Rag Trade to an extent that even Paris has a job to rival.

Thousands of girls on a limited budget will wear thousands of Bazaar copies turned out by the wholesale dress trade who know that as Quant thinks, so think Britain's Young Ones.

Quant ideas for Summer '63 include a dramatic use of non-colour. White, black and beige are mixed with the dazzle of a pools permutation. But though the colours are negatively neutral, the clothes as always are aggressively positive.

Perennial

Tunics, cheongsam-slit up the side, shift dresses, long hip-hugging pants, floppy hats, cheeky caps, knee-length shorts—these are the hallmarks of this season's Bazaar Look. And the Bazaar Look is becoming, in its way, as hardy a perennial as the Chanel Look.

BAZAAR '63 ITEMS PICTURED . . . Right: Tunic dress in heavy white cotton worn over black knee-length shorts. Dress £6 12s. 6d. Shorts £4 17s. 6d.

Left: Beige and white Plunketts (Mary Quant's husband and partner in Bazaar is Alexander Plunkett-Greene) worn with a black sleeveless high-necked top. Plunketts £6 12s. 6d. Top £4 7s. 6d. The cap— "far too expensive and we don't expect to sell many" —costs 7 gns.

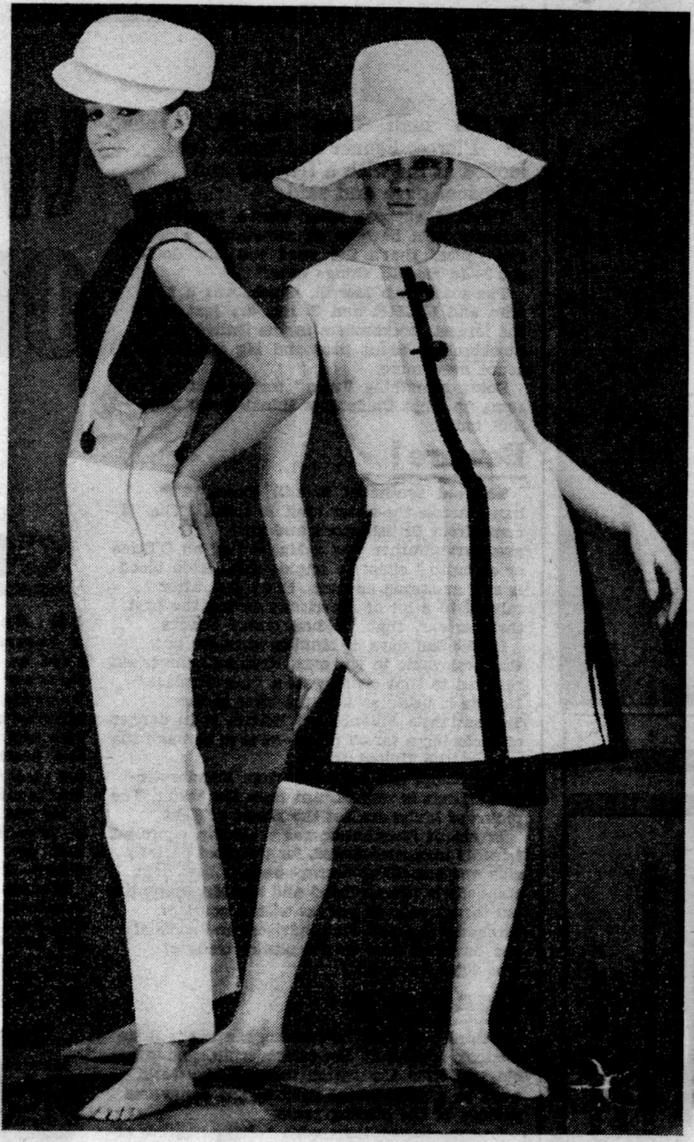

Picture by JOHN FRENCH

Personal verdict —by Mary Quant who designed the clothes

❛Clothes are a joke; clothes are impact; clothes are escapist.

Blue jeans with a well-worn highlight down the thigh are more sexually attractive than mink.

My formula for fashion: See something new, try it, and as soon as you're used to it, try something newer.

My clothes are stylish but NOT beat.

Most of my customers are between thirty and fifty.❜

Personal verdict—of 5 men

SOME people love 'em; some people hate 'em. But no one can ignore them.

JOE BROWN, 21, pop star, looking at the outfits photographed here, said:

"Don't like the long knicker-type things on the right. Like the trousers. But neither of the outfits seems sexy to me. They'd look ridiculous down at old Southend."

WILLIAM BROWN, 15, messenger from Abbey Wood, Kent: "I don't like the outfit on the right with the big hat. It looks silly. Don't mind the trousers outfit. It's sort of way-out and I like the cap. Crazy!"

DAVID FROST, 23, compere of TV's TWTWTW programme: "A load of irrelevant rubbish. Don't like the wilted geranium-type hat and also don't like the bare knees. If you are going to show knees, then you must also show the thighs."

SAM SMITH, 35, taxi-driver of Clapton, London: "Fabulous! I think these are stunning outfits. Especially the one on the left."

Forecast?

JAMES LAVER, 63, fashion historian: "I think these clothes are very attractive. The black and white shows a tremendous sense of chic. They are so covered up for beach clothes, it could well be a forecast that we will soon lose our brown-all-over complex."

These two pictures tell a dramatic story of how the new style of fashion photography brought black and white drama to the previously grey picture pages of newspapers. Perhaps I deliberately chose clothes in these dramatic black and white designs to make a maximum impact. But then boldness and drama were what the '60s fashions were all about. Daughters no longer wanted to look like mum and mum wanted to dress like her daughter – and designer Mary Quant's clothes were leading the pack. These dungarees and the tunic dress over shorts caused a near riot when they were first shown in Quant's newly-important King's Road shop. What I thought was needed was a man's eye view of this new radical look. So I asked a cross-section of men, from pop star Joe Brown and messenger William Brown to broadcaster David Frost, taxi-driver Sam Smith and fashion historian James Laver. These unlikely fashion commentators came out with some contradictory views – David Frost thought Quant's Bazaar looks were "irrelevant rubbish", Clapham taxi-driver Sam Smith thought they were "fabulous"!

JOHN FRENCH

The photographer who brought glossy magazine quality to newspapers

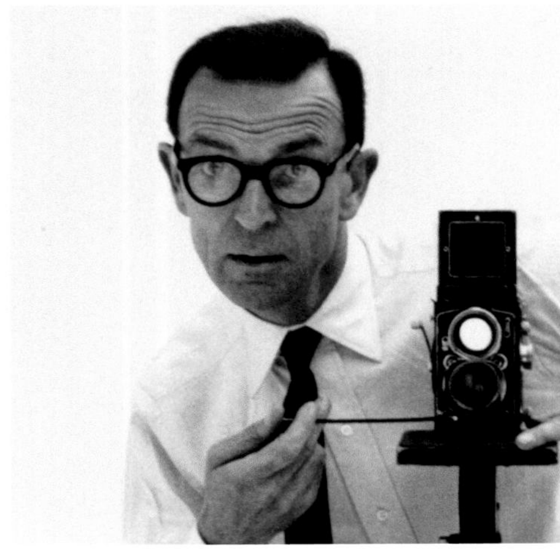

John French when I first knew him had a large white car, which I thought was awful. On the first occasion that I had the cheek and courage to ask him why he had such a vulgar car he replied, "It always comes in handy as a reflector of the light!"

Reflected light is the key to John's pictures. He told me he discovered it in Positano where he spent a great deal of his life. The light in Positano moves around from one white wall to another, eliminating all dark shadows, and turning the deepest of colours into pastel shades. John reconstructed this effect in his studio by bouncing a battery of lights off white boards placed around his models, burning out all the shadows, eliminating any blemishes from the girls' faces, and all the wrinkles from the dresses, making the girls and the frock designer very happy.

John liked his models to be ladies. He once sent a famous model home because she came to the studio wearing jeans. He would have quite a problem today, but it does show how much attitudes have changed. John was also changing. I asked him why he had given me the job as one of his assistants because I knew that he knew I was lying when I went for an interview and told him I knew about strobe light and how to load 10 x 8 slides. The reason I got the job was that he thought it was amusing the way I dressed in jeans and a black leather jacket.

John had style and a great sense of humour, the two things that always seemed to go together. John taught me many things, not particularly about photography, but how to move in life, more important than F stops or how to load a 10 x 8 slide for which I shall always be in his debt. Wherever John is now, you can be sure that he is basking in reflected light.

DAVID BAILEY 1984

FELICITY ON JOHN

Take a good look at the picture on the right... you're looking at a revolution that took place in fashion journalism. Photographer John French changed newspaper fashion pages with the same flash, bang, wallop that Mary Quant changed skirt lengths.

Those dramatic, simple black and white fashion images from the *Daily Mirror* pages in February 1963 are typical of a totally new standard of glamour and impact from the previously smudgy grey newspaper fashion pages.

John French knew nothing of technology. He did it all in his all-white studio with a bank of blindingly bright white lights reflecting on walls of white paper. On hand to load the camera came a string of talented assistants, including David Bailey, Terence Donovan, Brian Duffy and John Adriaan, all of whom became stellar photographers in their own right, and *Mirror* contributors in the '60s.

In those swinging '60s, every model loved working for John French. With his special magic he made each one feel special. Not only in the way she looked, but how she felt under those relentless lights that were the magical ingredient of his signature images. John's elegant charm also helped that magic. When the background and model were ready, Mr French entered centre stage, demonstrated to one of the swinging '60s top models precisely how he wanted her to stand, exited and let his assistant take the picture. He gave the model stage directions like a director gave to an actor. "Feel you have a string coming out of the top of your head, which reaches for the ceiling" he suggested – and immediately she grew three inches taller.

Under John French's direction, the previously anonymous model girls became famous personalities – among the starry best-known were Barbara Goalen, Anne Gunning, and Jean Dawnay – some of whom found fame, fortune and even a title. In the '60s came Jean Shrimpton, Tania Mallett, Celia Hammond, Paulene Stone and Grace Coddington, and all of them starred in the *Mirror*.

John French died in 1966, but today, almost fifty years later, his stunning fashion images remain a testament to his graphic fashion genius. As John himself once observed: "The best pictures are made when there's mutual understanding. It's really a flirtation between the girl, the camera, and the photographer."

Once upon a time fashion pictures in newspapers were sludge-coloured. Then came John French and it was as though he had switched the lights on illuminating these Mary Quant outfits

THE MOST EXPENSIVE C

It's the gentle London Line, plus handmad

by

FELICITY GREEN

Woman's Editor of the Daily Mirror

TODAY, for the first time, that top snob little group, the Incorporated Society of London Fashion Designers, are prepared to release to the world the secrets of their new spring styles.

The Society has eleven members. Seen here are outfits from seven of the more adventurous.

None of them, you will agree, would knock your eye out at twenty paces.

They whisper rather than scream of their haute couture origins.

And that, of course, is their strength, as well as their weakness, depending on what you want from your clothes.

Women who want excitement in their clothes don't dress in the London Line.

If they're rich they go to Paris.

Copies

If they're not, they go to Bazaar. Or to the wholesalers who copy both Paris and Bazaar in roughly equal proportions.

But since the Inc. Soc., as they're called, is doing very nicely thank you there must be enough rich and satisfied customers around to keep them all in business.

Are they, perhaps, women with difficult figures who can't buy ready-mades?

No, says John Cavanagh, one of the cleverest of the Group—he has been chosen by Princess Alexandra to make her wedding dress.

"It's not a question of having a 'difficult' figure. Some of my customers have exquisite figures—like the Duchess of Kent. There's no doubt that a woman feels **BETTER** in an outfit that is made for her."

Exclusives

Are they, then, "older" women, more interested in quality than fashion?

No, says Victor Stiebel. "I am designing for women from thirty to fifty, who expect beautifully - made clothes and don't want to see them in the stores."

There's a clue there. A successful wholesaler will fill the stores with thousands of copies of a number.

A couturier may make five—and he'll take a bit of trouble to see that great friends, or great enemies, don't choose the same dress.

What do they get for their money, the socialites, the tycoons' wives, the landed gentry and their deb daughters who may spend £1,000 in one go on four outfits for Ascot?

They get pure silk at £15 a yard. They get woollens imported at even more. They get linings in pure silk. They get hand-stitching.

Quality

They get hand-made buttons and belts. They get pop-studs covered in pure silk They get zip fasteners sewn in by hand.

They get quality with a big Q.

If they are choosey, they can get gentle fashion, too. Fashion that may not shake the world—but at least it won't look ridiculously out of date at next year's Ascot.

And even ladies who spend money at the couture rate must care a bit about that.

TOTAL VALUE OF THIS BUMPER FASHION BUNDLE

PICTURE BY JOHN FRENCH

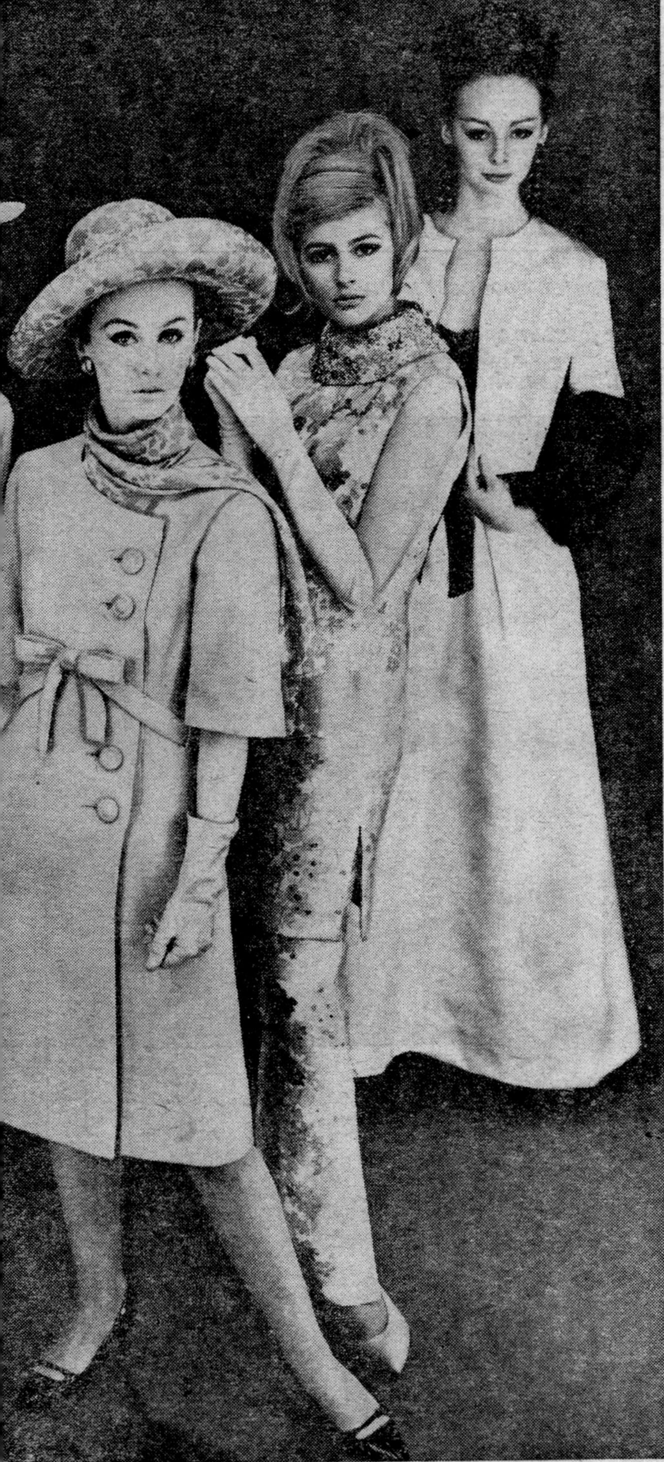

DAILY MIRROR, *Thursday, February 21, 1963* PAGE 13

OTHES IN BRITAIN

uttons and silk on the poppers

SHOWN here, left, just a sample selection of the outfits couture client Mrs. X might order for herself this spring.

Left to right: A beige and black tunic over black chemise dress by Michael, considered to be the most way-out of the group. Black dress and jacket by Hardy Amies. Red basket-weave two-piece by Mattli. Pale green suit by Cavanagh. Coral wool coat by Ronald Paterson. Printed silk evening dress by Hartnell. Black and white ball gown and jacket by Victor Stiebel.

Nerve!

How does this Mrs. X go about getting herself dressed by a member of Britain's top fashion team?

She gets an invitation to see the collection. (She has a friend who is a client, or, if she has enough nerve and money, just rings up and asks.)

She is given a programme, watches about sixty outfits and puts an "x" against the ones she fancies. (Some houses give the clothes numbers, some give fancy names—"Bonjour Twistesse," "Morning Glory," "Dinner with Auntie," etc.)

When the show's over she finds a saleswoman who's called a vendeuse and makes a date to view close-up, and, if she's the right model size, try on the clothes.

Statistics

At the first date she chooses the colour and has her measurements taken—all forty of them, some of which she didn't even know she had.

A first fitting comes a week later with, usually, a gent fitter for the jacket or the coat, and a lady fitter for the skirt.

Another fitting another week later to perfect the effect.

Another fitting another week later to improve the perfection.

And that should be it. But if it isn't, the fittings go on until it is.

And that's why it not only takes money to dress at the top houses. It takes time, too.

ABOUT £1,000

Every picture tells a story and this picture tells a story about money and clothes. Then and Now. The total cost of all the clothes shown here – on February 27, 1963, was £1,000. These clothes were the latest designs from the members of the prestigious Incorporated Society of London Fashion Designers. This was expensive stuff – precious fabrics, pure silk linings, handmade buttons, etc, etc. The fashions appealed to the rich and famous, royalty, society, the landed gentry and the wives of tycoons. And their daughters! They all wanted made-to-measure fit and a degree of exclusivity. Though on one preferably forgettable occasion, two titled ladies appeared at the same party in the same dress. Catastrophe! As Fashion Editor of the *Daily Mirror* in the '60s I felt that these designers, talented though they may be, didn't number many *Daily Mirror* readers among their customers, so their exclusive designs rarely appeared on my pages. This, however, was an exception worthy of note.

PARIS REPORT
* by *
FELICITY GREEN

Of all the dresses shown in Par
this is the one we'll be wearing

SHIFTY, that's the word for The Dress this season. Grand-daughter of the sack and second cousin to the gym-slip, it promises to be the one dress that no one can do without this summer.

In Paris it turned up in every fabric from a businesslike worsted to a floating chiffon.

A lot of shapeless dresses are going to be called Shifts this summer so it's just as well to know how to spot the real McCoy.

A Sixty-three Shift has cut-away armholes. It has no collar, or a flat Eton shape under which to tie a pussy-cat bow.

A Sixty-three Shift has **SHAPE** however subtle it may be. It fits gently over the bust, even more gently through the waist and comes to rest li on the hips.

As for length, it skims knees—just!

If you're planning an add to your wardrobe this Sp into-Summer, think Shiftly.

CLOSE UP:

Today a look at the new details

Talking Point — Dior's new Puff-top sleeve.

The coat that's almost Shifty. By St. Laurent.

The High-line suit with a narrow belt. Heim.

For the bold . .

The Less Front Dress by Michel Goma.

The Less Back Dress. By Laroche.

The Kite Line, a suit by Nina Ricci

The less dress look

EVERY season, some Paris designer takes his scissors and splits a neckline to the navel.

This season is remarkable only for the unanimity with which the top designers exposed their model girls' all.

Will the "less-dress" look catch on? Among the exhibitionist few, yes, it looks as though it will. Plunges are already selling in surprising quantities.

ABOVE, the Lessest-Dress of All by Nina Ricci. A bra-top cocktail dress in black silk.

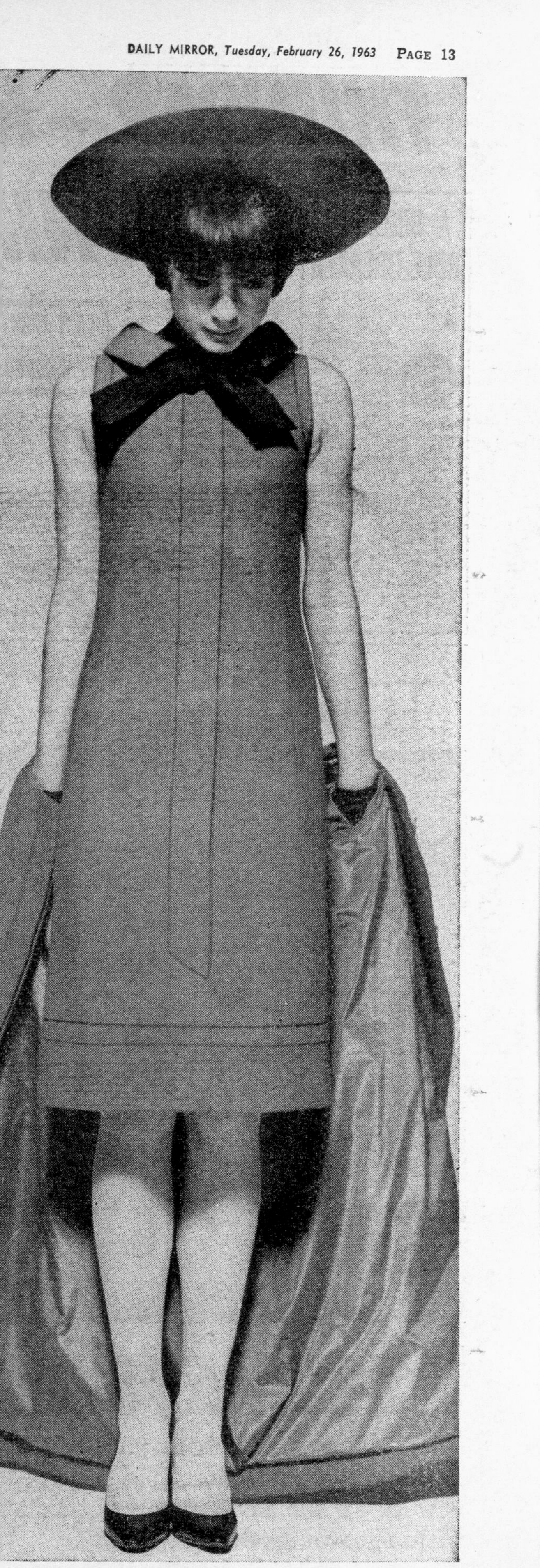
DAILY MIRROR, Tuesday, February 26, 1963 PAGE 13

Success Story No. 1—the Dior sleeveless shift in wool.

Don't bother to look at any picture on these two pages other than the one on the immediate left. It appeared in the *Daily Mirror* on 26 February 1963 and it was simply a quiet-looking sensation and the one we all chose to wear. It had many names to start with. At first we called it Shifty. I also described it as second cousin to The Sack, but in fact, it was much more subtle than that. The Shift was designed by Dior and it became The '60s Shape that swept the fashion-conscious Western world. International fashion centres knew a good thing when they saw it – so did women. The Shift flattered those of us who didn't have a perfect shape. The Shift could easily be copied by eagle-eyed manufacturers who saw a style that could be copied with a minimum of cost. The Shift has varied a little through the decades, but it's still with us fifty-odd years later.

FELICITY GREEN

THINGS HAVE TOUGHENED UP IN

SO you think it's a cinch to be a model nowadays? You think that all that's needed to rake in those fabulous salaries is a photogenic face, the necessary concave shape, and the ability to look at the camera as though it were a lecherous male.

Well, sorry, you're out of date. To be a Top Model today it helps to be a sort of cross between an athlete and a film stunt man . . . to take in your stride such feats as jumping fully clothed into Chelsea swimming pool.

You don't fancy it?

Well, what about riding a large white horse alongside the Life Guards down Constitution Hill . . . in a bathing suit?

You'd rather not?

High fashion—high up. Model Jill Kennington airborne in black chiffon alongside Queen Victoria's statue, Blackfriars Bridge, London.

All the best swimsuits are red, white and blue this year.

The hectic world o

Dizzy

Pity. Well, perhaps you wouldn't mind posing for some glamorous fashion shots, balancing sixty feet up in the air on a dear little platform the width of your wrist. In new slippery-soled shoes.

The mere thought of it makes you feel dizzy?

Me, too. Which proves, I suppose, that modelling today is not for the faint hearts, among which please do include me in.

All the above-mentioned feats, however, have been tackled with determination, if not pleasure by one of today's leading model girls, Jill Kennington.

Zany

And if you don't believe me, look closely at the pictures on this page and there she is, doing the lot.

Jill is typical of the Top Model, '63 version.

She's 5ft. 8in., 34-23-35, may look like a waif suffering just the teeniest bit from malnutrition, but give her a really zany job and she's off, prepared to swing from her teeth if asked.

Did she get danger money, I asked her, over and above the normal three-guineas-an-hour fee?

No, she didn't, and as far as she was concerned she didn't want it.

When models start asking for danger money, or mucky money or wet money or cold money, that was the end of professional pride as far as she was concerned.

'Gives'

"I don't mind doing anything crazy as long as I feel it's going to produce a marvellous, exciting picture," she assured me, delicately nibbling an asparagus tip.

"The thing about Jill," said photographer John Cowan, who took all the pictures of Jill shown here, "she's a **REAL** professional. When you want a certain sort of picture, Jill just gives and gives and gives."

Jill lowered her false lashes modestly.

Changed

Thinking of Jill's ability to give and give and give, I reflected how times have changed in the modelling business.

Once upon a time, when Barbara Goalen was Queen Bee, all a model had to do to reach the top—and sometimes catch a peer on the way up—was to lean against a white background, suck in her cheeks, and look haughtily, devastatingly gorgeous. In white gloves that were usually described as pristine.

Today's Give-Girl is as different from that hot-house orchid as a circus artist is from a film star.

Nerve

And if any young and attractive girl today has ambitions in the modelling world she had better have a head for heights, know how to handle a horse, and be prepared to dive in the deep end fully clothed.

There must be a less nerve-shattering way to earn a fortune.

DAILY MIRROR, Wednesday, May 29, 1963 PAGE 19

HOT-HOUSE OF FASHION

patriotic atmosphere supplied by the Guards.

Swimsuit by Marks & Spencer, 39s. 11d.

a photogenic blonde . .

E DRESS
AT LOOKS
T . .
TS WET

w rave fashion
is called cire
nounced seeray—
s as shiny and wet-
g as a seal. Even
dry. See left.
make it look even
r, Jill took a
r into Chelsea
ning baths.
ght.
ther model, even
game, performed
ame feat—and she
n't even swim.
is dress will soon
the shops at
9 gns. By
brand.

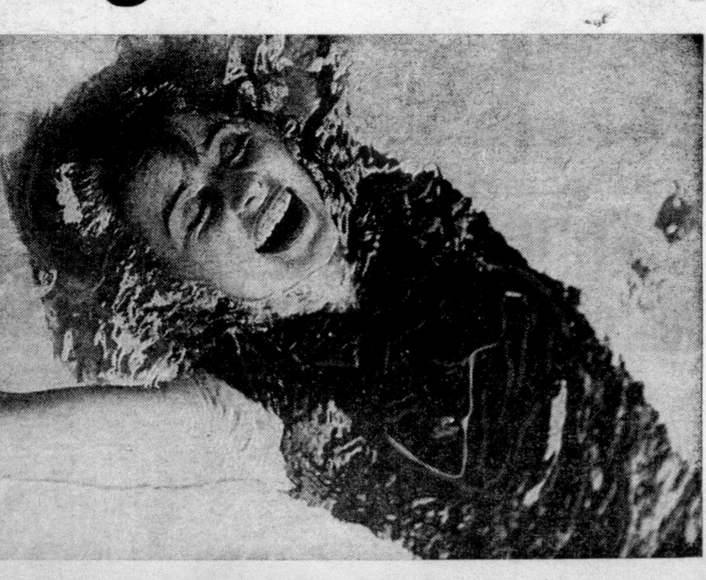

Photographer John Cowan was a hard taskmaster putting his muse and model, Jill Kennington through some highly unusual challenges that were definitely over and above the normal remit of a fashion model. Cowan, who said goodbye to the static studio shot, was part of a new generation of photographers who were changing the status quo. How was he able to accomplish this? For a start there were the edgy outside locations. Then there were the demanding action shots, which required camera skills on his part and agility, courage and good humour from Jill. Some of their more notable triumphs included Jill diving fully dressed into a swimming pool, climbing up alongside Queen Victoria's statue on Battersea Bridge and riding bareback in a swimsuit in front of the Life Guards down Constitution Hill. As I said at the time, there must be a less exhausting way for a model girl to earn a living.

What happens when a photogr
shoot some swimsuits outdoor

—They go to the local instead..

THE time: One morning this week.

The place: A fashion photographer's studio in Kensington.

The job: To take two model girls off to the nearest beach and shoot some pictures showing what's new in bikini-land.

Switch

But it rained. Showers alternated with downpours and the day looked like being a dead loss.

However, fashion photographers are nothing if not resourceful, so the location was quickly switched.

To the local.

There, the sensation caused by the appearance of one photographer and party lasted two minutes flat after which time everything reverted to normal.

Stoics

One gent wondered idly what his wife would say while the rest went back to their beer and the card game in hand.

This scene couldn't possibly take place in Paris, would never happen in Rome and would be downright unthinkable in New York.

British stoicism, it's marvellous.

Her suit may be trumps but the locals in the local concentrate on the game. And, really, it wasn't strip poker. Model Finola wears a red, white and blue bikini which costs 21s. and comes from Marks and Spencer.

DAILY MIRROR, Wednesday, April 3, 1963 PAGE 17

...her plans to ...nd it rains?

The French bikini modelled by Jill is brief. So is the interest displayed by stoic locals intent on their game of cards. The suit, for those who want to know, is in black and white cotton, costs 59s., and comes from Galeries Lafayette, London, W.1.

By Felicity Green • Pictures by John Cowan

These *Mirror* picture are examples of what happens when there's a special relaxed relationship between a brilliant and imaginative photographer like John Cowan and his models; seen here, near left his derring-do model muse, Jill Kennington and far left model Finola. So let's forget the carefully posed studio stuff and move elsewhere. This was the photographic freedom that was born in the Swinging '60s. If it rains, who cares? If we can't go to the beach, let's go to a pub. The locations on offer to the freedom-focused photographers could include everywhere from stately homes to the nearby docks. The controlled studio lighting was replaced by grey rainy days or brilliant cruelly harsh overhead sunshine. This was the real stuff, impulsive, on-the-day opportunism. This three-way relationship between the photographer, the models and the fashion editor back at the office resulted in the wonderful casual shots that arrived on the *Mirror* fashion pages in the '60s.

JILL KENNINGTON ON JOHN COWAN

The daring model muse on the action photographer who brought drama to fashion

When I arrived in London in the early '60s, I was a breath of fresh air. Life was so exciting and my energies were put to very good use when I teamed up to work with photographer John Cowan from early in my career. I had a close working relationship with John. Somehow it was always exciting. I felt from the start I could be myself, plus whatever ingredient was needed for the shoot. Amazingly, our work has become iconic and curiously hasn't dated. All the years I worked with him, John never tripped or fell though he clambered anywhere, including onto his Land Rover roof, to achieve a great angle. Luckily, I was born a mountain goat and many photographic adventures involved jumping or hanging off buildings.

Throughout the decade we achieved some highly original images, photographs in their own right that just happened to be fashion pages. Essential was the collaboration of a good fashion editor who, having shown us the clothes, was able to run with an idea, always allowing our creative input. Felicity Green at the *Mirror* was great to work with and John and I created some wonderful original work.

I was of the new wave – and all the boundaries had to be broken. One shoot, which I think was terrific, was bikinis for the *Mirror*. There was no budget to take us to the South Seas. It was cold, raining and winter in London. We were going to Chiswick, but filthy weather stopped us. John's Land Rover, which was often the dressing room, had make-up, the bikinis and photographic equipment, girls, assistant and fashion editor steaming in it. In desperation, we pulled over in the King's Road, Chelsea, at World's End and went to the pub for a re-think and it occurred to John, given permission, we could use this wonderful old pub, all wood panels and mirrors, as our location. Whose idea was it to stand on the tables? I don't remember! However, this is what happened. These workmen were easily bribed with pints of beer, not to look, to carry on talking to each other. So I remember doing my usual – only working for John, not taking notice outside that. There is a frisson about these pictures, free and abandoned and joyful in an unlikely setting and I'm happy to say we achieved high-voltage pictures.

"I was of the new wave – and all fashion boundaries had to be broken"

FELICITY ON JILL & JOHN

Fashion photography in the '60s fell in love with sexuality. Gone were the carefully-posed carefully-made up models of the past. The '60s girls were raunchy, but romantic, and their poses were nothing if not provocative.

The romantic relationships that developed between top models and the famous photographers made headline news and brought a whole new feel to fashion reportage. The romance between David Bailey, henceforth known as Bailey, and model Jean Shrimpton, known as The Shrimp, was the stuff of film star fame. Every girl wanted to look like his photographic muse. The Shrimp had hairdressers round the world straightening previously curly hair. The Bailey/Shrimpton trip to New York took the love story into the international fame stratosphere and the world was sad when the romance disintegrated and Shrimpton began a new romance with actor Terence Stamp.

Another unique twosome was the five-star fashion photographer Terry Donovan who teamed up with animal-loving, ladylike Celia Hammond – these pictures were deeply romantic, but static. But when model Jill Kennington and photographer John Cowan started to work together in the early '60s, a whole new world of almost acrobatic outdoor fashion photography came about. Jill leapt, dived, swam, rode, climbed stately monuments and frequently appeared to be taking her life in her hands as John set up these dramatic pictures and took those amazing shots. As a fashion editor determined to make fashion both fun and different, this combination was like gold dust. These pictures capture the feel of the daring '60s. We, the readers, loved it and we still do – as we ponder what a helluva long way all this derring-do was from the latterday world of glamorous supermodel Linda Evangelista, who famously said she wouldn't get out of bed for less than $10,000 a day!

Model Jill Kennington leaping around on the tabletop in a quiet King's Road pub and declaring war on the static posed fashion picture

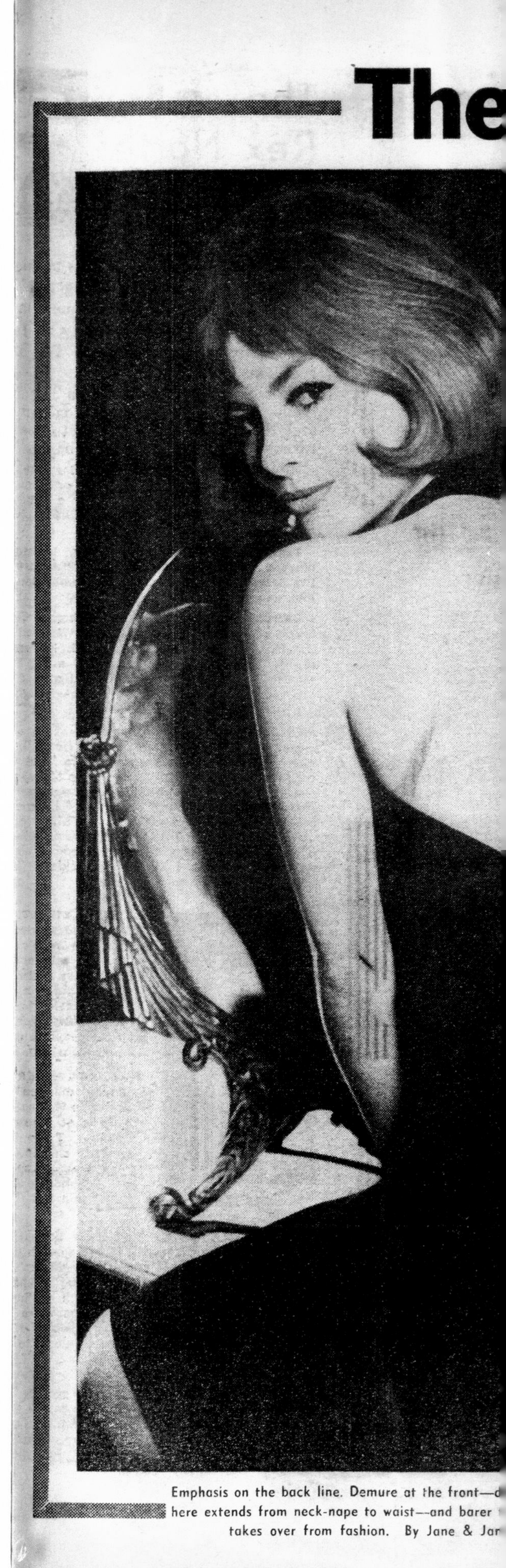

Emphasis on the back line. Demure at the front—d
here extends from neck-nape to waist—and barer
takes over from fashion. By Jane & Jar

Confession: the day after this page appeared in the *Daily Mirror* on Monday 24 June 1963, I got a letter of complaint from a male reader. "Dear Miss Green, there is no such word as Erogenic in the English language. The word, Miss Green, is erogenous." Yes, dear reader, I know this, but I thought erogenic sounded more modern, more technological. I would have written a letter combining my excuse with a semi-apology, but he didn't give me his address. Proof – a lot of men read the *Mirror*'s fashion pages. Specially ones that look like this.

shifting erogenic* zone

OR, WHERE IS THE EMPHASIS ON SEX-APPEAL TODAY?

FASHION PRESENTED BY FELICITY GREEN

THE idea that the female form divine needs the help of fashion to achieve the maximum impact is as old as the female herself.

Eve, as she reached for a fig leaf (do you have one in dark green in my size?), discovered the importance of the erogenic zone, and thus was the fashion business born.

CHOICE

How to reveal or to conceal just enough to arouse interest has been a fashion problem through the ages and it's a wise woman who manages to do sufficient of both with one well-chosen garment.

Today the crop of "erogenic zone" fashions is positively bewildering, but most can be traced back to the devastating effect Miss Lana Turner had when she first donned a white sweater. A tight, white sweater.

The bra business boomed, the knitwear industry enjoyed a new prosperity—and the age of the bosom was born.

WAISTS

Then came waists, a handspan above the burgeoning hips of Mr. Dior's New Look, which was to the wartime square-suited ladies what a set of seven veils would be to a destitute stripper. Manna from heaven.

BUT erogenic zones shift with the times and bosoms and waists haven't always had it their own way.

The 20's girl lived in the age when the erogenic zone chosen for emphasis by the fashion designers began at knee-level and worked its way down over curvy calves to a neatly-turned ankle.

Legs were in, bosoms were out—flattened out—by a bra which looked like a bandage and Jayne Mansfield would have made a fortune in a sideshow. Or frontshow.

Further back in the joint saga of fashion and sex-appeal, there were the Edwardians who loved a generous expanse of gleaming white shoulder and bosom while the Victorians, prudish at the neckline, were often bustle-happy at the back. (It didn't exactly **reveal,** but it certainly **suggested.**)

Then there were those sex-boxes of the 1800's, the damped-down ladies who wore chiffon and dunked themselves in water to get that clinging look. (So, when you think about it, today's trousered teenagers sitting in the bath, waiting for their jeans to shrink, are really not on to anything new).

UNTIL today the rules were clear. One age—one erogenic zone emphasised by current fashion.

Now the fashion designers are caught up in a sexy whirl where modesty plays second fiddle to impact.

Necklines plunge to new depths, armholes scoop down to the waist, and pinafore dresses are worn minus the other half. (Look, mummy, no blouse!)

In any one shop, on any one rail, a canny customer can find backless dresses, well-nigh frontless dresses, dresses slit to the thigh, dresses with peekaboo cut-outs scattered around like holes in a Gruyere cheese.

TREND

And as for bathing suits after the bikini, what?

Already an American swimwear firm is predicting a bottoms-only trend for the beach to allow for that all-over tan.

It seems inevitable, the way things are going at the moment, that clothes will soon be at such a minimum level that the lowest necklines will meet the highest hemlines at half-way mark and we'll all be back to fig-leaves.

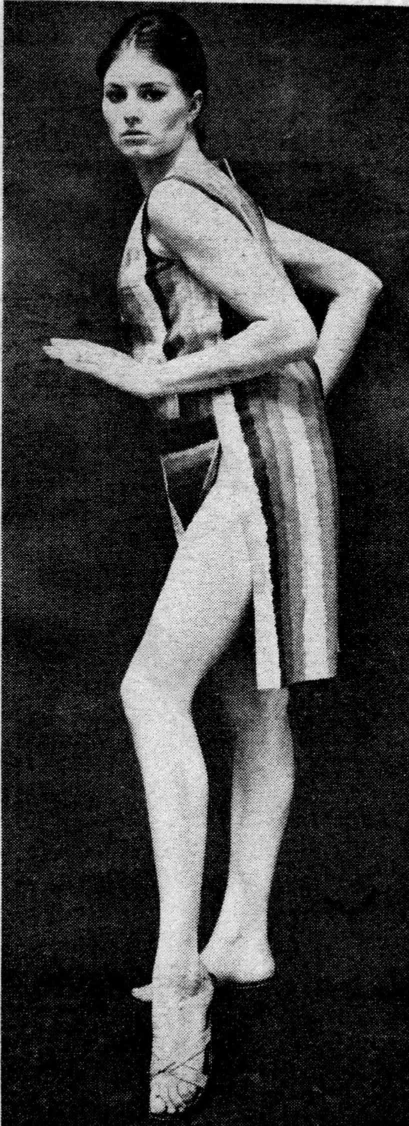

Emphasis on the leg line. Short skirts, tight skirts, split skirts. They all draw attention to a pair of shapely legs. Shapely legs here, exposed to thigh level in a split-side beach shift in multi-coloured cotton stripes. 7 gns. including matching top and shorts. By Fredrica.

Emphasis on the neck line. Down, down and even further down go the neck lines of the Sixties encouraged in the descent by enthusiastic Paris designers who put publicity-value before modesty. Seen here the plunge in a linen-look fabric in vivid turquoise blue. By Louis Caring, 3½ gns.

...ack! The erogenic zone ...s cannot be until nudity ...epe. £12 19s. 6d.

Pictures by John Cole and Gordon Carter

* **EROGENIC** . . that which stimulates sexual interest.

Two real powers rule Paris – and they couldn't be more different. It's Yves St Laurent's fourth collection since he left Dior and shot right to the top. St Laurent continues to frighten the natives of Paris, used to elegant clothes that confirm their ladylike status. Once Yves had arrived, he put a bomb under that scene with his collection that featured black leather in place of black velvet and jeans instead of skirts. And with this one collection he lowered the Paris style profile by thirty to forty years and changed forever the way Parisian women chose to look. But there was still the inimitable Chanel and where St Laurent had released a style bomb, Chanel was unshaken and irresistible. Her style remained ultra-feminine, but totally contemporary. With some strange design magic her soft femininity appealed to females of all ages who didn't want to frighten the natives with any black leather fetishes. Never has Paris had such two revolutionary differences of fashion opinion – and they both not only survived, but flourished. Which just goes to confirm the constant ability of women to flourish in their infinite variety.

COOL KID . .

A swinging Maid Marian . . . thigh-high boots in black crocodile, tweed tights, a tunic and a shirt — all topped with a black Robin Hood hat. —*Sketch by Ruth Sheradski*

Paris, Monday.

INTO a Paris that I was beginning to consider as Squaresville itself, Yves St. Laurent has brought the heady whiff of youth.

In his fourth collection on his own since he left Dior, this 26-year-old designer has really graduated to the top.

Tonic

His highly-contemporary collection has had the same exuberant effect on fashion as a shot of hormone might have on the bloodstream of an ambitious octogenarian.

Now let me present the St. Laurent girl, 1964.

She wears medium heels, thigh-high boots in black crocodile, teamed with black tweed tights, a black sleeveless tunic over a black polo-necked shirt, the stunning lot topped with a black Robin Hood hat.

In fact, she looks rather like a swinging Maid Marian.

For less strenuous activities, the St. Laurent girl wears pale tweed suits, dead simple, but souped-up with knitted sleeves and polo collar in black or bitter chocolate brown, with thick woollen knitted stockings to match (sorry, boys, but there it is).

Scare

She is female rather than feminine after dark.

Her cocktail suit in dull satin with jewelled

Felicity Green . . in PARIS

pullovers are gu
teed to scare the
out of any British
over the age of
who doesn't have
of the most sop
cated kind.

Widow-spider blac
virgin-bride white a
favourite colours,
whiplash flashes c
pink worn with pass
purple; or cool tur
with deep sapphire.

I'll bet my bottor
time that St. Laurent
boy to be the next b
of Paris fashions.

All those doleful
who keep asking "
ever will happen
Balenciaga isn't her
more ? " can now re

There's an heir-ap
fairly bursting with o
talent waiting on the
step.

At the end of Yv
Laurent's hit-show

CHANEL No 1

This frail-looking, steel-structure of a woman has done as much for clothes as Ford did for cars. . .

A rare picture of Coco Chanel with her big beaming smile. Beside her lie wool skeins . . . and she shows off one against her neck.

DAILY MIRROR, *Tuesday, July 30, 1963* PAGE 11

ning, I applauded
y along with the rest
ne crowd.
fact I shook reed-thin
warmly by the hand
said: "Formidable,"
n is the French equiva-
of "Super."
meone suggested I
lly kissed his feet
ch is, of course, not
I merely bent down
ck up my notebook).
is, I reckon, will be
most influential and
f the most copied col-
ns in the whole

Ahead

's be quite clear about
ort of girl St. Laurent
dear to his designing

lude yourself in if
e the type who prefers
black coffee to sweet
tea, and would
r listen to Ella than
uton Girls Choir.
h-it, I understand, is
ger a phrase used by
nes who are. So I
say Yves is.
settle for him being
ut and beat and so
in advance that Yves
well end up pulling
est of the designers
by their elegant
rings.

YVES ST. LAURENT . . . trims a flower stem in a dressing-room of his salon before presenting his collection. In the background, model hat-shapes on their stands.

HOT MOMMA

IT'S not supposed to be nice to talk about a lady's age, but it occurs to me that last year the indomitable Coco Chanel was supposed to be seventy-nine.

Yet today her collection was as relaxed and youthful as ever, with all the famous touches that have helped to make her one of the best known names in the fashion world.

What a character she is, this frail-looking, steel-structure of a woman who has done as much for clothes as Ford did for cars.

Ideas

Sitting, as always, at the top of her mirrored stairway she peers down at the prettiest-looking model girls in Paris dishing up the latest of the Chanel Look.

Which, you'll be glad to know, differs only slightly from the previous Chanel Look.

There was once a rumour that Chanel had changed her ideas completely. But it turned out to be merely that she had used a different type of braid binding . . . and the panic was over.

Always one for the soft look that makes young girls pretty and old men melt, Chanel says that an American business tycoon once told her she made the only clothes in Paris he didn't mind paying for.

And if Mr. Average Man would be frightened by all the black leather and beat business of this morning's St. Laurent show, then here's the stuff to cheer him up.

Tweeds

There are tweeds he loves to touch in pastel shades stirred up with swansdown.

There are Chanel's typical braid-bound suits, but with the heavy edging reduced to a thin line.

There are flirty pleated skirts just slightly longer than knee length, but nothing to get depressed about.

There are navy dresses with starchy white collars and cuffs—the sort of dresses that Chanel has been making with only slight variations ever since her first impact on fashion way back in the twenties.

There are pale tweed coats lightly quilted and lined in vivid silk with dresses to match.

And there are some very new-looking tweed coats edged all round with film star fox.

'Will these clothes look the same," said my neighbour, looking wistfully at the tallest, slimmest, prettiest models with the longest necks and legs to match, "if a customer is five-feet two and fat?"

The answer, regrettably, is: NO. To do full justice to the Chanel look you need to be what your admirers call slim and your enemies call skinny.

A Bet

Leaving aside the outfits I'd rather forget — red Mongolian lamb on heavy country tweeds, lame dresses with harem hemlines, black dresses in droopy silk—I quite agree with one of the zippiest fashion retailers in Britain who is sitting opposite me with a cheque for £1,500 which he's about to blue in on this season's Chanel.

He's nobody's fool. He knows that the woman who in her time has invented the flapper, the sweater and Chanel Number Five, is still one of the best bets in Paris when you're looking for ideas to adapt for the High Street.

This season's Chanel. A tweed coat in yellow trimmed with long-haired red fox. Chanel releases pictures immediately—unafraid of anyone who tries to copy her intricate cut from a photograph.

ull of
otami

FASHION PRESENTED BY **FELICITY GREEN**

Mary Quant . . . the Quant way is the way ahead.

What will clothes be like when Mary Quant is ten years older?

GIRLS WILL BE BOYS

SO you think the clothes on the right are way out, kookie and strictly for the beat birds?

Well, judging from the orders received by the makers, there must be sizeable outposts of beat birds . . . all the way from the West End of London right out to Glasgow and Edinburgh, taking in Stoke-on-Trent, Birmingham, Leeds, Manchester, Newcastle, Nottingham, Tenby, Wilmslow, Hull, Ipswich, Preston and Wrexham on the way.

To say nothing of even farther flung nests in America, Finland, Australia, South Africa, France and Switzerland.

Mixing

These clothes are part of a brand new budget-price range designed by the clever 28-year-old Mary Quant, the British girl who first gave the Chelsea Look its fashion status.

Mary's new range called the Ginger Group—two examples seen right—goes into the shops today for the first time. It comprises as many mix and match possibilities as a jigsaw puzzle has pieces.

Pants and tops, shirts, skirts, jumper dresses, pullovers, Bermuda shorts (sorry, fellers!), polo sweaters and Prof. Higgins long cardigans. The off-beat colours include prune, putty, black and—naturally—ginger.

QUANT clothes—often called Quaint clothes—are today a force to be reckoned with in fashion.

You may like them; you may wear them; you may despise them. But you can't ignore them.

The trickle of Quant-type clothes that took off at such a black-booted tangent from the main body of well-bred, serious fashion about four years ago has now become an avalanche.

Anguish!

Young designers everywhere are on a universal wavelength, creating In clothes for the young-minded, young-figured fashion-conscious wearer of any age.

They are also creating havoc and anguish for squarer-minded, squarer-shaped fashion shoppers.

Frankly, I think the outlook for the seeker of the c
suit is bleak and ge
bleaker. I believe the Q
way, the Beat way, whi
also incidentally, the Yv
Laurent way, is the way a

And given half a chan
the girls—who, anyway,
to dress as boys—and b
boys—whose dressing is
cidedly taking a turn fo
fancy—the fashion desi
for both sexes will pro
meet on common grour
about ten years time, a
then we'll all be dressing

Boys and girls in
boots, tights, snazzy t
Telling the boys from
girls at twenty paces w
well nigh impossible.

Heigh ho, perhaps by
time no one will care an

DAILY MIRROR, *Wednesday, August 21, 1963* PAGE 11

Two little numbers from the Ginger Group by Mary Quant. Left, a prune pinny in smooth worsted with laced front (7 gns.), worn with a cowl-necked shirt (4½ gns.). Right, a black and putty jersey pinafore (6 gns.), matching muffler (2½ gns.), polo sweater (3 gns.).

Picture by John French.

Unbelievably when this fashion picture was taken of the latest Mary Quant range in 1963, Quant the fashion revolutionary had been in business for nearly ten years. With Bazaar, her shop in the King's Road, Chelsea, the Quant name became famous round the world. And then the fashion world split in two. The Beat generation loved it. The Traditionalists hated it – and dismissed it as a decadent passing phase. Well they were wrong. The Quant genius – and yes, she was one – enchanted the young ones, whatever their age and even their shape. The Quant mini-skirt was a worldwide winner. But there is more to Quant than the mini: in 1963 she introduced her less expensive Ginger Group and this hugely successful collection took the Quant name up, up and away not only throughout Britain but around the increasingly fashion-conscious world.

Hairdressing was one of the cults of the '60s. First, or course, came Vidal Sassoon (top row, fourth from left) who cut hair like cloth and was leader of the pack: a regiment of talented men – and one woman, Rose Evansky – who gave hairdressers a whole new role in the way women looked. Suddenly they were in the spotlight. Straight hair was definitely in and perms were frequently used to straighten hair rather than curl it. Vidal Sassoon was the hairdressing superstar of the '60s. Among the first clients lining up to have a Vidal Cut were model Grace Coddington, on whom he launched his famous Five-Point Cut, designer Mary Quant, and film stars Nancy Kwan and Mia Farrow. Both here and in America clients couldn't wait to have their Vidal Cut. Another couture cutter pictured here is Leonard (top row, third from the right) whose inspired crop cut transformed the girl from Neasden into world famous Twiggy. It was Leonard's friend and Twiggy's boyfriend and manager, former hairdresser Justin De Villeneuve who made this momentous introduction and the resulting boyish crop is still as stylish as ever – fifty years later. One photograph and a star was born – and so was a hairstyle.

What
FELICITY GREEN
thinks about the Mayfair style-and-setters

THEY are a phenomenon of today. They are the top-flight Mayfair hairdressers through whose moneyed and talented hands pass all the best-turned-out heads in the country.

Mostly they are snazzy dressers.

They drive large and/or fast cars.

Generally speaking, they do not admire each other very much. At least, I have never heard one make a complimentary remark about another, although, of course, I cannot swear it has never happened.

Together or separately they wield more power over more women than most women would admit.

THEY can cajole, bully, placate and please their clients in direct proportion to their success.

They take themselves very seriously as befits a group of shrewd tycoons who aspire to be "creative artists" rather than just hairdressers.

"It's a minor art form," says one of his daily stint with the brush and comb.

"We combine a sense of the aesthetic with imagination and technical perfection," says another.

"Hair is closely linked with a woman's emotional attitude," says a third.

No wonder the relationship that exists between hairstylist and client is a very special one.

After all, he's the third man in her life. The only one, other than her husband and her doctor, whom she allows to see her at her very worst. And she knows that thanks to his "art form" she will emerge from his hands looking her best.

As I said, it's a very delicate relationship between a man and a woman and no one's surprised there are so few females among the Big Names in hair.

Thirteen men

What they think about themselves

MICHAEL OF L'ELONGE

1—We aim for good taste in everything and manners to every woman who comes in. V out to create a friendly and relaxed atmospher we don't have any client that we can't count a friend.

ALAN SPIERS

2—We try to combine a sense of the aestheti imagination and technical perfection. We method of four-dimensional cutting becau believe no two heads of hair can be cut or t in the same manner.

JOHN OF KNIGHTSBRIDGE

3—We believe in a relaxed atmosphere tolerance and understanding towards hair problems. Hairstyles should never be un ing, unfeminine or gimmicky.

VIDAL SASSOON

4—To me the training of hairdressers is th important thing. I would specially like youngsters entering hairdressing because they as a minor art form rather than being pus parents who are dazzled by high financial re

woman—and for your who's who guide to the picture see the chart on the left.

SON

very client should be considered separately, nd a hairstyle suiting not only her looks but er personality should be chosen. A swinging yle is fun and really gives a woman confidence.

IARD OF RAPHAEL AND LEONARD

ur aim is hairstyling at the highest level— achieve recognition throughout Europe that n is the centre of creative hairstyling.

OR OF DUMAS

/e believe in the absolute basics—that a oman's hair is her crowning glory and that if ir is a mess she will look and feel a mess. The hould never be treated as something isolated the clothes and personality.

/e believe in hairdressing as a creative art, eparate, but complementary to fashion and an sion of personality. Almost an art form in

E

/e set out to give our customers the best of verything—the best of available materials, a atmosphere and creative hairstylists. I regret ecline of art in the profession. It is too easy ople with no hairdressing skill or knowledge en salons.

ROSE EVANSKY

10—We know how closely hair is linked with a woman's emotional attitudes—her hair is her whole appearance. We search for a woman's personality and help to express it in her hairdo.

GERARD AUSTEN AT CARITA

11—We feel that harmony between fashion and hair is most important and we try to give this feeling by adapting Parisian ideas to suit the beauty and style of English women.

DAVID SANDLER OF LEON SANDLER

12—The hairdresser is one of the last bastions of the custom-built rather than the mass production job. I believe that every client is entitled to an exclusive design.

FRENCH

13—Hair must reflect modern living. I don't like terribly exaggerated hairstyles which always remind me of padded-shoulder suits. The client is the star of our show. She comes in to relax, to be pampered, to be discreetly fussed over and waited on not just for a shampoo and set.

BERNARD OF ANDRE BERNARD

14—We believe that a woman should look like a woman and not like a freak. We do not like to see hair tortured into an exaggerated shape.

THE HAIR RAISERS

Seen in London yesterday . . the
of a girl called Emmanuelle Kh
designer who dares to say 'I

FELICITY GREEN LOOKS AT THE FIRST KHANH CLOTHES IN LONDON

THE name is unusual. Emmanuelle Khanh. She is French. 25 years old and already a wow in the Paris wholesale fashion business.

Now two enterprising British firms are going to produce Khanh clothes over here and I predict a big success for this girl whose talent is as unusual as her name.

Yesterday I saw the first Khanh range of spring coats—and very exciting they are, too.

In an age of the Kookie, the Beat and the Way-Out, Khanh clothes manage to be all of that but also feminine and unfrightening to men who prefer women to look like members of the sex that's still opposite.

Fellers, Khanh (pronounced Karn) is on your side. Only sometimes does she go wild—see far right.

But take heart because she hates boots, heavy coats, wool stockings, the Little Boy Look and no waists.

She likes clothes to be subtle and feminine.

Supple

The Khanh clothes I saw yesterday — narrow figure-skimming coats in fabrics that follow the curves they cover but don't conceal — seem to have the best of both designing worlds in their clever cut.

They combine the simplicity of that well-known fashion disciplinarian, Balenciaga, plus all the supple femininity that has made Chanel the darling of millions.

Says Hans Jacoby, head of the British firm of Cojana who are making the Khanh coats: "She is full of wonderful new ideas and her things are causing a great stir."

I agree. You'll hear more about Emmanuelle.

KHANH drawn by herself . . . this is her spring coat line, all curves and cling.

At 25, Emmanuelle Khanh is already an influence in the fashion world. Seen here at home in Paris in her outsize spectacles, T-strap shoes and divided skirt.

Inspired by Garbo and the 'thirties,
typical Khanh suit and pull-on h

Joan Harrison in Paris talks to the girl behind the clothes

EVERYTHING about Emmanuelle Khanh spells Paris, 1963.

It was typical of her that she chose to meet me in a crowded Left Bank cafe, full of young people all talking hard.

She was wearing a simple sweater with an easy boat neckline and three-quarter-length sleeves trimmed with crochet scallops. Unusual, but not Beat.

Tiny, with straight black hair and round owlish spectacles, she moves with the ease of a fashion model. As indeed she was for four years — two with designer Balenciaga and two with Givenchy.

And there, perhaps, lies the key to her personality and talent for design.

"If I hadn't been a model in a top Paris dress house," she said, "I wouldn't be a designer today.

"It was reaction to
wearing stiff, dr
up clothes. I neve
feminine in them.

"Walking up
down, my hair
back in a chigno
enormous helmet
on my head, I us
feel that what I
wearing had nothi
do with being a w

"During my last
at Givenchy I des
and made myself a
which hung fron
hips. I wore it w
went to pose for
magazine.

Impact

"When I told
fashion writer t
had designed it
she asked if she
photograph it.
that's how every
started."

Emmanuelle ha
training as a de
and had never se
in an art school.
of which has det
from the impact sh
made on Paris,
they know style
flair when they se

DAILY MIRROR, Wednesday, October 30, 1963 PAGE 17

plosive talent
, a way-out
etest boots'

Nothing if not unusual, Khanh's designs are sometimes real traffic stoppers, specially by night. Example, above, this chain mail evening top—designed, please note, to wear over an evening dress.

Emmanuelle Khanh was a one-off. This '60s Paris designer had been a model for both couture designers Balenciaga and Givenchy when she rebelled against what she called their "stiff and dressed-up" clothes. So brave Emmanuelle went her own way with a collection of sporty styles for the French Youthquake generation waiting in the wings. When she brought her collection to London it was obvious that in her culottes and outsize glasses, Emmanuelle, like Mary Quant, looked just like the girls she was designing for. Her first collection introduced culottes before Courrèges and chain mail before Paco Rabanne. Back in 1962 I bought an Emmanuelle Khanh shirt dress in tiger print velvet, which I absolutely adored and I wish I still had it because I would happily wear it today. No wonder she was often called the French Mary Quant.

First came Dior, then came St Laurent, but Paris in the '60s was no longer Top Chien. Marc Bohan had followed St Laurent and the temperature dropped more than somewhat. His clothes appealed to the French mature ladies, but Swinging London was making the international headlines with the New Generation designers, eg. Quant for a start. But for me, Paris in the middle of the night was truly exciting. So turn over to pages 72-73 for further details.

Pages 72-73: This picture by John French was shot at 2am. Why? Because it was the only time the "hot" numbers from the Paris Collections could be prised away from the hordes of international buyers and rushed round to the studio under protective white sheets to shield them from the "pirate" fashion photographers hoping to catch a glimpse of something they might sell illegally to a lurking manufacturer. Paris was certainly a 24-hour fashion festival! To get this unique group shot of top models looking their elegant best in these couture clothes – on which fashion buyers from all over the world would spend millions of pounds even in those pre-inflationary days – took the skills of photographer John French. Mr French was master of the group photograph and an unparalleled expert at making every model not only look her best but feel it too. As you can tell by just looking at them.

I SAY! THIS IS RIPPING NEWS FROM THE SPRING SHOWS

Dior puts the clock back thirty years . .

THE word I would use to describe the Marc Bohan collection at Dior yesterday was "ripping."

Ranging most firmly on the side of the young designers who like a dash of fun with their fashion, Bohan served up a collection reminiscent of the time thirty years ago when Jack Buchanan in white "ducks" was asking hopefully, "Anyone for tennis?"

BRIMMED

Miss Dior today comes to us straight from the early 1930s. Short, waved shingle, upturned cloche brimmed hat, long jacket, low belt, pleated skirt, T-strap sandals and all.

Getting in the mood for what he calls "the new way of life," Bohan has designed clothes for "air travel, yachting parties, and small select country house parties."

For air travel, women wear Oxford bags—no crease, please, in the wide flapping trousers—and a matching jacket. For yachting, it's a long, navy blazer and a white, pleated skirt with a halo hat to match.

For those select country houses, it's a floating, ankle-length evening dress with a divided skirt, and here's to central heating

TOUCHES

Other touches of the '30s more keyed to a down-to-earth existence and designed for a successful life among the copyists: Edge-to-edge coats fastened with one button just under the bust, bishop sleeves, cowl necks, bias-cut evening dresses.

Miss Dior—and there will be a thousand replicas of her around before you can say foxtrot—likes a long-jacketed, hip-belted suit, probably in navy, with a white halo or cloche hat, or maybe a printed shirtwaist dress with a pleated skirt worn under a bright green or navy blue jacket.

She is also partial to a back-belted coat with a broad-brimmed straw panama, or perhaps a one-button edge-to-edge coat with big white lapels and a white cloche beret.

In the evening she knows there is nothing more sexy for a girl to be wrapped in—unless it's her boy-friend's arms—than chiffon. So she goes in for lots of drifting sheers in black, and sometimes, navy blue.

She likes skirts that swirl—short skirts for cocktails and long, just above the ankle skirts for grander occasions with which her life is obviously filled.

She likes lace, too, and little beaded jackets over clinging ankle-length sheaths, even if she

clanks like a knig
armour when she
She has redisc
macrame — that b
string stuff from
Aunt Ethel was f
making doilies —
wears it crochetec
stockings, blouses,
and hats.

MAGNETIC

I don't think th
collection is any lor
the class by itself
once was, but Dior
the most magnetic
in fashion.

Sober-sided pr
clients may be a bi
tant about spendin
to finish up looking
Gertrude Lawrenc
her heyday, but I
the manufacturers
go for the gimmic
this collection in
way, and undoubte
is going to be a
copied look in the
streets everywhere.

CLINGING

Thick sweaters are out, and the new "pulls," as they are called, look as though they've had a long session in the washing machine with the dial set to "hot wash."

These sweaters, which are ribbed, are as clinging as a sock with skimpy armholes and tight sleeves.

So, if you're in a knitting mood, reach for the 3-ply, number 10 needles, and make with the two-plain, two-purl—in a size too small.

Picture by Murray Irving.

Trend 1

A NEW all-elasti
bra designed at D
give "perfect adhe
flattens and separ
the point of non-exi
But then bosoms
the cult of the '30
way.

Trend 2

EYES still domina
lips for face intere
you have mastered
of the eyeliner, try
trick.

Draw another
line — with grey e
liquid or a non-
dark grey shadow—
the crease at the
the lid.

A wow at twenty
a bit alarming at tw
terrific for maxi
effect in mini
lighting.

DAILY MIRROR, *Friday, January 31, 1964* PAGE 13

Where all the flowers have gone

Flower prints have been conspicuous by their absence in the fashion shows this week. All the s were abstract or geometric, when a few flowers did bloom, weren't the kind easy to ify by anyone except an expert. here the flowers have gone is to see. They have turned up all over the prettiest bras and girdles now on sale in the Paris undie shops. These duets are liberally scattered with all the flowers of the field—roses, daisies, and the like.

Very pretty, too, and there is no doubt the floral touch helps to turn the purely functional into the also glamorous. Flowers are blooming, too, on the beach, and one range of swim suits by Sports-Plage, a leading French beachwear manufacturer, is a veritable hothouse of blossoms.

Get a suntan all over if you must this summer, and here's hoping for the opportunity to do so. But keep your legs pale or you'll be in dead trouble, fashionably speaking. All the best-dressed legs in Paris are wearing nylons so pale they look like sheer versions of the surgical stockings they put on you in hospital before an operation.

Still tricky to track down in Britain at the moment, but I understand they should be in better supply by the time we all get out of our boots.

IT'S BLAZERS AND FRILLS

THINK of a 1930 line worn by a 13-year-old schoolgirl and you have the Dior suit look (right).

The long jacket ends way down on the hips and has a collarless blazer front and a low belt.

Note the schoolgirl-pleated skirt and the deep pockets.

This suit was in navy blue wool, worn with a navy blue chiffon cowl-necked blouse and a white halo hat.

For after dark—Miss Dior grows up. There is nothing little girlish about this frilled black organza cocktail dress (left).

Its V-neck plunges almost to the waist. The waist is put back in its natural place and held there by a narrow belt.

The dress has wide sleeves that end in a trumpet of ruffles.

Sketches by Ruth Sheradski.

THIS IS PARIS

You have
ALL the

Commentary by FELICITY GREEN

YOU have never seen a picture of Paris fashion quite like this. It was taken at the dead of night—the only time the clothes could be wrenched away from Paris's top designers, who were frantically busy all day long showing them to the world's leading buyers.

They had to be returned in the early hours, heavily swathed in white sheets, in case fashion spies lurked in dark doorways.

The model girls — two British, four French, one American, one German, and one Swedish—burned the midnight oil to provide this unique line-up of all the fashion winners that tell the complete story of Paris for Spring and Summer '64.

These are the couture clothes on which buyers will spend around £70,000,000 which is the sum that goes tinkling into French fashion coffers every year.

Pricey

To start with there's Chanel. Each suit and blouse now costs £650, so you could either buy half a dozen Chanels or a small house.

Second from the left there's Balmain, who makes clothes for all the best-dressed Princesses and Empresses.

He also makes stunning simple evening dresses, and this season goes for the strapless tunic over an ankle-high hemline, a surefire copying success if ever I saw one.

Third from the left there is a cape-dress from St. Laurent, which is really two dresses for the price of one—a sheer loose tunic over a slim sheath.

At £450 this may not be a breath-taking bargain, but copies at £15 will interest all fashion shoppers with an eye for the sexiest look for after-dark dressing.

Goma at Patou likes plunge necklines and big romantic collars. So does

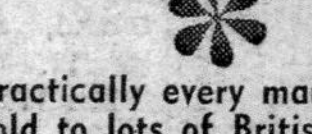

practically every man. Patou sold to lots of British manufacturers, so it seems safe to assume that British men will be happier about Paris fashions than they often are.

Relaxing in her chair is the Courreges girl dressed in the white trousers and camel jacket that this designer suggests women wear for jet-age travel.

The long black evening dress with the big white organdie collar is from Crahay at Lanvin.

Then there is the "Butch" suit from Ricci with the turn-up hemline and the contrast tweed jacket.

Next, Cardin's loose tunic with the navel-low neckline filled in with a navy blue modesty vest.

And lastly the Thirties girl from Dior, in her navy chalk stripe suit, with its pleated skirt and long jacket.

Pinch

These clothes are the prototypes for thousands of dead-spit copies and many, many more "adaptations" or "inspirations," which is the fashion trade's polite way of admitting that they pinch the idea without buying the original.

Aggravating for the designer and maddening for those 21,000 rich women who total the private clientele of all the Paris fashion houses. But lovely for you and me as all those near-as-dammit Diors start turning up in our High-street any day now.

Picture by JOHN FRENCH

☐ Nine Paris winners, left to right: 1, A pastel tweed suit by Chanel, worn by Danielle; 2, White lace evening dress by Balmain, worn by Enid; 3, Black organza cape-dr… by Mildred; 4, Pale blue e… Patou, worn by Ingrid. ☐

ever seen a picture quite like this before: it gives hion news that matters in one wide-angle view..

Laurent, worn ss by Goma at nter the world of high fashion: 5, A camel and white travel suit by Courreges, worn by Sophie; 6, Black evening dress with white organdie collar by Crahay at Lanvin, worn by Babette; 7, Contrast jacket suit by Ricci, worn by Anna Lena; 8, White wool tunic over navy by Cardin, worn by Melvina; 9, Navy chalk-stripe suit by Dior, worn by Miriam.

The chair was designed by Bertoia for Knoll International.

DAILY MIRROR, Saturday, February 29, 1964 PAGE 9

magazine MIRROR

FELICITY GREEN in PARIS

CLOTHES IN THE CAVIAR CLASS

BALENCIAGA is to Paris fashion what a pot of caviar is to a well-stocked larder. He is a treat, an acquired taste and so expensive that if I were a buyer instead of a journalist, I'd have to pay £1,000 for seeing today's grand final of the current fashion season.

For that kind of money I'd be able to choose two linen patterns to take home to copy by the dozen for women who like the Balenciaga look at High-street prices.

I'd consider buying a navy, double-breasted reefer coat, back-belted and tabbed at the shoulders. My younger customers would go for this look. They would also like a boxy, seven-eighths coat in crinkly, white nylon worn with navy and red check stockings.

And for the best-dressed Beats in town, I'd consider a brown, leather raincoat with sou'wester hat to match. (They would need brown and black dark stockings for this one.)

Subtle

For more conservative clients, I'd choose one of the boxy top coats that looks from a distance like a classic, raglan-sleeved raincoat, but is so subtly cut that it would give the average British tailor a fit of apoplexy if he tried to copy it.

Other possibilities for my list: **a collarless suit** in white cotton or beige linen with the new, narrower squared shoulder line, or one in cotton gaberdine with a loose jacket over an easy skirt that would look fine in the country.

I MIGHT go for one of the **silk shantung dresses** with cape sleeves slit along the shoulder seam to show a lot of under as well as upper arm. (I'd have to warn my customers about showing a lot of bra, too, as this is one habit even Balenciaga hasn't overcome.)

Brass

And I'd order all my Spring and Summer materials, which would include cloque, waffle organza, linen and camel hair, in shades of neutral from white to desert sand.

I'd settle for a barrel full of brass buttons and use them on navy, serge, white linen and blonde camel.

Then I'd tell all my most fashion-conscious customers to wear pale beige lace-up shoes with a medium heel with all their day clothes, and quite high heels for the afternoon and evening.

For the more energetic customers, I would consider **sheaths** beaded neck to hem with such abandon that they would just have to dance all night, as sitting down once would ruin about £75 worth of beads as well as their decorum.

Rumours have it, as rumours will from time to time, that Balenciaga, now sixty-seven years old, is about to retire.

I don't believe it. I won't believe it.

Today's show was as youthful as any I have seen. A shot in the arm for womankind in a week when the newly discovered elixir of youth turns out to have a "men only" label.

PRACTICALLY no one in the fashion business has laid eyes on the elusive M. Balenciaga, a shy Spaniard with a highly developed distaste for publicity.

But I have it on the best authority that he is a kind, considerate, painstaking friend to his best clients.

Gone

One of whom went home recently to change from one Balenciaga outfit to another, but found that her favourite coat had gone.

Where was it, she asked her maid.

M. Balenciaga had it, she was told.

So Madame H. rang the Balenciaga salon.

"M. Balenciaga saw you walking along the other day and didn't think the collar was quite right, so he asked us to send for it so he could make it perfect."

That's what I call really haute couture.

STRAW

IT'S only a straw in the wind, and I don't want to go raising any false hopes. But . . .

- At the Givenchy show on Thursday, one model girl measured 38 round the hips if she measured an inch.
- At the Patou show a month ago, designer Michel Goma, who likes to make his collection on the thinnest model girls in the world, told me he was bored by "sparrow arms."

Could it be the dieters are out?

Andre Courreges, one of the new and important names in French fashion.

The man with a revolution in mind

Paris, Friday.

IT would not be exactly true to say that fashion designer Andre Courreges wants to change the face of womankind.

But he does have some ideas about the way we look that, if accepted, could bring about a profound alteration in our appearance.

M. Courreges, a new name at the top of the Paris fashion world, had one of the biggest successes of the current season.

Stunning

Buyers and Press fell about in admiration at the sight of his pique twopiece for morning wear, his jersey twopiece for an afternoon's stroll around the park, his ribbed, cotton twopiece for holiday wear and his glamorous lace twopiece for a grand evening.

The surprising thing about all these stunning outfits is that where most twopieces have a skirt these have pants.

They are mostly in white, they are worn with flat, white boots and, where appropriate, the ensemble is topped off with a huge flowered pot hat.

WAS M. Courreges serious about the pants-with-everything idea? I asked him as we talked in his sun-filled salon in Paris.

Did he not feel it was a bit unfeminine, and did he think women really wanted to wear the trousers literally as well as figuratively?

"Something has to happen to women's clothes. They are no longer designed for the life you lead," he said. "You run. Can you run in high heels?

"You drive. You need a special pair of flat shoes in your car.

"All women want to look young, and short skirts help you to do so, but skirts cannot get any shorter and still be decent.

"As for trousers, they are comfortable and practical for living today, and, if they are beautifully cut, can flatter a woman's figure and be every bit as feminine as anything else she wears."

THE Courreges trousers are certainly beautifully cut and, as a white cotton trouser and tunic outfit with a short matching coat cost about £700, this perfection isn't surprising.

The legs are tapered not only to the ankle, but right down to the floor with a clover notch on the instep to make them hang like a plumb line.

But can any trouser outfit ever be feminine?

"Femininity," said M. Courreges firmly, "has nothing at all to do with what a woman wears. It is what she is."

He may be right—and, in fact, I think he is—but I am sure the major proportion of the male population of the Western world would die of fright if expected to take a girl to the ball when she was wearing the Courreges outfit pictured here.

AND THIS IS THE WAY ANDRE COURREGES WOULD DRESS YOU

A new idea for evening—a white guipure lace evening suit with a tunic top fastened only at the neck with a bow and low hip-slung pants by Andre Courreges.

Picture by Hatami

DAILY MIRROR, Saturday, March 14, 1964 PAGE 11

magazine MIRROR

TOP SECRET

PICTURES NOT TO BE PUBLISHED UNTIL SATURDAY, MARCH 14

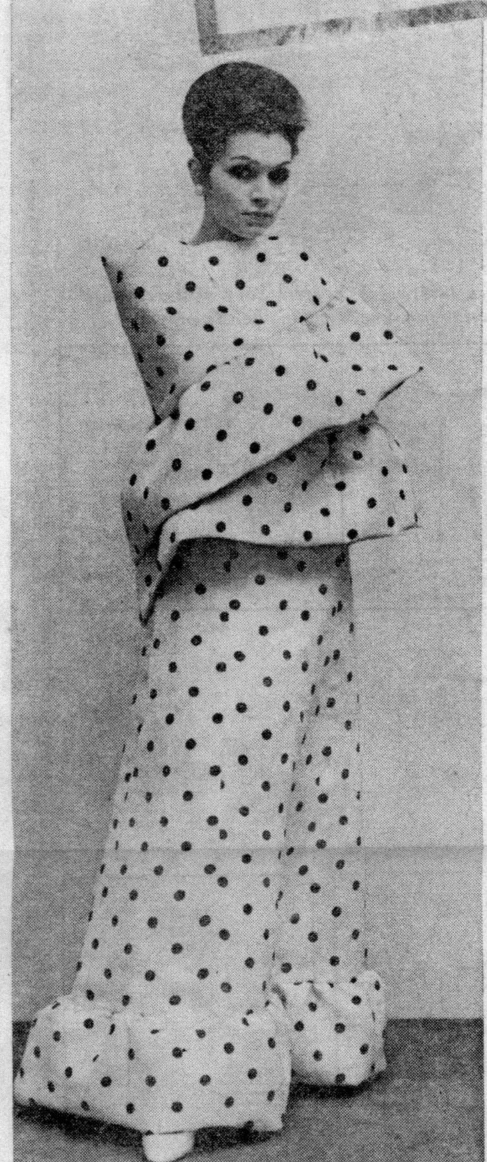

● A genius with many octaves in his fashion register, Balenciaga goes from the Beat Look for day to great and often gaudy grandeur at night. Some of his evening clothes are so way-out that you'd have to be way up in the exhibitionist class to get away with them. (Shocking silk pants under floor-length white lace, black tulle ruched in like a Christmas cracker.) But always in every collection there are the simple elegant dresses that have delighted the ladies of the Best-dressed Lists who buy Balenciagas like you and I buy a new pair of nylons. In such a category is this stunning number in white silk taffeta, coin-dotted in black.

Revealed today—the world's most exclusive (and expensive) clothes

IF by some mischance these two pictures had been published before today, there was a distinct chance that your erring correspondent would be found languishing in a Paris jail trying to explain in pidgin French that it was all a terrible erreur.

You see, although both outfits may look perfectly ordinary, if charming, to you, they represent to designer Balenciaga what the Budget secrets mean to Mr. Maudling. Details may in no circumstances be released before an agreed date.

by FELICITY GREEN

Today is the agreed date for Mr. Balenciaga, and we all know about Budget Day and Mr. Maudling.

Rules

The reason for the secrecy—and I signed a legal document to say I'd abide by the rules—is just as essential in one case as the other.

The fashion secrecy is necessary because manufacturers pay a great deal of good money to see the Balenciaga collection and to choose what they will actually buy.

Minimum purchase in this, the most exclusive fashion house in the world, is £1,000. So no wonder most buyers are a granite-faced crew.

Copies

When they have chosen what they hope are their lucky numbers, they go home to try to fill in the time until the garments and/or the patterns arrive by running up as many near-as-dammit copies from the collection as their highly-trained memories will allow.

But even for buyers who have seen the clothes close to, trying to copy a Balenciaga garment without an actual pattern is like trying to knit a Fair Isle sweater in the dark.

So it's only when the customer has his pattern and the designer has his money that pictures can be shown. The exchange usually takes about a month to six weeks — which brings us to today.

Pirates

The careful secrecy thwarts those fashion pirates who wait, foot on the treadle, scissors poised, to run up a couple of dozen near-Balenciagas from any and every advance picture they can get a look at.

As one who has seen the real McCoy made from a real pattern alongside the rough-and-too-quickly-ready replica, I'm glad about that form I signed to say I would observe the rules of the release date.

And anyway I don't think I'd like to languish in a French jail.

● Balenciaga may be the greatest designer in the fashion-conscious world—and most experts agree on this—but he's also as Beat as the occasion demands. At 67 years of age, he is as young-minded as any kookie Chelsea designer, and a great deal more technically brilliant than most of them will ever be. This suit, from his new collection for spring and summer 1964, is made in navy blue poplin with a white over-blouse. The coat and hat is in shiny white vinyl and the stockings are in red and black plaid.

Pictures by Hatami.

PLAIN JANE?

ARE you a Plain Jane or a Fancy Nancy? Just as one man's meat is another man's poison, so one girl's favourite dress is another girl's choice for the outfit she'd prefer not to be seen dead in.

Some girls who are the Fancy Nancies of today like frills—and why not?

Other girls, who would rather be Plain Janes any time, go for the stark and simple and think frills look better on cakes.

by

FELICITY GREEN

Fancy Nancy likes sugar pink spiced with white; Plain Jane prefers khaki jollied up with black.

Fancy Nancy goes to parties in chiffon slashed to the navel. Plain Jane feels at her most seductive in her husband's hand-knitted, knee-length sweater.

THIS season's fashions might have been designed with these two types in mind.

FOR PLAIN JANES, there is navy disciplined with white, sleeveless black and rows of military-minded buttons.

FOR FANCY NANCY there are flower prints galore, ruffles and scallops and drifting sleeves.

But the gap that divides the Fancy Nancies from the Plain Janes is clearly defined at all fashion levels.

At hairstyle level, we have P.J. all sleek and straight while F.N. runs to soft bangs and drifting wisps.

AT foot level, P.J. chooses sturdy heels and elegance; F.N. likes strappy sandals and sighs for the exciting stiletto.

But the real acid test that divides the two groups starts at skin level and takes place in the undie department.

Look carefully at the next-to-nothings on this page and then decide — always presuming you don't already know — whether you're a P.J. or a F.N.

Is it red, white and blue stripes that appeal more, or white lace tricked up with baby blue?

Easy, isn't it—especially if there's no man around to influence the choice?

If you're a Plain Jane by preference, you'll choose undies on the simple side. This red, white and blue striped girdle costs 29s. 6d., and the navy bra 19s. 11d. All undies from Fenwicks, London, W.1.

DAILY MIRROR, Friday, April 24, 1964 PAGE 17

FANCY NANCY?

... high - waisted ...eveless dress in ...ue and white ...rtical mattress-tick... stripes. By Young Jaeger, 8½ gns.

This hip-belted pinafore dress has a double row of white pearl buttons. In French navy. Frederica, 7½ gns.

A Liberty print dress with lavish frills at the neckline of a high - waisted dress. Marlborough, 5½ gns.

There are frills round the hem and sleeves of this pink gingham shift. Bernshaw, £5.9.6.

Pictures by John Adriaan
Sketches by Barbara Hulanicki

If your taste in undies is for the absolute in femininity, you're the Fancy Nancy type and will go for these. Bra 14s. 11d., suspender belt 8s. 11d., pants 6s. 11d.

Are you a Plain Jane or a Fancy Nancy? A perfectly good fashion story and a perfectly good reason to put two perfectly lovely model girls in two contrasting underwear styles at a time when variations in our underwear were making the fashion headlines. Bonus: Early sketches by soon-to-be-famous fashion artist Barbara Hulanicki of future Biba fame.

by FELICITY GREE

Four girl
and business ide

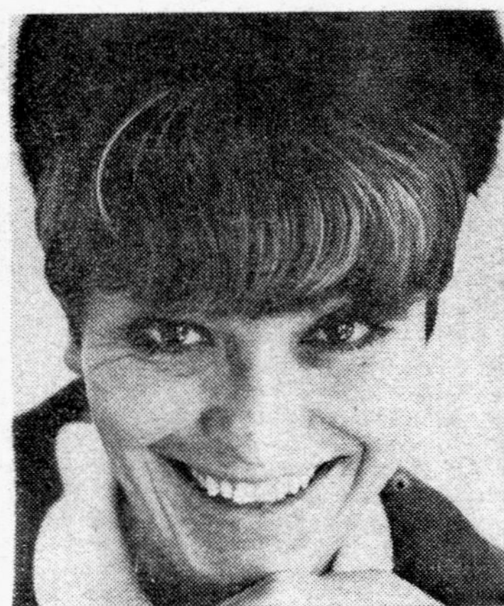

THIS IS LETIZIA

SHE DESIGNS AND IMPORTS HANDBAGS.

Letizia, married to film designer Ken Adam—Dr. Strangelove, Dr. No—found friends drooling over the bags she had made to her own design in Italy, her homeland.

So if everyone liked them and wanted them, why didn't she organise it so they could have them?

She lined up the workmen in Rome and Florence, provided them with the necessary sketches, and suddenly she was in the handbag business.

Now imports them in quantity and has them on sale in the THE most exclusive West End shops. Expensive—from 22 to 120 gns. "But chicissimo" says Letizia, "and just what women want."

THIS IS SALLY

SOON SHE'LL HAVE HER OWN COUTURE BUSINESS.

Some time early next month ex-model
Simpson, who confesses to being bored rigid
two years before the camera, opens up he
couture business, "Vanilla."

Her task—designing and making to m
clothes for fashion-conscious clients with an e
the exclusive and a bank balance that d
balk at a starting price of £30.

The styles will be young and pretty and de
by Sally and her partner.

Why "Vanilla"? "Everyone asks that,'
Sally. "so it obviously makes an impression.'

The dress that started it all. You are looking at a *Daily Mirror* picture that made both fashion and mail order history in 1964. It was used to illustrate a story about career girls who were making a financial success of their burgeoning fashion businesses. And then I had an idea. I admired the way one of these girls, fashion illustrator Barbara Hulanicki dressed. Barbara was struggling with the fledgling Biba mail-order business she had set up with her husband, Stephen Fitz-Simon. So I had another idea. I asked Barbara to design a simple summer dress with a headscarf to match that I could offer to the *Mirror* readers for twenty-five shillings. And that's how this simple design in pink gingham set the Biba Postal Boutique on its first firm footing, paving the way for the Biba success story. I estimated we'd sell two to three thousand. In fact we sold seventeen thousand, plus another five thousand in blue gingham – we had emptied the UK of pink gingham.

rove that beauty can go together

IS IS MARIE LISE

HE'S OPENING A BOUTIQUE FOR "WIGS AND PRETTY THINGS"

Monday of next week the ground floor of of London's newest and most glamorous ressing establishments—it's five floors, so can't call it a salon—will be taken over by Lise.

at will be on sale? Shoes, scarves, belts, lery and handbags, all designed by the h-born boss herself. Also hair pieces de- d in collaboration with her husband, wig- r Simon Boyle.

think people want pretty, individual things— not too expensive, either," says Marie Lise. hair pieces, for instance, will start at 4 gns."

THIS IS BARBARA

NOW SHE'S A DRESS MANUFACTURER AS WELL AS A FASHION ARTIST.

One of the most successful fashion artists in the business, Barbara went to a party in a long skirt she had made herself. A fashion editor saw it, adored it, and wanted a similar one for her readers. So Barbara got a friend in the cheaper end of the rag-trade to make it up in quantities at a next-to-nothing price.

Hundreds of people sent for it. Now she designs specially for newspapers and magazines on a mail-order only basis. On the right a "Barbara" summer shift designed exclusively for Daily Mirror readers. For more about this, read on. . . .

. . and this is one of her designs. Interested? It can be yours for 25s including the kerchief

✻ If you're in the market for something cool and shifty . . .

If you think gingham is an "in" fabric . . .

If you like the idea of the headscarf to match . . .

If you feel twenty-five bob isn't a fashion fortune—and it isn't . . .

This is your dress, with its figure-skimming lines, softly rolling neckline and keyhole back.

It has been designed and made specially for the Daily Mirror by Barbara Hulanicki.

If you would like one, send 25s., plus 1s. 6d. for postage and packing, to Biba's Postal Boutique, 35, Oxford-street, London, W.1.

In pink gingham. Sizes: 10, 12, 14.

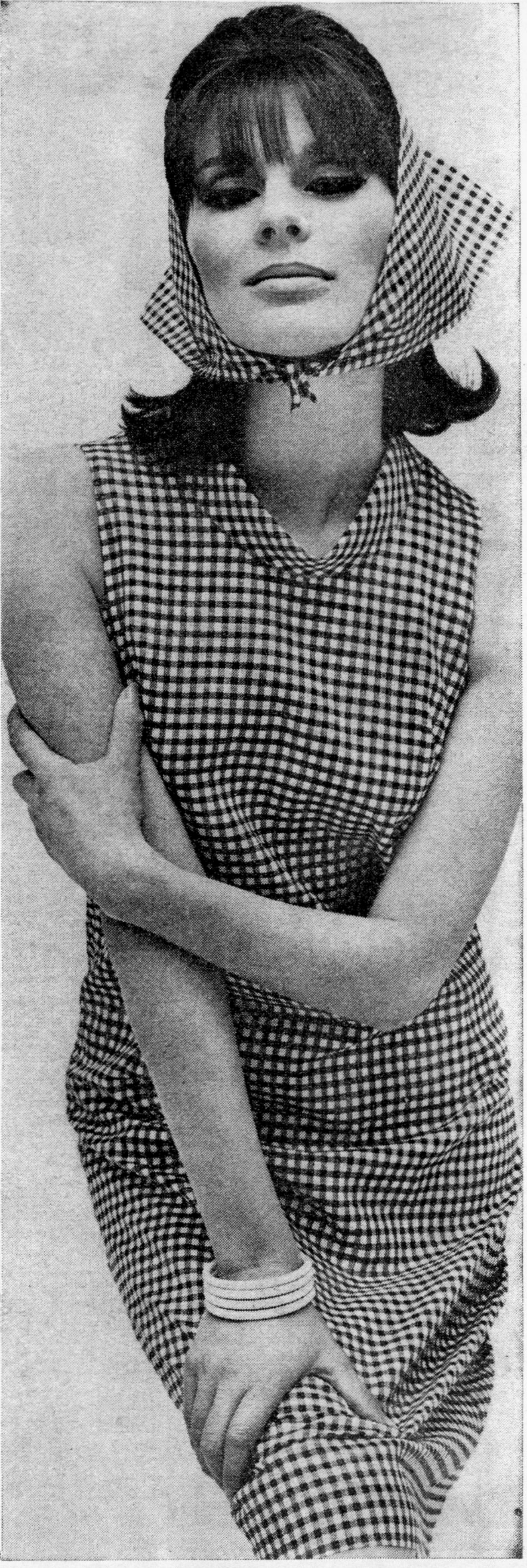

DAILY MIRROR, Friday, July 24, 1964 PAGE 13

Like it or not, these are the men who decide what women will wear..

Felicity Green

REPORTING ON THE EVE OF PARIS

There is no fashion dictator in Paris any more and no one designer can be bossy enough to influence all of the women all of the time.

But there's still a front rank of big names who will be making news when the autumn shows open there next week.

Like it or not, the sum total of what they will be saying about necklines and hemlines will undoubtedly add up to The Look for 1965.

Seen here are seven of the leading faces in the Paris fashion limelight. In addition, there's also Balmain and Heim. And the emigrant Italian, Capucci. And the husband-and-wife team of Simonetta and Fabiani.

Among the designing women there's the indestructible Chanel. And a new name, Real, the fashion house run by Helen Vager and Arlette Nastat.

And, if you're interested, no, I don't think any designer worthy of the name will show topless dresses.

If I'm wrong, I'll eat my bra.

ANDRE COURREGES
Basque, age 41. The man who wants women to wear the trousers. All the time. Preferably in white. Thinks skirts are out of date.

MARC BOHAN
French, 38. No matter what, Dior — where Marc designs—is still the biggest name in Paris. Likes womanly women who are young and gay.

JULES FRANCOIS CRAHAY
Belgian, 46. Moved last season from Ricci to Lanvin and scored a smash hit. Likes clothes with a dash about them—specially after dark.

MICHEL GOMA
Spanish, age 32. Likes feminine clothes and bright colours, low necks, small waists and jazzy accessories.

PIERRE CARDIN
French, 41. Great designer. Clothes so fluid, it's often hard to see where they begin and the girl ends.

GERARD PIPART
French, 28. New name at old house of Nina Ricci. Young, gimmicky and very easy to wear. Also to copy.

YVES ST. LAURENT
French, 27. The boy who brought the Beat Look to high fashion. Used black leather—crocodile, of course—instead of black satin. Is more in line with youthful thinking than many of his rivals.

After Dior died in 1957, there was no longer any dictator, but the Big Names were still masculine – well male. It's true they were younger – St Laurent brought the Beat to Paris and Courrèges loved white leather. But where was the woman's voice? There was the fabulous Chanel whose softly tailored suits brought femininity into Paris tailoring, then young, primarily London designers – Quant, Hulanicki, Foale and Tuffin – took over the world. Hurrah!

Opposite page: The Topless Trend began in 1965 and the man responsible was 34-year old California-based designer Rudi Gernreich. He had what he thought was a Small Idea – a topless swimsuit, which would be just a one-season fashion novelty. He "thought" it would sell a maximum of four or five. It sold 1,000 the first month and 2,500 the second. "I never meant it to sell like this," said the apologetic Mr Gernreich. Hmm...

PICTURE OF A MAN WITH A BOMB IN HIS HANDS . .

GERNREICH in London . . . sketching his secrets for next season.

by FELICITY GREEN

WHAT do Frankenstein and Rudi Gernreich have in common?

They both had a good idea that got out of hand.

Frankenstein had his monster and Gernreich started the to-do over Topless.

[For the record, it was Emilio Pucci, the Italian sportswear designer, who first **predicted** the trend a couple of years ago—but he pitched it ten years into the future. Mexican sportswear designer Ruben Tores took up the idea this year, gave an interview on the subject in New York, and planned a topless dress show in Paris to prove what you might call his point. He then lost his nerve and filled in the gaps with whatever seemed suitable at the time. Like sequins.]

But it was Rudi Gernreich, 33-year-old Californian designer, who first got this doubtful starter off the ground.

Diminutive and smiley, Mr. Gernreich passing through London this week, talked to me about the bomb he let off when all he had in mind was a fire-cracker.

Nudity

"I was talking to a girl I know on a fashion trade paper a couple of years ago and I said I thought nudity was on the way in. She quoted me in just a small story but, my heavens, the reaction!"

The reaction included T.V, radio and Press coverage and eventually a request from "Look" magazine to make a topless suit and show the world what all the fuss was about.

"I said 'No,'" continued Mr. Gernreich, "but then I rang back and said 'Yes' because of the publicity. After all, if I didn't do it, Emilio would.

"I thought we might sell four or five. Actually we sold 1,000 in the first month and 2,500 the second. Now I've lost count."

"Look here, Mr. Gernreich," I said sternly, "don't you think this nonsense has gone far enough?

"Don't you think women should not be encouraged to make fools of themselves with trousers at one end and no top at the other end?"

Mr. Gernreich swung an elegantly tailored leg over the other—and in tapered trousers with 14in. bottoms this was no mean feat. Adjusting his just-below-waist-length, collarless jacket with the new skinny look, he set about explaining his fashion philosophy as it relates to the Topless Trend.

Trend

"It IS an important trend," he repeated. "If not it wouldn't have caught on like this. But I NEVER meant it to be worn in PUBLIC. I meant it for private parties and yachts and personal swimming pools."

I mentioned the ladies who had been arrested for following the dictum too enthusiastically, the pub-keepers offering free drinks and the thousands of hastily concocted topless dresses that were nothing more than ordinary dresses with strategic bits removed.

"Horrible! Ghastly! Awful!" agreed Mr. Gernreich. "But I NEVER meant the Topless Look to be worn in the evening. It was just for the beach."

Dust

Earlier this week when I was walking through Great Portland-street, one of the main arteries in the heart of Britain's wholesale dress world, I saw three fashion windows still showing topless cocktail dresses.

But the pink plastic untipped breasts were gathering dust and the atmosphere was sad and run-down.

Did Mr Gernreich agree with me that the worst—or best—was over? Most emphatically he did not.

"My new resort collection will have four topless swimsuits. And in the meantime I have a marvellous new idea for Autumn. It's the trouser suit with the transparent top. 'Vogue' have photographed it for their next issue."

"Show me," I said, inwardly groaning. He executed a lightning sketch.

"It's black satin with a sheer chiffon top—and of course you **could** wear it over a bra. But it should look erotic and sensuous."

"Where would you wear it?" I asked.

"It's for married women," said Mr. Gernreich, "to wear at home. For their husbands or their lovers. It costs £300."

But, of course, it will be worn in public and even from here I can hear the whirr of the sewing machines in Great Portland-street and the other wholesale dress centres whipping up budget-priced copies for over-enthusiastic disciples of an idea that started as a minor gimmick and has far from finished as an international sensation.

"Please, don't be afraid of me," said Mr. Gernreich as we parted.

I smiled weakly.

He obviously was a nice, kind man—but then so was Frankenstein, and look what he unleashed.

What he is sketching: The trouser suit with a transparent shirt . . . "you *could* wear a bra, of course."

PRESENTING A MALE VIEW OF PARIS FASHION CHO

Aided and A

SEVEN REASON WHY A MAN

LOVE IT! THINK IT'S SMASHING —BUT DON'T WEAR IT AT THE ZOO

A zebra-striped knicker-bocker suit in fur by Heim.

TANTALISING, THAT'S THE WORD FOR THIS LOT. MY EYES GOT TIRED, JUST LOOKING.

A white robe, helmet, sequin pants—and no bra—from advance-thinking designer Courreges.

ITS ALMOST PURITANICAL SIMPLICITY MAKES THIS DRESS STRANGELY EXCITING.

A low-necked evening dress and separate feather-lined hood in pink. Michel Goma at Patou.

TWO COATS FO
WHO DON'T

Russian Look.
by Real. Right:

BY PETER STEPHENS

ed by FELICITY GREEN

There are some 5,000 outfits shown in Paris each season. This season—the year of The Topless and The Trouser—the good ideas outnumber the ghastly by a healthy proportion.

But which lucky seven of the most sizzling outfits to pick for turing today—the first day when ALL the secrets can be published? uld we print the Courreges suit or the Cardin dress? Or both? What ut the Dior coat? And the Lanvin wrap?

ook a man to solve the problem.

er Stephens, Chief of the Mirror Bureau in Paris, offered to help: "Why 't you let a male choose?" he said. "After all, we're far better red for the job. We can look at clothes dispassionately. We can e them the cool, measured once-over. And, anyway, how many women r choose a really smart dress without the advice—or consent—of their lmate?"

sounded convincing for all sorts of reasons. Women dress to please n. Men pay the bills. Men are interested in what women wear.

K," I said, "I'm convinced. You go ahead and choose what you nk are the best ideas this season."

/hoopee!" he said.

e results of his exuberant selection and his comments about them are n on this page.

NOWS BEST

OME WOMEN G SQUEEZED.

lynx-trimmed, mink by Dior.

POWERFUL STUFF, THIS. I THOUGHT THE GIRL WAS STARKERS.

Actually she's in flesh pink tights under a transparent black robe. By Lanvin.

IF YOU DON'T WEAR THE BOW, YOU'VE GOT A TOPLESS

The stiffened bow is fixed to a bra and the dress actually IS topless. In bright green silk, beaded at neck and hem. By Pierre Cardin.

PHOTOGRAPHED ...

● Pierre Cardin, age 40. Wanted to be a designer even before he knew what a designer was. Became a designer at Dior and also worked for the theatre. Five years later, in 1955, he took the lead among the young couturiers—and has held it. He likes Maxim's, the smartest restaurant in Paris, and the little cafes. Says he hates coarseness.

● Andre Courreges, age 41. Wanted to become a painter. Became a road engineer. Spent eleven years with top Paris designer Balenciaga. Showed his first collection in August, '61. America raved about it. Likes Roquefort cheese, Bordeaux wine, the 17th century and real jewels — and lots of white. Hates fussiness and swank.

SKIRTS v. TROUSERS

The experts thrash it out on French TV

CARDIN SAYS: Women will always be women, mysterious, sensitive and refined. Without them we would be as good as dead. Comfort? Comfort is secondary to fashion. When Dior revived the wasp waist corset, women wore them with pleasure. Trousers may be practical—but they are certainly not beautiful. Good for cold weather? When one wants to please, one is never cold.

● Fade-out shot: I know REAL women.

COURREGES SAYS: The unreal flower-like woman is dead. Today's woman is active, sensual and down to earth. Her problem is that the way of life is constantly changing. In 1920 women wore corsets and umpteen petticoats. Today's changing social habits have altered all this. Women now work, drive and dance. Trousers are now a basic need for a woman. Anyway, women are cold in winter.

● Fade-out shot: You don't KNOW women.

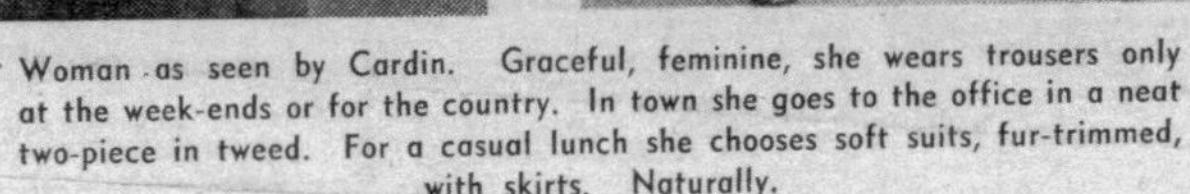

Woman as seen by Cardin. Graceful, feminine, she wears trousers only at the week-ends or for the country. In town she goes to the office in a neat two-piece in tweed. For a casual lunch she chooses soft suits, fur-trimmed, with skirts. Naturally.

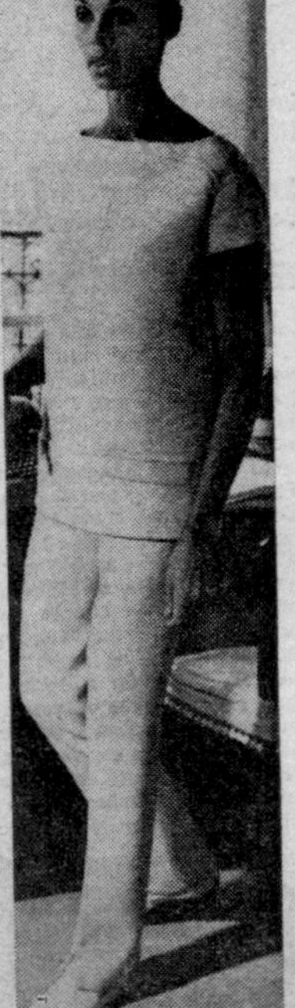

Woman as seen by Courreges. She wears trousers all the time. Seen here, trousers in gold brocade for the evening. For the office, trousers in crisp white whipcord.

DAILY MIRROR, *Friday, September 25, 1964* PAGE 9

✻ Blonde-Bombshellery

Feathers, satin, platinum blonde hair and no bra.. thanks to Jean Harlow, yesterday's queen of glamour, there's a brand new image for today's sex symbol

Already a rage in America, this is the first Harlow look in Britain. Here actress Barbara French wears a Harlow-inspired dress in soft grey satin. Cut on the cross for extra cling, of course. The shoulder straps are made of rhinestones. This dress, price 10 guineas, will be on sale at the Marble Arch and Knightsbridge branches of Wallis Shops at the beginning of November.

Picture by Philip Stearns at Image Studios.

STAND by for a new sex symbol. Or rather the reincarnation of an old one.

The prototype will arrive in Britain next month when the new multi-million dollar Paramount production, "The Carpetbaggers" comes to town.

As played by Carroll Baker, she's platinum blonde, likes soft satins, clinging crepes and lots of feathers. As you can see from the picture on this page she bears a distinct resemblance to the original sex symbol herself, Jean Harlow, who died just twenty-seven years ago.

Fever

In America, the spiritual home of so many sex symbols, Harlow fever already runs high.

Two films are being made of her life story and a book about her private life has stirred up great interest among a whole fashion-conscious generation to whom Jean Harlow was only a name.

Whether the current Paris trend, also highly 1930 in feeling, preceded the Harlow craze or caused it to happen, will be something for the experts to argue about.

In the meantime, a fashion report from New York tells of a swing back to Blonde-Bombshellery.

There are sultry negligees, lavish with swansdown.

There are slinky dinner gowns, plunging dangerously, worn with ostrich feather capes and boas.

The lingerie buyer of a Fifth Avenue store has described it as "A whole new way to separate the girls from the boys. Real 24-carat glamour is fashionable again, and this is only the beginning.

"The 'Jean Harlow Look' is going to be the strongest influence on fashion in the coming months."

Bra-less

Coming in, too, is the Harlow face with its pale and interesting look. For the first time in years, girls are buying ruby red lipsticks.

Amidst all this enthusiasm, there is one black cloud. It hangs heavy over the heads of the bra manufacturers, just reeling back from the body-blow of the topless scare.

Harlow never, ever, wore a bra. She said they were "constricting," and did nothing for that famous bosom of which she was so proud.

Those would have been fighting words indeed in a nation that now spends millions of dollars a year on achieving the maximum in uplift and separation.

But I have a feeling that, bra manufacturers notwithstanding, girls with good enough figures to get away with it will be going bra-less this winter.

FELICITY GREEN

Jean Harlow, sex symbol of the 1930s, with her platinum hair and clinging clothes could influence the way we look today.

Carroll "Baby Doll" Baker in a Harlow-type satin outfit she wears in the new Paramount film, "The Carpetbaggers."

DAILY MIRROR, Saturday, October 17, 1964 PAGE 11

MAGAZINE MIRROR previews the Body Stocking that is to today's bra and girdle what a Spaceship is to a horse and buggy

YOU ARE LOOKING AT A REVOLUTION!

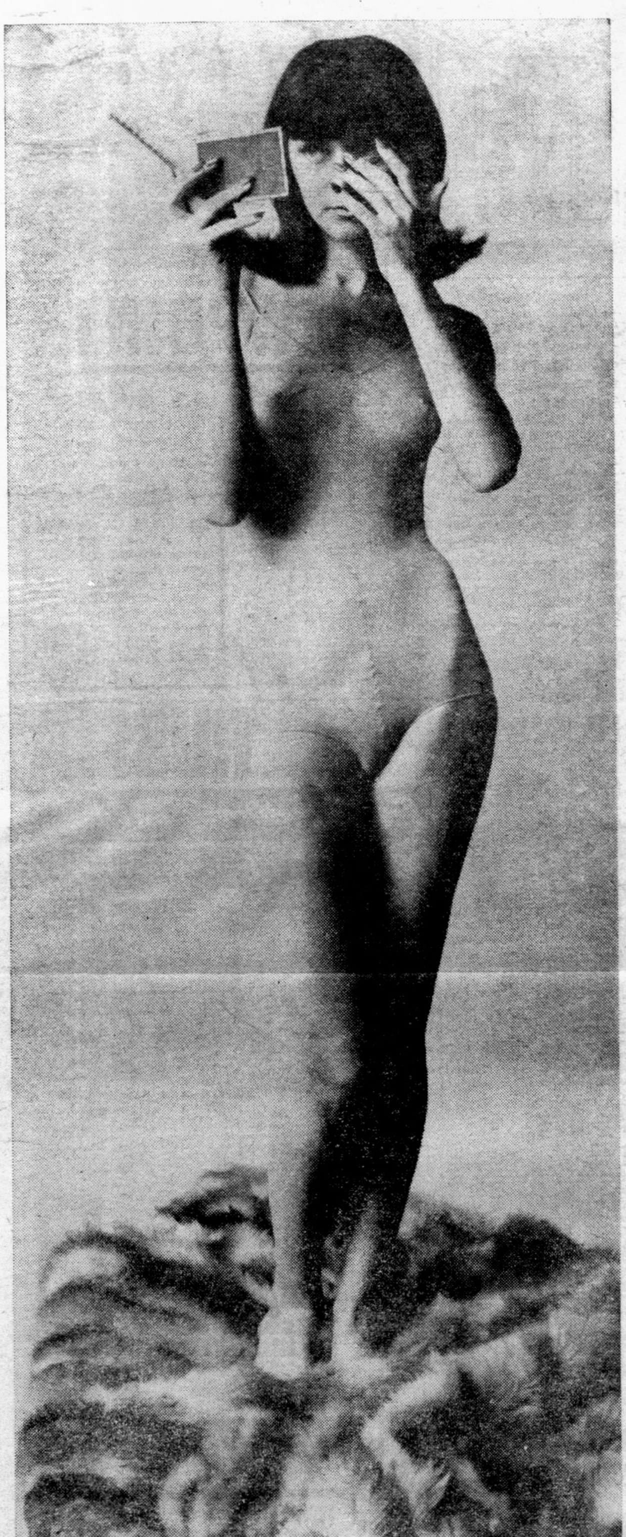

The now-you-see-it, now-you-don't look in undies. Called Body Stocking, it's doll-sized and it stretches to fit the average doll, costs the equivalent of £4 and is the colour of flesh. Of course.

THE girl in the brand-new high-fashion crepe dress slides sexily across the room. As she moves, every curve of her stunning figure is clearly revealed in all its feminine glory.

Equally clearly revealed is the edge of her girdle, the outline of her panties, the bumps on her suspenders and the fastening at the back of her bra.

Oh dear, it won't do at all. Undies are supposed to fulfil a useful function, but not to show.

As fashion gets more and more revelatory and fabrics get more and more slinky, so foundation garments have to get into the same near-nude mood. (Unless, of course, girls are to go undie-free and thereby wreck a £70,000,000 a year flourishing business.)

by FELICITY GREEN

So, with the Jean Harlow craze as their inspiration, the bra and girdle barons have now solved the problem of the invisible bra and the all-gone girdle.

They have just introduced the all-in-one garment that stretches to fit and clings as closely as if it were sprayed on and weighs under half an ounce.

Made by Warners, it will be introduced in America on November 1.

Called the Body Stocking, see left, it is knitted on a hosiery machine and was born when a stocking manufacturer realised his idle plant could be usefully employed making bra cups instead of heel cups.

Invisible

Also on the invisible undie scene is Rudi Gernreich, the man who invented the Topless and is now busy studying ways of covering up what he once wished to expose.

His no-bra bra, due to be shown for the first time next week, is made of sheer nylon net. The shoulder straps are string-thin, and it is being made in three shades, all transparent.

Answers to questions that will undoubtedly be asked:

No, you can't buy Body Stockings here yet. It is so new that the London office of Warner's saw the samples only last week. However, a spokesman said it should be available by December.

Hold-up

No, there are no suspenders on the Body Stocking. If an American girl wants to wear stockings she can keep them up with Ultra-Hold, the "garter in a bottle." She rolls some colourless liquid round the top of her thigh, sticks her stockings on to it and they're there for the day.

It works. I know because I tried some. It hurts a bit when you pull the stocking off.

I only hope that it, too, will be available over here soon or we'll all be in dead trouble with those wretched suspender bumps.

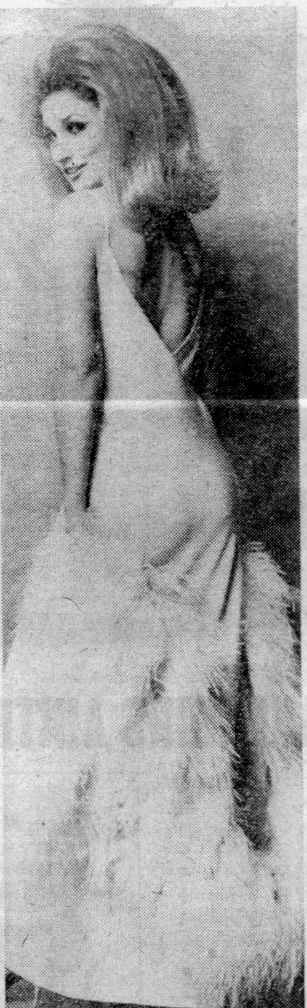

The Harlow-inspired dress in which an ordinary girdle causes more bumps than a pound of peas.

DAILY MIRROR, *Friday, October 30, 1964* PAGE 9

NINE WAYS TO HELP THE EXPORT DRIVE

Meet the new pop group . . the one that makes clothes not discs

PREVIEW of next week's first-time fashion line-up from the new Associated Fashion Designers. All prices are approximate and all the clothes will be available early in the new year. Left to right: White linen-type dress and coat with embroidered flowers—by Mark Russell, 12 gns.; Culotte pleated skirt dress with navy flower-printed top—by Marlborough Dresses, 6 gns.; High-waisted dress with navy printed bead-edged top—by Ann Tyrrell for John Marks, 7½ gns.; Navy linen-type dress with see-through crochet midriff and cuffs—by Hildebrand, 5 gns.; Grey wool suit with zip front and circle pockets—by Andre Peters, 14 gns.; Pink-check suit—by Mono, 9 gns.; Dress with white top and pleated spotted skirt over white knee-length pants—by Rhona Roy, £9 19s. 6d.; Skirt and over-blouse in sailor blue linen-type—by Ricki Reed, 8 gns.; Trouser suit in sugar pink linen-type with navy blouse—by Carol Freedman, 13½ gns.

✱ WE LIVE in the Group Age—Pop Groups and Fashion Groups.

Top Group in the fashion charts just now is the Fashion House Group of London who are showing for the twelfth time next Monday.

With twenty-eight members—some sizzling, some staid—they put on champagne-level dress shows twice a year and this season hope to bring in about £4,000,000 of export orders.

Taking place one day later—when about 1,000 well-heeled, overseas buyers are in town, cheque books at the ready—is a first-ever show by a rival group, which plans to nose its well-dressed way into the fashion limelight.

Drive

This new group, the Associated Fashion Designers, comprises nine of the brighter sparks in British ready-to-wear fashions whose clothes are already favourites here and who now feel there's room at the top of the fashion export drive for some new blood.

The man behind the group is John Marks, a shrewd 35-year-old manufacturer who calls himself "one of the older, young designers." He bases his hopes for the A F D on a hunch that the young British look is as much in demand abroad as the British sound made by the Beatles or the Rolling Stones.

"Buyers are coming here now for young clothes—not for classics. We will be the first group to specialise in really young clothes."

With their production know-how they can avoid with ease the pitfalls of too many of today's lone-wolf young designers who are full of good ideas that go wrong for all sorts of reasons. Perhaps their workrooms are inadequate. Sometimes their technical knowledge is non-existent. And their cash resources are usually slim to nil.

So next week A F D is born and the rival groups get set to bid for the fashion favours.

Fine

How does Raymond Zelker, chairman of the Fashion House Group of London feel about the newcomer?

"Fine," he says. "In fact, we're rather flattered that the new group has chosen our Fashion Week for its first show.

"And, anyway, the more there is going on here for buyers next week the better it will be. It will create more interest and more business."

Says John Marks: "There's a big demand for young British clothes all over the world now.

"Buyers come here to buy the sort of young clothes that appear on the pop T V programmes. But it has been hard to find them in previous seasons. That's why we've started the group."

As all the clothes in both shows will be available not only abroad, but at home, too, this state of healthy competition can mean only one thing; even better and brighter styles for you and me. So let battle commence.

MEANWHILE, BACK AT THE ESTABLISHMENT..

NOT ALL is totally trad, though, in the well-established London Fashion House Group. Among the heavily classic, mink-trimmed prestige numbers that will sway their dignified and pricey way down the catwalk next week will be a healthy proportion of swinging styles to catch the discerning buyer's eye.

There will be trousers by the bagful, dazzling, printed linens for high summer, and crisp, cavalry twills for spring suits.

There will be more than enough goodies to go round for all the buyers from forty-one countries coming here for a super spring spending spree.

Seen here, a three-piece trouser suit with a rib-baring top. Designed by Digby Morton at Reldan, it will sell for about 10 gns.

WORDS By FELICITY GREEN **SKETCH** By BARBARA HULANICKI **PICTURE** By DOREEN SPOONER

If you want to see how much women have really changed, just look at these corset ads *

*** In the days when bras were called bust bodices and girdles were stays—1924 to be precise—girls looked like this and were considered daring, to boot.**

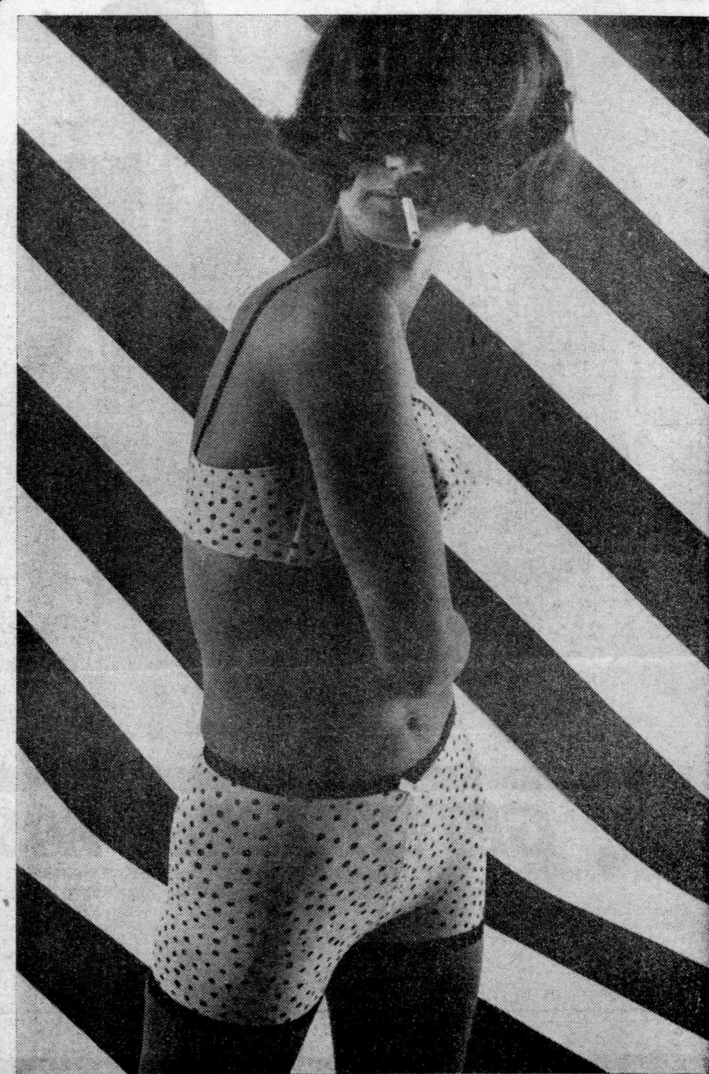

*** Today's girl in her Ban-lon bra and suspender-free girdle looks life—and the camera—straight in the eye. Only her roughed-up hairdo gets in the way.**

by FELICITY GREEN

THERE are more in some pictures than first meets the eye. These two for a start.

They're both corset advertisements with a 40-year time lag between them.

At first glance they show how bras, girdles and suspenders have changed since the days when they were called bust bodices, stays and hose supporters.

But at second glance nothing has changed more than the girls themselves.

On the left Miss Foundation Garment 1924, carefully Marcel waved, clasps a posy and coyly suggests it's all rather daring and whatever would Daddy say?

On the right Miss Foundation Garment 1964 replaces the flirty flowers with a fag —I'll just bet it's a Gauloise—and suggests that she doesn't give a damn what anyone says. Including Daddy-O. Far from covering up her thighs with a couple of demurely placed flounces she exposes her navel with all the aplomb of a successful belly dancer. Or, perhaps, just a modern-minded girl used to wearing even less on the beach any summer.

Her hair has today's roughed-up look that irate husbands and/or fathers say looks like a floor mop and expensive hairdressers charge a fortune to create.

Funny isn't it? The more we spend on getting a good shape—£70,000,000 a year at the moment—the less superstructure is needed to do it.

18 NOV. 1964

What sort of undies go best with the new trouser suits?

Trouser-type undies, of course

* Not so much a fashion, more a way of life. That's the trouser suit to the young stride-ahead set. Ideal for scooting around, ideal for week-end wear, ideal for girls who want to get ahead in fashion while an idea is still new enough to be controversial, the trouser suit looks like top favourite for winter warmth in 1964/65.

For extra winter warmth what's more logical than trouser-type undies? (Same slim-legged silhouette, no additional bulk, no problem about a topcoat—see?)

Seen here, grey flannel trouser suit by Emcar. 6½ guineas at Fenwicks, London, W.1. Its undercover friends in scarlet wool and Bri-Nylon are by Lux Lux, vest 17s. 6d., pants 29s.

PICTURES by PETER TEBBITT

VIDAL SASSOON

'60s hairdresser whose precision cut changed the way women round the world wanted to look

Felicity Green was as much responsible for putting the swing into the '60s as any of us, including Mary Quant and me! Felicity's vision was extraordinary and she would often have ideas far ahead of the rest of the press.

Fortunately for me, Felicity was blessed with a real sense of fun – and that's how she became my No.1 shampoo girl for Paris designer Emanuel Ungaro's first show since he had left the great Balenciaga. The fashion world was buzzing with anticipation. On the eve of the great event, Felicity, who was staying in the same Paris hotel, spotted me and my team on our way to put the finishing touches to the haircuts for tomorrow's show. Felicity's eyes gleamed and I knew she had An Idea. "Surely, Vidal, you must need an extra shampoo girl?" To dispel any of my doubts she reassured me. "Don't worry, with an apron on I can easily look like one of your team." So that's how Felicity became my shampoo girl, and a good time was had by all, including Ungaro who enjoyed this little bit of fashion fun. And Felicity kept her promise to me not to break the strict embargo that ruled the Paris fashion scene at that time. If she had published her Ungaro story a day ahead of the rest of the press, it would have caused mayhem among them, and wouldn't have helped Ungaro – or me!

What a marvellous group of young British journalists followed Felicity's '60s example. Before this, unless a style came out of Paris or Rome, it didn't have the necessary cachet. The British press changed all that and suddenly London was Number One in the world.

When Felicity, who was a main board director of the Mirror Group at the time, left the *Mirror* she joined me as Managing Director, Europe. But I knew she missed the pace and excitement of the newspaper world, so I wasn't surprised when the world of print welcomed her back. I miss Felicity as a lovely human being and someone who could put her vision into practice for me as she did for the *Daily Mirror*.

PS Felicity always said if she hadn't been a journalist she could have been a hairdresser.

She was probably right.

VIDAL SASSOON 2012

"Under Vidal's genius the curlers, rollers and waves just disappeared. Vidal cut hair like a tailor cuts cloth"

FELICITY ON VIDAL

Vidal was to hair what Mary Quant was to fashion – they were the '60s revolutionaries. Under Vidal's genius the curlers, rollers and waves just disappeared. Vidal cut hair like a tailor cuts cloth. To be first among all the Vidal disciples, the big starry names – including Mary Quant, model Grace Coddington, and Hollywood star Mia Farrow – waited in line for his magic scissors to render them first among Sassoon-cropped equals.

From the time Vidal the apprentice in Mr Adolf Cohen's East End hair salon took up a pair of scissors, he was determined to cut hair not only better, but differently from any other hairdresser ever. He was determined to be a Star. And that's exactly what he was.

His wonderful way with hair was pictured in the *Daily Mirror* throughout the entire swinging '60s and every hairdresser did their best to do a Vidal.

Note: I loved Vidal. Vidal loved me. He never cut my hair.

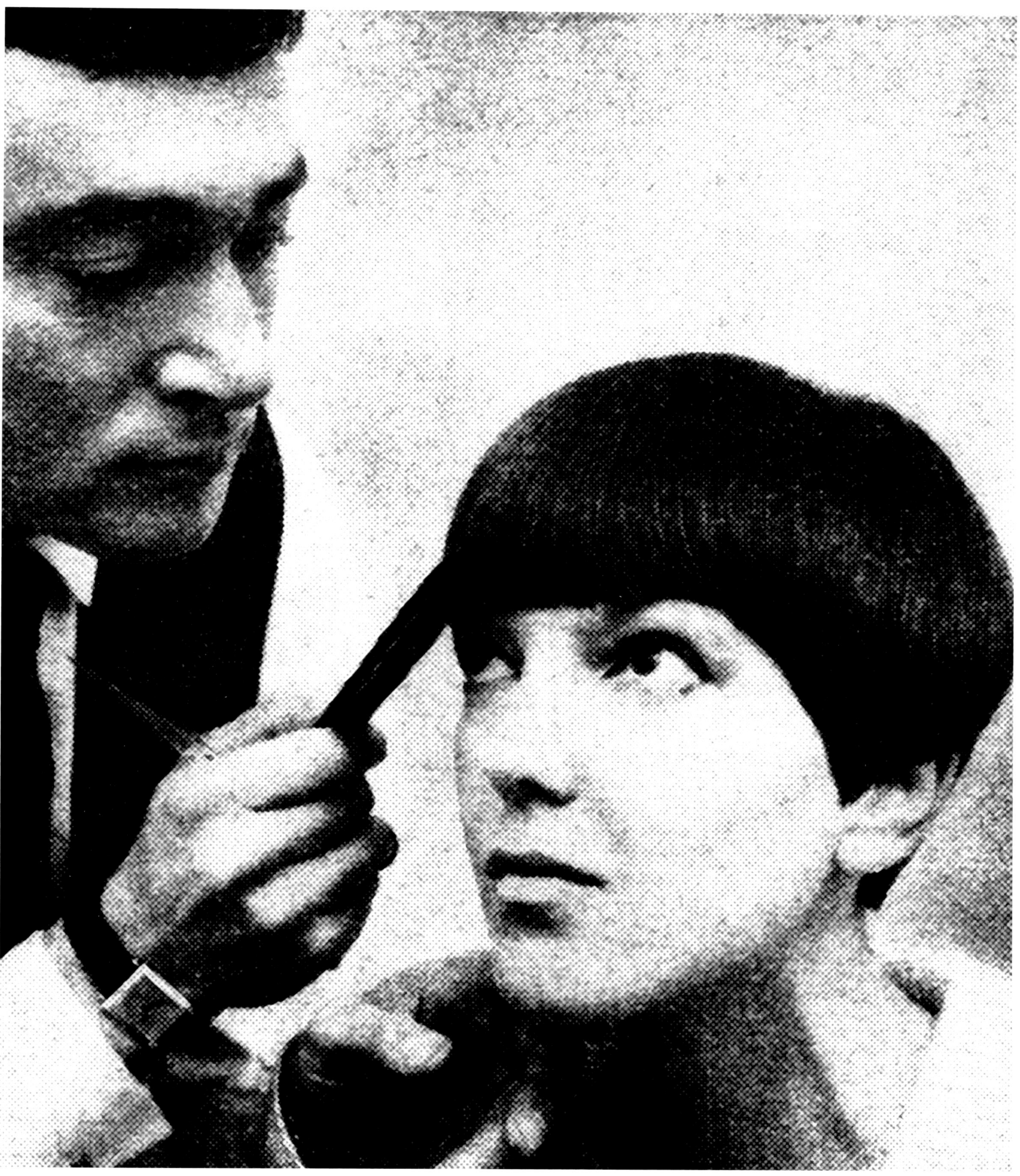

Two of the biggest and brightest stars shining in those Swinging '60s – Vidal Sassoon gives Mary Quant his famous Five-Point Cut that swept the world

For me, these pages are momentous. Never before in newspaper history had the front and back pages of a national newspaper been given to a Fashion Editor to fill. Hugh Cudlipp, Editorial Director of the Mirror Group sent for me and said felt he was out of touch with Britain's Swinging '60s. He felt there was a lot going on in the whole of the London scene – what he called this "with-it" world. He thought I knew more about this than he did and he felt it was important. So to fill the gap in his knowledge and update any of our less hip readers he instructed me to fill this gap. And in order to pass my knowledge on, he planned a *Daily Mirror* first. He planned to give me the front and back pages to bring our 15 million readers up to date with the clothes, the hair, the music, the youth and this New World Order. Gosh! Well I tried. With the help of top fashion photographer, John Adriaan I chose two views of two of the '60s sensational fashion stories. The Topless Trend that was adopted among the young enthusiasts, in London immediately, if more slowly further north. It's hard to remember now the one-piece swimwear that was bottoms only pioneered by American sportswear designers Rudi Gernreich and Reuben Torres. Trousers – and trouser suits – for women were almost acceptable almost everywhere except the Dorchester Hotel. They even asked Raquel Welch to leave when she turned up in trousers for my interview, and anachronistically my editor at the *Mirror* wasn't too sure about them either. But Paris designer Andre Courrèges was absolutely sure – trousers were the modern way for women to dress. How did my male colleagues regard this revolutionary idea, a woman filling these important pages of the mighty *Mirror*? If they minded it, I never knew it.

PS The news story in the left hand corner of the front page arrived in the middle of the night and the first I knew about it was when I saw the paper the next morning!

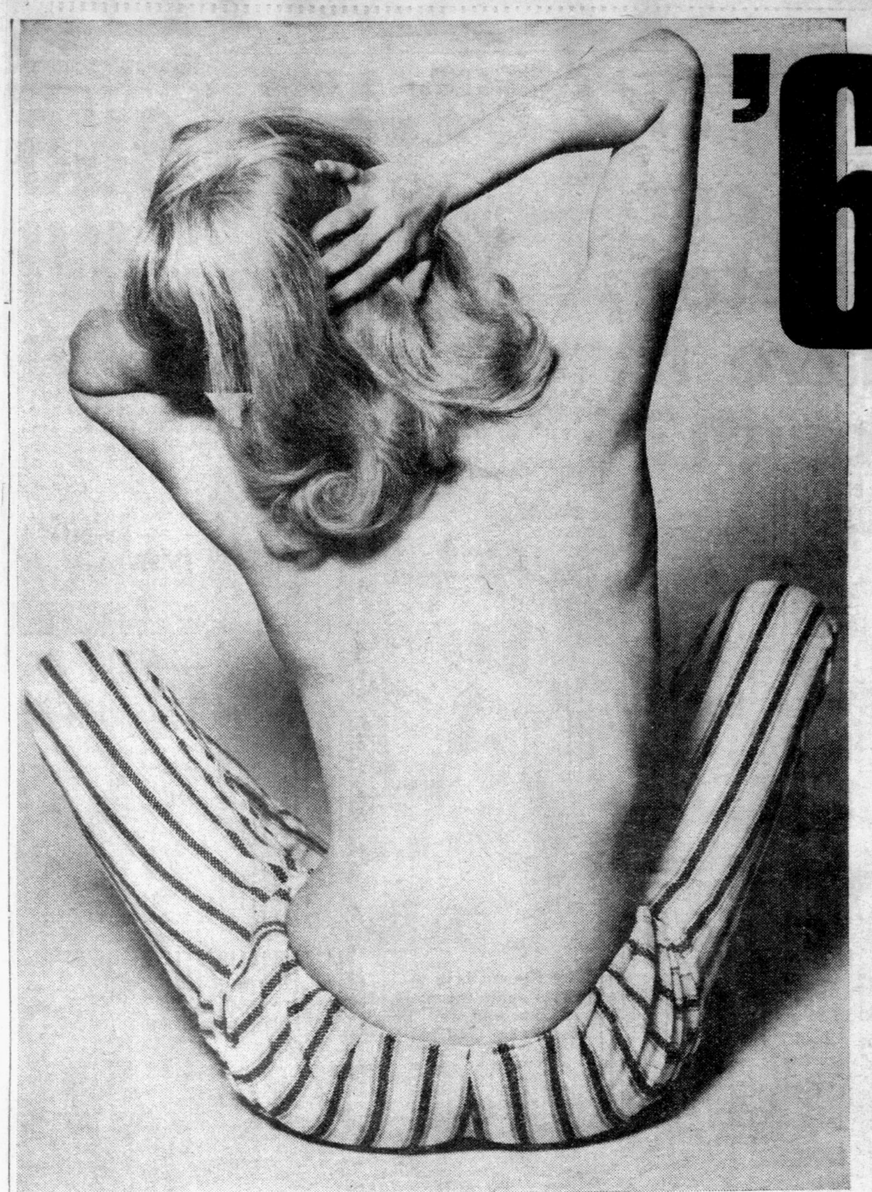

If you want to go topless, good luck to you! If you want to buy the suit, it's by Raymond of London and costs 11 guineas. The picture is by John Adriaan.

'64

by FELICITY GREEN

IF Miss 1964 took (the jacket of h new two-piece trous suit, she might w have been bare fro the navel up.

Trousers and Tople . . . these were the b fashion stories of t year.

The trouser-suit sto came from Paris whe designer Andre Cou reges decreed th skirts were out of do and pants for roun the-clock wear we part of modern life.

Two Americ sportswear designers Rudi Gernreich a Reuben Torres—inve ted the bottoms-or swimsuit and wh started as a seasi gimmick soon turn into a world-wide co troversy with everyon but everyone, getting on the act.

IN RUSSIA a week newspaper denounc topless as a reversion barbarism and a sym tom of the sickness American life.

IN BRITAIN, r only swimsuits, b dresses, too, went to less.

Enthusiastic follow of fashion wore t new trend at a Lond night club, on We minster Bridge, Brands Hatch, at Harrogate Hotel advertise a tracti engine rally, in Pic dilly and at a mine gala in Doncaster.

But after a colour and action - pack career, which led to couple of arrests, topless trend now see to have burned its out on the launchi pad.

NOTE FOR NE YEAR: Mr. Gernre is busy designing tra parent bras.

ALL-OUT HUNT FOR CHILD-KILLER

By TOM TULLETT and BARRY STANLEY

A MASSIVE hunt was on last night for child-killer Frederick Alfred Smith.

He escaped from a gardening party at Wormwood Scrubs yesterday by tying two hoes and a piece of bent pipe together.

He used the pipe as a hook and climbed over the wall at about 1.20 p.m.

Smith, known as the Babes-in-the-Woods killer, was sentenced to death in 1947 for the murder of seven-year-old Eileen Gaff. He was later reprieved.

Eileen was found dying in Manor Woods, Guildford. Her nine-year-old brother Leslie was dead by her side. At his trial, Smith pleaded guilty to murdering Eileen. A charge of murdering Leslie was ordered to remain on the file.

It is known that Smith was a violent prisoner. He received psychiatric treatment in prison.

Watch

The house at Worplesdon, near Guildford, where Smith, of gipsy origin, lived with his mother has been demolished. Last night police were keeping a close watch on the area.

They were also searching gipsy encampments in the South.

Scotland Yard flashed a description to all police stations with the warning: "This man must be recaptured."

They said he wears a hearing aid, is just over 6ft. tall, balding with an oval face, and was dressed in grey prison "battle dress" when he escaped.

Later they issued a new description which said his hair is "receding at the temples" and that though 38, Smith looks 50, with drawn features. He may be wearing a blue raincoat missing from the prison.

Frederick Smith . . . as he was in 1947.

THE DAILY MIRROR NEWSPAPERS, Ltd., at Holborn Circus, London, E.C.1, and at Mark-lane, Manchester, 4. Tuesday, December 22, 1964.

Daily Mirror

'64

A SOUVENIR ISSUE FOR THE MIRROR'S 15,000,000 READERS

d. Tuesday, December 22, 1964 No. 18,975

KRUSHCHEV SACKED. CHINA EXPLODES ATOMIC BOMB. MOSCOW AND PEKING MOVE POLES APART IN THEIR PRIVATE DEEP-FREEZE. TORIES TOPPLE, BRITAIN GOES WITH WILSON. JOHNSON RIDES HOME ON A LANDSLIDE, GOLDWATER GOES WEST. NEHRU DIES, SHASTRI (5ft 2in) SHOULDERS THE DESPAIR OF 441 MILLION. CATHOLICS BEGIN AN

THE YEAR THAT CHANGED ALL OUR LIVES

AGONISING PURSUIT OF TRUTH IN THE MODERN AGE. THE POPE VISITS HOLY LAND AND INDIA.

AND, OF COURSE, SKIRTS GOT SHORTER, BOYS' HAIR GOT LONGER, SMART GIRLS WORE THE TROUSERS, THE TOPLESS WENT BUST AND THE BEATLES (WHO ELSE?) WENT EVERYWHERE . .

▲ SEE BACK PAGE

PAR

by Felicity Green

There's about as much unanimit
the Paris fashion scene at the mor
as there is on a stormy day in the H
of Commons.

Arguing highly in favour of femininity
Trad Party put forward a policy of ple
waists, swirling skirts, chiffon and curly hair

Giving the veto to so much nostalgia is
radical Courreges who says it's for the b
feathered species. Women should get Twen
Century-minded, he campaigns, starting
their wardrobes. Time marches on and the only way to keep up with it is in trousers, or a skirt 3in. above the knee.

Other designers may finish their collections with a full-scale, sigh-provoking wedding rig-out, veil and all.

Courreges whams in with the navel-exposing get-up shown above, right, the veil replaced with sun goggles.

The international fashion trade paper Women's Wear Daily describes the two looks for '65 as Bodysoft versus Tough Chic.

Over to you to make your choice. Or you could, of course, stay a floating voter.

Pictures by HATAMI, RELANG and DUFFY.

PLEATS, PLEATS, AND MORE PLEATS

For connoisseurs of such things Paris '65 has a plethora of pleats in the following varieties: box, sun-ray, knife, cartridge, unpressed, inverted, bias cut, and accordion. For the uninitiated, it's enough to know that any old pleats will do this summer as long as they swing when you do. ABOVE: flat pleats on a beige herringbone print suit with turban to match, and a white overblouse. By Dior. TRIO BELOW, left to right: knife pleats on a white check and plain grey suit from Real; biased-cut and unpressed pleats in orange silk from Ricci; box pleats on a grey-flannel, white-waistcoated suit from Goma at Patou.

THIS IS THE DIOR TUNIC

Softest and slinkiest of the soft looks—a tunic-line dress in printed green chiffon, by Marc Bohan of Dior. The tunic has long sleeves, a collarless neckline, small jewel buttons, and slit sides. Underneath is a matching skirt, softly gathered. On top—a turban. India, you may have guessed, is where Marc Bohan is finding his inspiration. Both tunic and turban are Trad there.

CARDIN

Waists are in.
do an exercise
who still fanci
dress in black
to the hips and

DAILY MIRROR, Monday, March 1, 1965 PAGE 13

S 65

There are now two distinct looks to choose from . . . One is soft, the other's tough. One is Trad, the other Mod

…HIFTY

…go on a diet,
… follow Cardin,
… . This coat-
… falls straight
…in a low flare.

TAKE COURREGES

Don't underestimate the influence of Courreges. One American department store chain selling £50,000,000 of dresses a year says his influence on casual and sportswear is "terrific." Before you say, "It's fine, but not for me," just think how the two outfits above—both black and white—would look without the boots. Without the hats, maybe. And just an inch or so longer. Most fashion-conscious women could wear them. LEFT: not an outfit for the Black and White Minstrels, but the new Courreges trouser suit, trimmed sexily in black with a razzle-dazzle striped lining. Note the toeless boots.

DAILY MIRROR, Monday, March 29, 1965 PAGE 9

Case of the Missing Model

IT was to have been an all-star spectacular picture. Only in this case the main star didn't arrive.

The scene she should have graced was the studio of fashion photographer John French who was all set to take one of the pictures of the year—Britain's top ten models, as chosen by the leading art directors, fashion writers and photographers.

For the second year running Jean Shrimpton was placed first. But it's no good looking for her famous face in the group on the right.

Tied

Released today, this picture shows the leading model girls in Britain—from numbers two to ten.

The reason there are ten girls in the picture, even without Miss Shrimpton, is that two girls, Vicky Hodge and Primrose Austen, tied for place No. 10.

What had happened to Jean Shrimpton? Her failure to be on time was just not done in a world where a model never, but *never*, lets the side down!

The organisers of the poll paced the studio floor and started a slight case of ulcers.

JOHN FRENCH, a long-time and staunch friend of Miss Shrimpton, said he was sure she *would* arrive. She had said she would.

The other models, who were being paid by the hour, waited, at least profitably.

At 7.15 p.m., one and a quarter hours after the job was due to start, a message was received. From the secretary of the photographer Miss Shrimpton had been working for earlier that day.

Miss Shrimpton had been on location. She was on her way back when she had a flat tyre. In Harlow New Town. She couldn't get back.

So, regretfully, the picture, minus star, was taken.

Safe

The next morning Miss Shrimpton came clean, to Mr. John French. "I'm sorry I let you down. It was nothing personal," she told him. "I decided I don't hold with polls any more. I don't think models ought to be graded."

It's a safe view to take, one can't help feeling—provided you're No. 1.

Felicity Green

Left to right (with the number of points they scored in the poll): 9th Marie-Lise Gres (49); 10th Primrose Austen (44); 4th Sandra Paul (144); 5th Paulene Stone (105); 8th, seated, Susan Murray (81); 10th, standing, Vicky Hodge (44); 3rd, seated, Celia Hammond (153); 2nd Jill Kennington (176); 6th Tania Mallet (104); 7th Grace Coddington (96). Jean Shrimpton's score was 184.

Jean Shrimpton

BRITAIN'S TOP MODELS FOR '65

(No's 2, 3, 4, 5, 6, 7, 8, 9, 10 & 10)

IN THE TOP COLOUR SCHEME: BLACK & WHITE

SEEN HERE are the girls who represent the cream of the modelling world for 1965.

Newcomers to the Top Ten include Susan Murray, Marie-Lise Gres and Vicky Hodge who has been modelling for only six months. Paulene Stone, No. 5, was missing from last year's list because she was having a baby. Jill Kennington, No. 2, was recently involved in a serious road accident and had to undergo plastic surgery on her face. One who almost made it, but not quite is Pattie Boyd, girl friend of Beatle George Harrison.

To connoisseurs of fashion rather than girls, details follow of the black and white outfits seen above: left to right, pique dress, Courreges-inspired, by Bernshaw, £4 9s 6d.; mesh-topped dress by Jean Varon, 6½ gns.; Tricel slacks, 4 gns. and Arnel print shirt, £5 9s. 6d by Majestic; tablecloth check evening dress, by Simon Ellis, 4 gns.; baseline sweater by John Craig, 32s. 6d., pleated Tricel skirt by Majestic, 4 gns.; towelling beach dress, by Angela at London Town, 4½ gns.; chalk-striped cotton dress by Lee Cecil, 5 gns.; spotted rayon dress, Polly Peck, 6 gns.; linen dress, Susan Small, 10 gns.; dress with wool skirt, string top, John Stephens, 6 gns.

For where to buy the dresses, write to Fashion Department, Daily Mirror, 33 Holborn, London, E.C.1.

This picture by photographer John French was supposed to have One More Model. But The One who disapproved of ranking models by numbers was of course the famous Jean Shrimpton – so she didn't turn up. But The Show Must Go On, the judges needed ten girls so another more easy-going model was shipped into the line-up. Above and opposite: The enduring favourite colour combination in '65 and favourite today – and tomorrow and the day after that! Black and white combining with the '60s Op Art craze for maximum style impact.

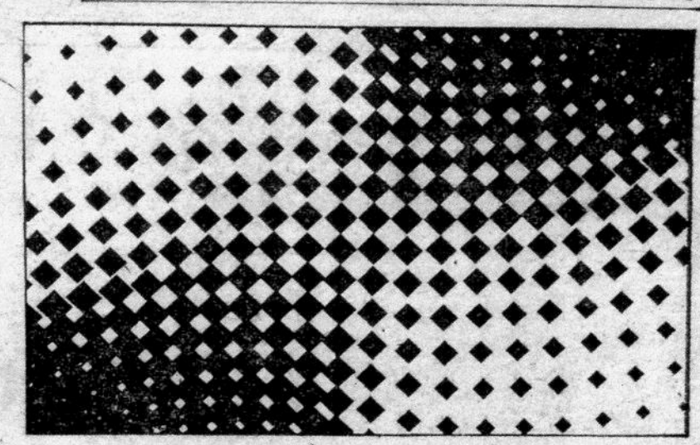

Two Op art paintings by British artist Jeffrey Steele. One is at the Grabowski Gallery in Chelsea, where they say: "It will sell for several hundred pounds." The other is in a private collection.

THE WORD IS 'OP'..

it's short for optical illusion • Op art paintings are selling for hundreds of pounds • Now Op art is hitting the fashion world with a supersonic bang

● Op art circles dazzle on a short towelling shift. In black and white. By Angela at London Town: £4 19s. 6d.

TAKE one whiter than white background. On it, place a vibrating pattern of black lines, squares, dots or circles—anything, in fact, that's dazzlingly geometric in shape.

If the resulting pattern dances about before your very eyes, you have a reasonable facsimile of Op art, the craze that is as much a part of to day's scene, on both sides of the Atlantic, as the Mods, the Beatles and Jean Shrimpton.

Serious Op artists are not all that happy to be inspiring such items as sweaters, blouses, bathing suits and curtains.

As one American art critic put it: "Putting Op art patterns on clothes is only one degree less perverted than putting a reproduction of Rembrandt on a wastepaper basket."

by FELICITY GREEN

But the less art-conscious fashion and fabric manufacturers, happily using Op art vibration effects for summer '65, are ignoring this cry from the heart.

Smart

In America, where there is a new and highly successful Op art exhibition at New York's world-famous Museum of Modern Art, smart stores on Fifth-avenue have quickly followed suit with Op art fashion windows.

In the furnishing sections, Op art curtains and upholstery fabrics look like paintings by the yard.

Among the merchandise ideas there now and coming soon are Op art dresses, blouses, sweaters, hats, handbags, shoes and jewellery.

In London, Op art paintings vibrate on the walls of all the most go-ahead galleries and tempt the connoisseurs at prices up to £1,000 a time.

Here, too, the fashion and furnishing world is moving in.

Summer dresses and sportswear are getting Op art treatment. Shoes are available. So are cushions.

Force

And much as the Op art painters may object to seeing a spitting image of their latest work all over someone's 36-24-36, there's nothing they can do about it.

Op art is now a force in the fashion world and we shall all be seeing a great deal of it. I hope we don't get eye strain.

● Op art squares against an Op art background create the essential dazzle. The eye-catching beach top is by Emcar. There are trousers included in the price—5 gns.

OP ART FASHION DRAWINGS ON THE LEFT ARE BY GERRY RICHARDS

DAILY MIRROR, Wednesday, May 12, 1965 PAGE 17

A PICTURE THAT COULD ONLY CLICK WHEN A BEATLE MEETS THE WORLD'S TOP FASHION PHOTOGRAPHER

HAIL, RINGO

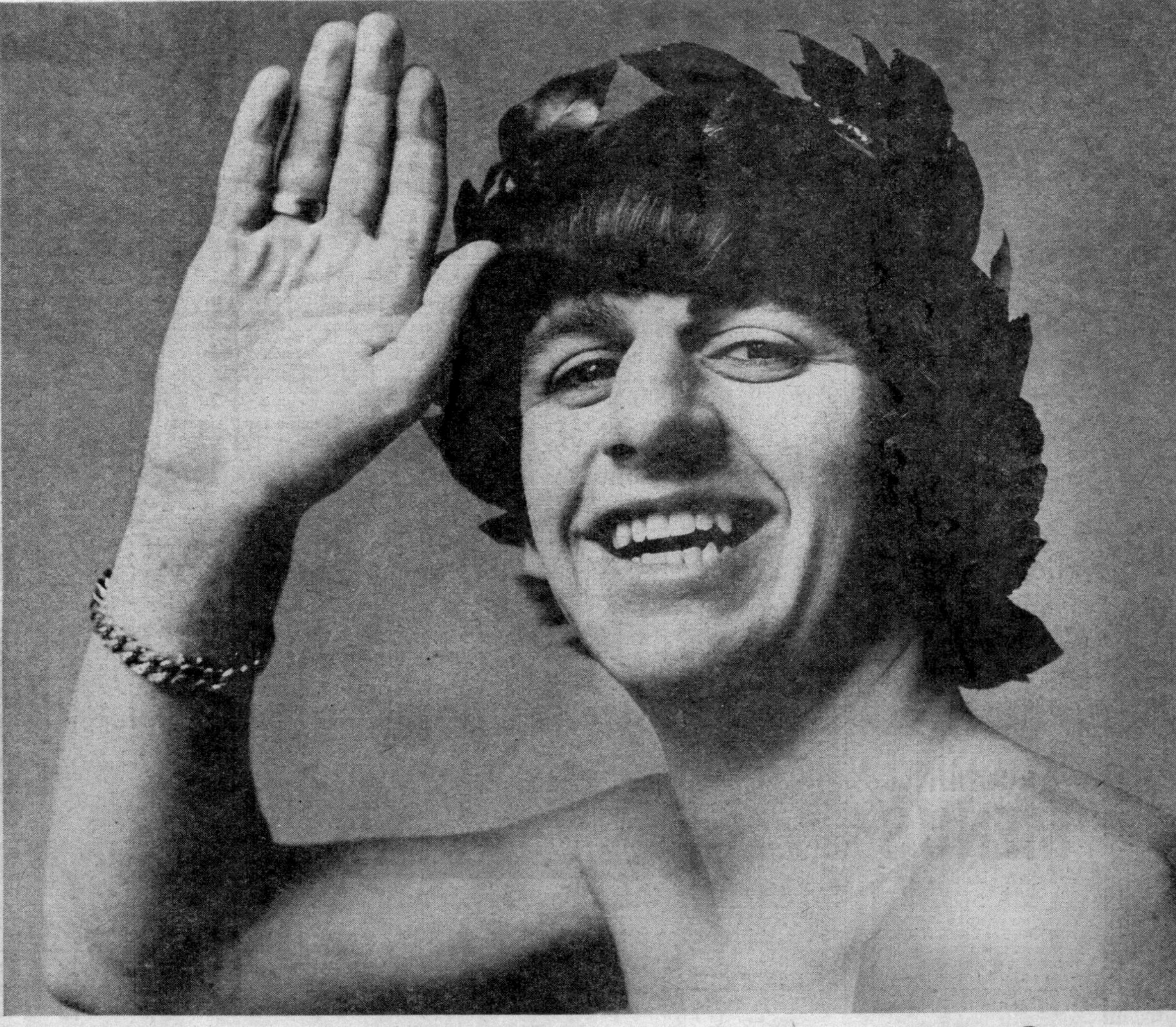

THIS is Ringo. The Beatle who isn't the best-looking one. The one with the funny, lovable face that arouses such deep feelings of passion, and mother-love among women of various age groups.

This is Ringo, 25 on July 7. Who weighs 10½ stone, stands 5ft. 8in, and says he likes fast cars, his parents, and anyone who likes **him.**

This is Ringo the near-monosyllabic Liverpudlian drummer who inspired a songwriter to compose a hit called "Ringo for President."

This is Ringo who, when the pop bubble finally bursts, could be the Beatle with the career as a comic.

This is Ringo, three months married and an expectant father and who, say those who know the Beatles best, is the **nicest** one.

This is Ringo as seen by Richard Avedon . . . And when Mr. Avedon had finished photographing Mr. Ringo Starr, Mr. Starr photographed Mr. Richard Avedon. The result is seen below.

Said Mr. Starr: "I must've jogged the camera."

—AND THIS IS AVEDON by RINGO

"A touch of Chaplin, a bit of Harpo and the Great God Pan"

—RINGO by RICHARD AVEDON

FOR BEATLE FANS this is a vintage picture. It's Ringo, their beloved drummer boy, laurel-wreathed to look like the Emperor Nero.

It was taken in a London studio in the dead of night—"to avoid the crowds; only the charladies were there"—by Richard Avedon, the famous fashion photographer, for a recent issue of American Harper's Bazaar.

Avedon, who had been asked to edit a special edition of this super glossy magazine, was in London to gather atmosphere and picture ideas for his pro-British theme.

A 41-year-old, slim, dark pixie of a man, he met the Beatles at the "Ad Lib" club and invited Ringo to pose.

Ringo, like Bardot, and Maugham, and Monroe, and the Windsors, and Judy Garland, and a hundred other personalities of our time, was happy to oblige—for Avedon.

Said Avedon of Ringo: "I found him charming, co-operative and inventive. He talks as much with gestures as with words. He reminds me a little of Chaplin, Harpo Marx, and also the great god Pan.

"He communicates not with language but with his whole body when he wants to reassure or reach out. Ringo . . . his very name flies from the tongue like an exultation—or a cry for help.

"To get the shot I wanted I must have taken about 100 exposures. But this is my favourite. It's Ringo the Emperor, Ringo the Winner. That's why I thought of the laurel wreath."

Said Ringo: "It's great. It was taken by the world's best fashion photographer, wasn't it? I don't normally like pictures of me without a shirt on.

"With a figure like mine—you've got to watch it. You can lose fans that way."

Did he feel a bit silly posing like this? Said the Beatle drummer: "Why? What's the difference between wearing a hat and a laurel wreath?"

The picture above of Beatle Ringo Starr was taken by the famous American photographer Richard Avedon whose work was more likely to appear in such glossy magazines as US *Vogue* or *Harper's Bazaar*. But I thought I'd try to get it for the *Daily Mirror*. I called him, he answered. I sang the praises of the *Mirror* and he said yes. I was thrilled. I rushed out to tell everyone in the newsroom what a coup this was. No-one in the whole room had ever heard of Richard Avedon. Good grief!

DAILY MIRROR, Tuesday, June 15, 1965 PAGE 15

There will be about 15,000 hats making the scene at Ascot this week, but I doubt if any will top these

HEAD-GEAR

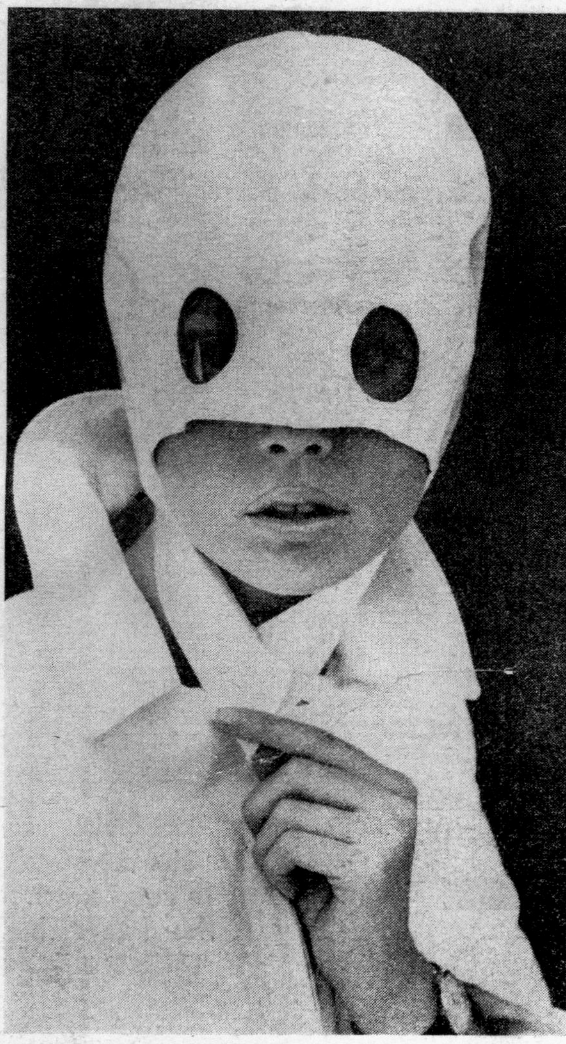

THE Beatles may or may not deserve the M B E.

But if the hatters of Britain were in a medal-giving mood, then they should surely pin one on J. Lennon, Esq.

From the day, back in January, 1964, when the undeniably masculine, aggressively contemporary John took off from London Airport in a black leather girl's cap bought from Mary Quant's Bazaar in Chelsea, headgear and the young-in-heart got together for the first time in a generation.

Swinging

It was the moment when young girls discovered the swinging wash-and-dry hairdo's that owed nothing to the hairdresser's gentle art of backcombing.

Unlike the bouffant beehives, their hair was flat and shiny to start with, so there was nothing to squash, and simple, boyish hats were suddenly In.

THE millinery trade, already doing nicely to the tune of about £24,000,000 a year with their over-thirty customers, stopped weeping into their beer about why they couldn't sell anything to anyone under twenty-five.

They called in young designers, concentrated on line rather than trimming, and looked for new materials in which to make new shapes.

Leather

Leather took over from tulle and skidlids became a fashion as much as a protection.

Fuss went out in a flurry of feathers, and the new pared-down shapes went with the new pared-down clothes

SEEN here is an advance look at what the hat business has in mind for autumn and winter 1965-66.

In Ascot Week when mad hats will be the order of the next three days, these are madder than most.

They're strictly not in the fete-opening class and they would make the Gainsborough lady clutch her gracious sweep of plumed straw and ask herself whatever is the country coming to?

What it's coming to, in my opinion, is the best year the hat business ever had and it's beside the point that the moon-dotted Space helmet, right, seen lying on my desk by a male colleague, was mistaken for a chihuahua's kennel.

REPORT
FELICITY GREEN
PICTURES
JOHN FRENCH

MEANWHILE, BACK IN SPACE

WHAT the hat business needs is a good gimmick. For 1965-66 they have chosen the best one of all. Inevitably, it's Space and those larger-than-life helmets worn by astronauts in orbit will be seen circling around town very soon. Shown here: the capsule line by Edward Mann. Above, two Space shapes for Moon maidens. One, in black felt with white moons, £6 19s. 11d. The other, with half, costs 59s. 11d. Below, more Moon maidenry in white swansdown. Left, a helmet, £6 19s. 11d. Right, with visor veiling, 4 gns.

ED WHITE . . . IN 1965

A TOUCH OF THE AVIATORS

SPACE wasn't always stratospheric, of course. There was the time when Those Magnificent Men—and girls—in Their Flying Machines took to the air in a nice close-fitting helmet and goggles. Like Amy Johnson's on the left. This, too, has its counterparts in contemporary headgear, as can be seen from the white plastic hood above. This costs 29s. 11d. and we should, I think, ignore the fact that the designer says it was inspired by a hangman's hood.

AMY JOHNSON in 1936

The Swinging '60s were a good time for hats, in 1965 we were already spending £24,000,000 a year on the serious stuff – feathers, flowers and veils – all suitable for Ascot. Then a whole new generation of Youthquake customers took to hats of a more crazy and casual kind. Berets and caps were the No.1 choice, but outstanding favourite was the black leather cap that John Lennon bought from Mary Quant. Never ones to miss a trick, the hat trade went all Space Age with these unwieldy and undoubtedly uncomfortable helmets – guaranteed to squash even the most buoyant Vidal Sassoon crop. They didn't last.

PAGE 10 DAILY MIRROR, *Monday, August 30, 1965*

Revealed today: the Paris look for '66

IT'S A DIC

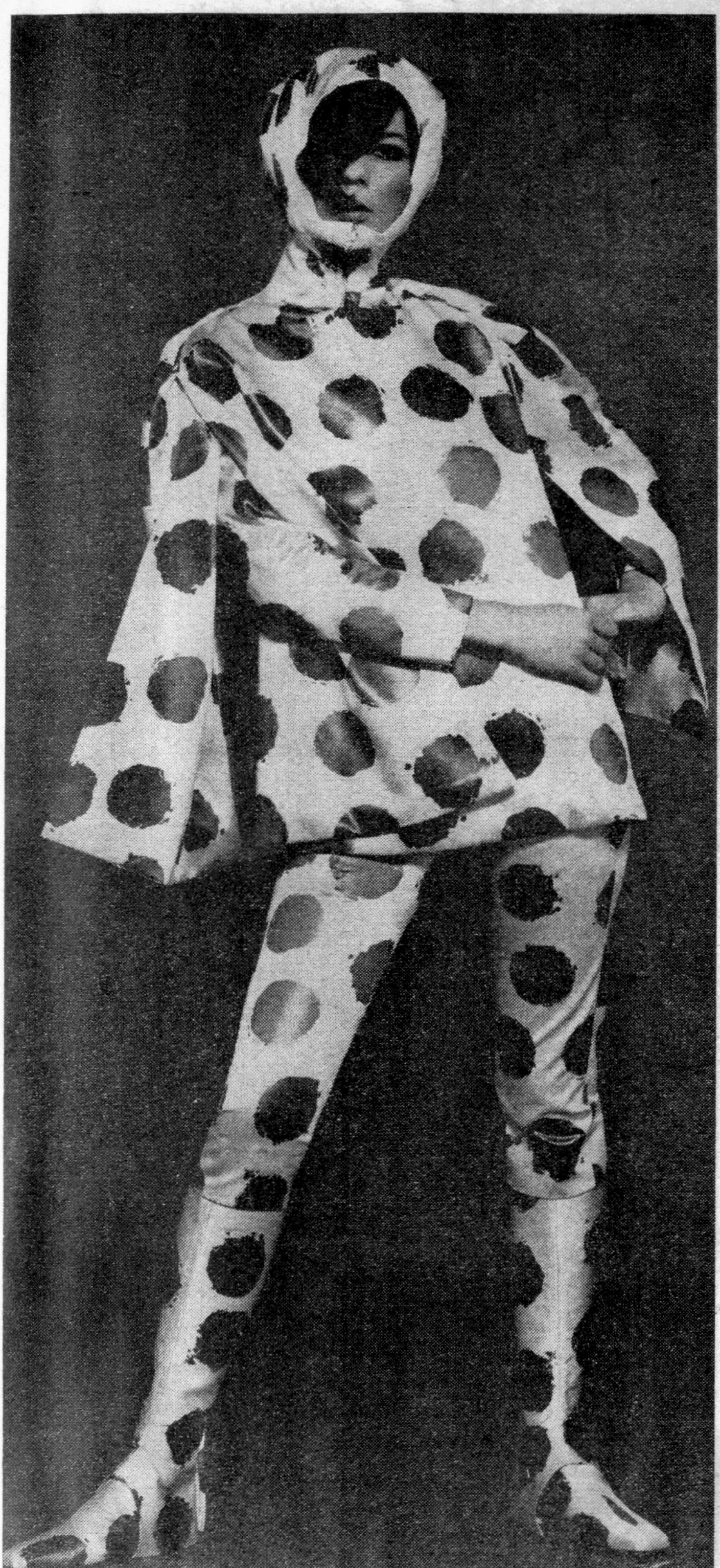

The astronaut look—from new designer Ungaro, who worked for Courreges who really invented this look. A suitable garment for stoking hell-fires, it's in white satin with blood red splashes. It comprises matching helmet, cloak, tunic, trousers, gaiters and shoes.

One of the shortest skirts in Paris—a tunic and dress by Ungaro. They're not boots, they're shoes and matching gaiters.

A real but-when-would-you-wear-it outfit. In brown harlequin-printed jersey by Heim. The coat is made from tiger skin.

by
FELICITY GREEN

DICHOTOMY means divided into two—and that just about sums up Paris fashion this season.

The clothes that have made the current collections the most profitable ever for the French fashion capital are as dichotomous as can be.

On the one hand, there are those designers who see us as female astronauts, striding into the twenty-first century, all sinister and swinging and prepared to show our knees and thighs at the sound of a countdown. Gear, fab, and all that sort of thing.

On the other hand, there are those designers who think this Space age stuff is strictly for the too way-out birds. They're happier making styles for more conservative birds who think their thighs should remain a secret between them and their knee-length skirts.

The result of all this difference of opinion is a very nice mixture indeed.

There's something for everyone, say the manufacturers happily gathering ideas to copy for the High Street.

They must be right. American buyers alone have doubled their spending and to date have placed orders for about £350,000.

Which is as good an answer as any to those prophets of gloom and doom who say that Paris fashion has had it.

Seen here, a selection of stars from the current shows. On the left, the way-out lot, on the right the more wearable ones.

Which side of the dichotomy are you on?

Pictures by John French

DAILY MIRROR, *Monday, August 30, 1965* PAGE 11

OTOMY *

● Even in Paris, Op-art runs riot. Seen here on a wrap skirted suit from Pipart at Ricci. In black and white.

● Feathers are favourite at Dior. Here fluffy black feathers make a collar and cuffs on a scarlet silk coat.

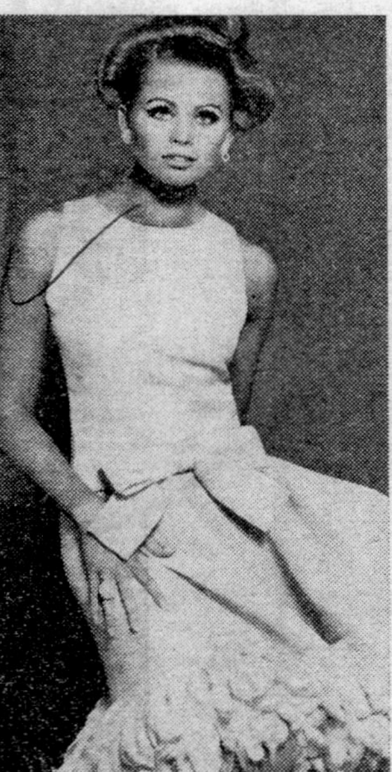

● Not real feathers, they're fabric petals on the swinging hem of a short evening dress. By Goma at Patou.

● A nice sensible suit from Bohan at Dior. In black and grey dice check. Artists' bow, big black dramatic hat.

● If chiffon has more appeal than plastic, if you'd rather slink than stride—then Pierre Cardin's your man. Seen here, his acid-green dance dress with a rose at the frilled hem.

* IN OTHER WORDS, THERE ARE TWO DISTINCT IDEAS ABOUT WHERE FASHION IS GOING . . AND THEY'RE BOTH RIGHT

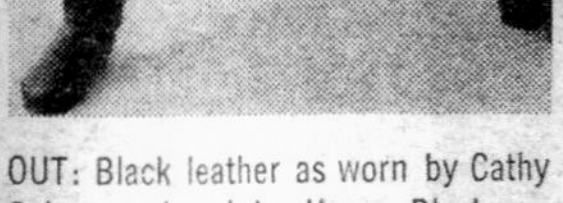

OUT: Black leather as worn by Cathy Gale as played by Honor Blackman

IN: Black stretch jersey as worn by Emma Peel as played by Diana Rigg

Launched this wee

ENTER EMMA

The question, the morning after, will undoubtedly be: Did you see what Emma wore—and where can I buy it?

LET me introduce you to Emma Peel, internationally-educated daughter of a wealthy shipowner and youthful widow of a famous test pilot.

Emma is Steed's swinging new girl-friend, and you'll meet her this week when "The Avengers" return to the telly.

And if Emma herself—as played by Diana Rigg, a stunning 27-year-old from Leeds—doesn't knock you sideways, then I'll bet her wardrobe will.

Realising that the Cathy Gale black leather boom is over, the experts at ABC-TV decided to give Emma a wardrobe specially created for "the swinging girl of today and the forward-looking woman of tomorrow."

Working to this idea, trend-setter John Bates has designed a whole range of "Avengers" styles—accessories as well as clothes—which will be on the screen one night, in the shops next morning.

There are hipster trousers galore, and thigh-high skirts.

Licences to make these killer-diller clothes have been issued to a limited number of manufacturers.

"And anyone else who tries to copy them will have a writ waiting for him in the morning," said Mr. Bates, in real "Avengers" style.

IN the first episode this week, Emma poses as a village schoolmistress, wearing the trouser suit shown right.

In a later episode, set among the kilted lairds in a draughty Scottish castle, Emma wears an ice blue Lame trouser suit, with only a bra between her stiff upper lip and her hipster bell bottoms.

Fighting

"I've been so inspired by these clothes, that I've slimmed down until I'm nearly a size 12," said the king-size Diana, who stands 5ft. 9in. in her black stretch-jersey fighting suit.

"Why bother?" as the man in the office said when he saw the picture on the far right.

ALTOGETHER John Bates has designed three dozen "Avengers" outfits, and fittings are in progress for many more.

However, several episodes were already filmed before he was called in, so for the next few weeks Emma will alternate between the new look and the best the studio could provide.

There will be no prizes for guessing which is which.

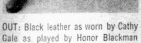

Felicity Green

ON THE subject of his new girl-friend and her clothes, **Patrick "Steed" McNee, impeccable as ever, says: "The clothes are great. Diana's great, too. A real comedienne in the Kay Kendall class."**

ABOVE: The Avengers' girl as you'll see her in Episode 1. She wears a black and white tweed suit by Reginald Bernstein. With belt and blouse it costs 24 gns. The target-crowned beret costs 17s. 11d. The gloves, watch and boots are all available, too.

Picture by Norman Eales.

RIGHT: For a draughty week in a Scottish castle, Emma we another hipster trouser suit, time in ice-blue lame, bare to navel. On sale to other week enthusiasts for 29 gns. Watch this outfit in Episode 5, sched for the week of October 24th.

Picture by Terry O'N

DAILY MIRROR, Monday, September 27, 1965 PAGE 15

The new 'Avengers' girl

Actress Diana Rigg's impact as Emma Peel in *The Avengers* emphasised the far-reaching influence of television on '60s-style culture. Popular television shows mirrored the new fashion zeitgeist, picked up on the key trends then served them back to the viewers. And it wasn't only music shows like Granada's *Ready, Steady, Go!* hosted by style pin-up Cathy McGowan, which sent viewers in search of the fashion they'd seen on the screen. Emma Peel was an original, very '60s style – all-action heroine – lithe, beautiful, independent, intelligent – and sexy with it. Her wardrobe, much of it designed by John Bates and then by Alun Hughes, was an integral part of the series, guaranteed to be a talking point and a fashion influence. Rigg's TV partner, John Steed, played by Patrick McNee, enigmatically cool in his immaculate three-piece suits, was the perfect foil for Peel's fashion-forward gear. But the real fashion flair was reserved for Emma Peel – and the designers went to town. Black stretch jersey catsuits, pixie boots, thigh-high mini-skirts, hipster-belted trouser suits in lamé with matching bra-top and bare midriff – all calculated to set the cash tills ringing. This prime-time drama series was a sartorial must-see. But it was also a real commercial first, with John Bates designing a spin-off capsule collection based on Peel's TV wardrobe – available in the shops the next day.

DAILY MIRROR, Saturday, October 16, 1965 PAGE 11

In town today, Mr Topless introduces a burlesque look for the beach

WHATEVER he does, wherever he goes, way-out Californian fashion designer Rudi Gernreich is known as Mr. Topless.

This pains him, he says, since his career as a sportswear designer of international standing was clearly established long before he showed the world's first bottoms-only bikini back in June, 1964.

"I feel the whole Topless idea got really out of hand," he said yesterday, during a brief visit to London to collect a Sunday Times fashion award.

by FELICITY GREEN

"Do you know, in California there are still some cafeterias where the waitresses have bare bosoms. I tell you, it's awful."

Putting aside memories that may be painful, but undoubtedly helped to bring him world-wide fame, Mr. Gernreich concentrated on current successes.

Great

"I'm just introducing my new burlesque look for the beach," he said, showing me a sketch of a black jersey swimsuit with black mesh stockings attached to it by red patent suspenders.

"Also Exquisite Form, who make my No-Bra bras have just brought out The Band Bra.

"It's great under skinny dresses. Gives a very natural looking line. Uplifts, too."

Funny when you think that the man who appeared to be banishing the bra altogether is now the white-haired boy of the bra business.

So much so that Mr. Erwin Roseman, one of the vice-presidents of Exquisite Form, who is also in town to share the Gernreich triumph, said:

"We are so delighted with Rudi's efforts in connection with the foundation garment industry, we have just renewed his contract and are letting him roam loose on Intimate Apparel."

So we can now expect No-Bra bras to sleep by.

This is Rudi's Peggy

IN town with Rudi Gernreich is his favourite model, 26-year-old Peggy Moffitt. Peggy, seen here wearing one of Rudi's casual dresses in green, black and white jersey with stockings to match, is the Californian girl who bravely agreed to pose in the original Topless swimsuit.

"A hoot, really," she said. "Rudi really had to talk me into it as I'm about the most modest girl in the world."

At the time we talked, she was wearing red tights, a Gernreich black and white check suit with a thigh-high skirt and, for a touch of facial uplift, white powder and bright red eye-shadow.

"In America," said Peggy, "everyone stares at me in the street and says things like 'Who do you think you are?'

"Over here, they're much more polite. They don't say anything. Anyway, as I'm so shy, I just look at the floor all the time."

Her dress will be on sale here in November.

GERNREICH thinks of everything. The black mesh stockings on this black jersey burlesque - on - the - beach outfit have a rubberised finish to make them waterworthy. The suspenders are red—and so are the motifs on the knees.

Drawing by BARBARA HULANICKI

After the No-Bra bra —The Band

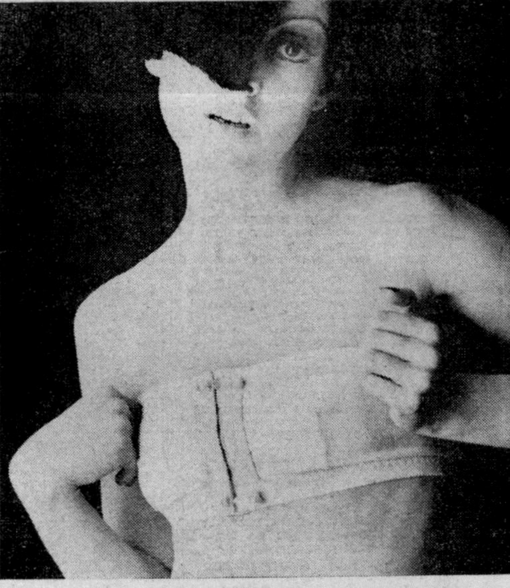

THIS is The Band that Gernreich sees as a follow-up to the No-Bra bra. He says it gives a natural shape with a little uplift. I say Hmm. It sells in America for four dollars, has a front fastening and is made of fine elastic. Exquisite Form who make it are still considering whether to sell it over here as well.

Underwear in the '60s was very big – or very little, depending on how you looked at it. Californian sportswear designer Rudi Gernreich was big news in the Swinging '60s. Gernreich introduced the word Topless into our fashion vocabulary – he designed the first topless swimsuits, thereby creating an international shock-horror reaction and bottoms-only swimsuits were big on beaches round the world. He took the same shock tactics into underwear. When he wasn't exposing the breasts, he was binding them up, or down, in his new No-Bra bra – the Band. The Gernreich burlesque swimsuit illustrated here by Barbara Hulanicki combined heavy mesh stockings suspendered onto a rubberised, waterproof swimsuit. Not a big seller at Marks and Spencer. Gernreich made headlines with his model muse and what Jean Shrimpton was to Bailey, so Californian model Peggy Moffitt was to Gernreich. Famous not only for baring her breasts, Peggy made headlines with her shock-tactic make-up: dead-white face and bright red eyeshadow. Very Japanese!

But would you answer the door to the milkman in this?

—after all, it IS supposed to be a nightie and negligee

It's official, so, if it has been worrying you, you can all now sleep easy in your beds. "Sexy Lingerie," says the headline in the fashion trade paper, "is Here To Stay."

Whether it really stays remains to be seen, since nothing ever does in the dizzy world of fashion, but here it undeniably is.

Nice

Suddenly there's a surfeit of the sort of undies that used to be available only in a Certain Sort of Shop where nice girls didn't go, and nice gentlemen went to buy their Christmas presents.

Shop windows in even the most conservative shopping areas are decked out in The Latest Look in Lingerie and might well be mistaken for the wardrobe department of the nearest strip club.

WHAT has happened, one wonders, to have increased the supply and demand in this way?

Why, suddenly, in 1965 do we all want more sexy undies than we did in 1964? One explanation is that sexy undies are an antidote against the severity of our outer garments. As clothes get more aggressively plain and geometric, so undies give the necessary counter balance.

WHAT'S
WITH
WOMEN
?
DAY TWO

We may be wearing boots and a Courreges shift on top but it's comforting to know our bra is covered with forget-me-nots or there's a pink lace insertion on our black lace mini-slip.

Drift

"I spend so much on fabulous looking undies," said the pretty 18-year-old shampoo girl at my hairdressers, "that my mother is really worried."

She needn't be. Her daughter is just reflecting the drift towards what the trade calls "black lingerie."

"What we mean by this," said one store buyer, "is anything sexy as long as it's refined."

To cope with this new and ever-increasing business, underwear firms are rapidly re-thinking.

Some who used to make nothing more titillating than a see-through nylon nightie—and the fact it was transparent was considered something of a sales drawback—are losing their restraint quicker than you can say ruffled suspender belt.

KAYSER BONDOR, one of the largest underwear firms who made their fame and fortune with the sort of simply-cut undies that even the vicar's wife wouldn't mind getting run over in, are styling up quite saucily.

Their newest bedtime outfit is just a bikini made from four frilly triangles—two at the top and two at the bottom—and a sleeveless, see-through jacket that is a sort of dressing gown

Sweet

It's called "Three Piece Sweet," is made in five colours including Red Hot and Tickle Pink, and costs 59s. 11d.

The outfit on the left is another modern equivalent of yesterday's nightie and dressing gown.

It's a bedtime bikini and stole made by Elizabeth Hayes.

"We sell a lot of this sort of thing nowadays," their sales manageress told me. "Perhaps it's because you can't tell the boys from the girls when they're in their daytime clothes, so they don't want any mistakes when they're undressed."

Whatever the reason for wearing this little lot in the bedroom, it would certainly take a plucky little woman to wear it to open the door to the milkman.

FELICITY GREEN

PICTURES: GORDON CARTER

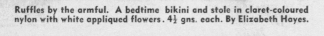

Ruffles by the armful. A bedtime bikini and stole in claret-coloured nylon with white appliqued flowers. 4½ gns. each. By Elizabeth Hayes.

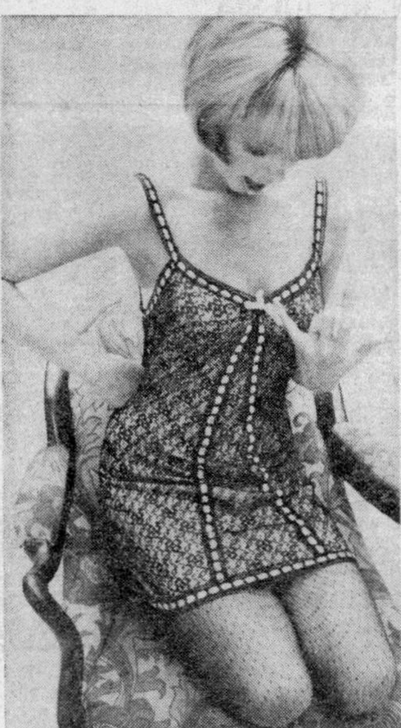

The thigh-high black lace mini slip for mini dresses. By Neatawear. 29s. 11d.

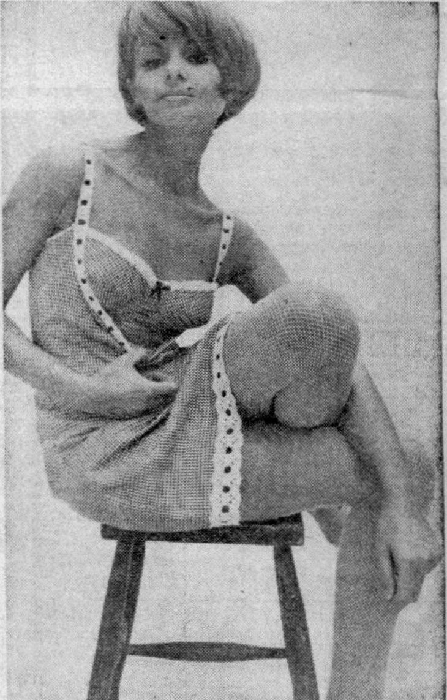

The topless gingham slip and peek-a-boo bra. 39s. 11d. and 27s. 6d. By Peter Pan.

Surprise, Surprise! The big news in the underwear world in October 1965 was that sexy undies were here to stay. Store buyers and manufacturers were reporting soaring sales of the type of undies that were previously sold in shops where nice girls didn't go and City gents bought their Christmas presents.

These two outfits illustrate an international culture clash when famous top model Jean Shrimpton, named The Most Beautiful Girl in the World, was pictured wearing a mini-dress at Australia's Melbourne Cup. Shrimpton went to the races and unwittingly sparked a style disturbance when she appeared in this short white sleeveless mini, which was a whole four inches above the knee. She also appeared sans hat, gloves and stockings and was warned by the stuffy Australian authorities to change her outfit. This, they said, was no dress for a lady! It was a dress that wouldn't turn a hair in London, but Miss Shrimpton had to go home and re-think her outfit for the next day's events. This couldn't and wouldn't have happened in London.

WARNED

One verdict: 'Wonderful, the way she dresses'

Here is the beautiful Miss Shrimpton in the four-inches-above the knee shift dress that caused all the trouble on Saturday. But Lady Casey, the 73-year-old wife of Australia's Governor-General, says, "The way dresses is wonderful."

And Melbourne should note of that single brooch thick watch strap. They already classic in London.

OFF!

Look what they've made me wear, says the Shrimp . . I just don't feel like me any more

om NICK DAVIES
elbourne, Tuesday

:EAN SHRIMPTON, the world's top model, was ordered by the Victorian Racing Club of Australia ' dress properly " for the Melbourne Cup meeting ay.

o Jean, who had outraged Melbourne's lady race-
:s by her shift dress on Saturday, attended today's
ting in a three-piece grey-and-beige tweed suit.

e also wore—as ordered—a hat, gloves, and stockings. But
nemline stayed—4in. above
knee.

ook what they've made me
" the 23-year-old British
l told me. "I just don't feel
Jean Shrimpton any more.
ve been disciplined! Last
, a committee member of the
rian Racing Club told me offi-
that I was not to appear at
acecourse in the same clothes
did on Saturday."

Saturday, Jean, who is in
alia to model man-made
, wore a simple white shift
four inches above the knee.
wore no stockings, hat, or
s.

Gloomy

lay, despite the bright sun-
Jean was gloomy. She told
"I hate wearing all these
sories. The hat was bought
ne in Melbourne last night
with the gloves and stock-
It's just not me. I feel
ful in them.

it I wore the accessories to
urteous. I am a guest of the
g Club and that is why I
lied with their demands."

MR. Frederick Gilders, a
club committee mem-
aid: "I told Miss Shrimpton
ner sponsors, Dupont Indus-
that she must dress correctly
ip Day.

er attire on Saturday was dis-
ful. There was a storm of
t from the committee mem-
wives.

warned her that if she did not
properly she would not be
ed to present the prizes in our
n contest.

am glad to see that she has
d our wishes."

Behind

y Casey, 73-year-old wife of
alia's Governor-General, com-
d: "I think Miss Shrimpton
utiful.

saw a picture of her dress
aturday and thought it was
tful."

er today's meeting, Jean, who
ccompanied by actor Terence
), commented: "I feel Mel-
e is not yet ready for me.
ms to be some years behind
n."

n DID present the fashion
and she saw Light Fingers,
1 chance, win the £30,000
urne Cup.

Mr. Frederick Gilders . . . He warned the Shrimp.

NONSENSE!

says JEAN DOBSON in London

IF the dressy ladies Down Under were expecting Jean Shrimpton's London Look to be the sort of fancy dressing-up that goes on at Ascot — then no wonder they were surprised.

Currently named the Most Beautiful Girl in the World, what the Shrimp — and thousands of British girls—wears today the rest of the world wears next year.

Hers is the look that is creating a world demand for British fashions bringing in millions of pounds in export orders.

The gear that appears unconventional on a spectator at Melbourne races would pass unremarked in a London street. The Shrimp's leggy look is the fashion that is in the shops of every High Street in Britain.

Fussy

Short skirts, low heels and high necklines are IN among the smart young set.

What nonsense all this fuss is, you Melbourne critics.

What would upset ME at a well-dressed function would be a rash of Melbourne's fussy hats, low necklines and loud prints.

As the Shrimp says "Melbourne isn't ready for the new look yet."

The more's the pity.

Her protest: 'I've been disciplined'

The Shrimp dresses for the part. Kitted out in a grey and beige three-piece with ice-blue Breton hat, beige gloves and shoes, chocolate suede bag, she looks every inch a top model. Unrepentant about her short hemline, but wearing stockings the Shrimp went on to present the prizes at a fashion contest at the races yesterday. This outfit looks good on her. Anything does. But . . . "I've been disciplined!" wails the Shrimp.

TERRY O'NEILL ON JEAN SHRIMPTON

The '60s Superstars: the famous Photographer on the original Supermodel

To this day I remember when I first met Jean Shrimpton and I'll never forget it. I was with Bailey in his studio in early 1963 or maybe late 1962 come to think of it.

Jean was there for a fashion shoot and I was mesmerised by this beautiful coltish girl with the most fabulous legs and smile.

You have to remember Marilyn Monroe had just died and with her went the hourglass figure and the big-ticket bosoms.

Until then girls had wanted to look like women and dressed like their mothers. Suddenly women wanted to look like girls – and wear clothes they could wear to the office and still go dancing in or clubbing or dining out without having to go home and change.

Jean had the best legs I've ever seen on a woman and of course this was the dawn of the mini-skirt, gamine, girlie easy fashion. It was as if the world had changed overnight. Jean Shrimpton was the poster girl for this generation of girls. She was dating Bailey at the time, he was the new working-class hero at *Vogue* and she was the magazine's new cover girl – stood to reason they'd be an item for a while.

Next thing I knew, Jean was dating Terry Stamp, a mate of mine and we got talking and I found out she was just a farm-girl – or at least the daughter of a farmer and I went home with her for a day or so and I photographed her at home with her parents, horses, pigs, whatever.

Jean was in her element and that's when I realised why she was so alluring. She was just an ordinary girl with extraordinary looks. She never adopted any airs and graces. She was the girl next door, more at home on the farm than at a fashion show.

She was a natural – she didn't have to strike a pose, she just had it, all the camera and the photographer had to do was shoot – she was the easiest girl I ever photographed.

I've always admired Jean because one day she just suddenly stopped at the top of her game and instead of trying to fight time, fashion and age and stay relevant she just said "enough, I'm off" and disappeared.

If only they all did that. Fashion, a look, has its time, it has its moment and when the world's ready for something new, move on while you're on top. Now, of course, celebrity keeps the models in the public eye for longer than they deserve and their fall from grace becomes a public spectacle. But Jean knew the secret to eternal beauty. She didn't fade, she just quit.

Jean was undoubtedly the first SuperModel and there's never been another like her.

"She was a natural – she didn't have to strike a pose she just had it"

FELICITY ON JEAN

First a confession: I never met Jean Shrimpton – just admired her from afar and I did interview her once on the telephone. But I would have had to be on Mars not to realise the impact that this country girl had on every aspect of the international fashion world at that time.

Her stunning beauty was undeniable, her legs longer than possible. According to every photographer who ever came into contact with her in the studio, she emanated her own special magic whenever she was in front of the camera.

However, she didn't do this all on her own. Her romance with photographer David Bailey made fashion history not only in this country, but round the world. Every famous photographer was occupied capturing The Shrimp – a nickname she hated, which was a pity because it was bestowed as a popular term of endearment – well lots of us hate our nickname.

The Shrimp and Bailey were the first famous couple in the '60s and together they changed everything. Bailey captured the Shrimpton look and made her a star. The Shrimp's influence was not only on fashion, but also on make-up and hair, on shape and style. Girls just wanted to look like Jean Shrimpton with her long sexy legs.

Among all the impact and the excesses of the '60s there was this quiet girl – never drunk or disorderly. She had an innate sense of elegance and of having been well brought up. Certainly Jean Shrimpton's was the favourite face of the Swinging '60s – right around the world.

International supermodel Jean Shrimpton creates a stir in her mini-dress, which was declared unacceptable at Australia's 1965 Melbourne Cup – the fashion furore made headlines around the world; she was sent home to change

DAILY MIRROR, Tuesday, February 22, 1966 PAGE 13

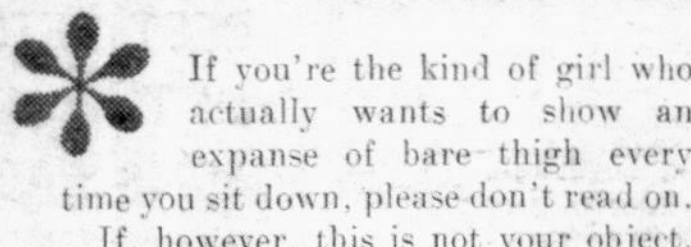

PROOF!

You can't be decent in a short skirt unless you're wearing tights

If you're the kind of girl who actually wants to show an expanse of bare thigh every time you sit down, please don't read on.

If, however, this is not your object, then may I ask you a leading question:

How short are you wearing your skirt ?

If you're among the dowds who cling to knee-cappers you haven't a thing to worry about—except looking even more dowdy.

But if you've raised your hems by two to four inches—let alone more—the chances are that you give a leg-show every time you sit down.

Worry

No matter how you pull up the tops of your stockings with short, stubby suspenders, or how frequently you fuss with the hem of your skirt, there's no way to sit without the worry of over-exposure.

There is only one solution: Tights. Not longer stockings. Not panty-girdles. Just tights.

There is no leg line tights do not improve, no leg position so awkward they can't disguise it.

More than 420,000,000 pairs of stockings were sold in this country last year. At least half of that number ought to be tights this short-skirted year.

Then we'd be sitting pretty.

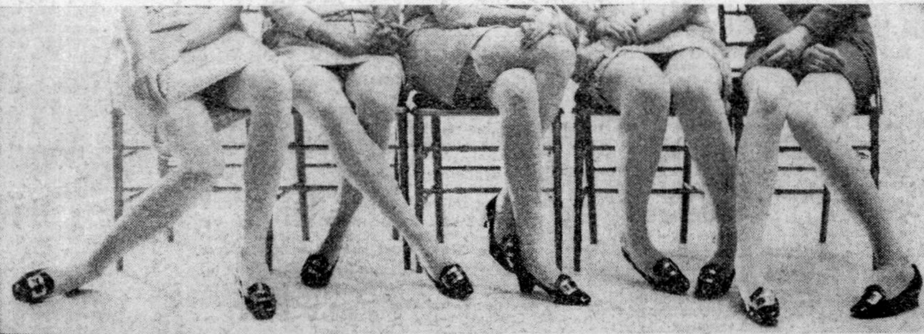

PROBLEM How to present a decent view and avoid the worry of over-exposure when your new short skirt rises to stocking-top level.

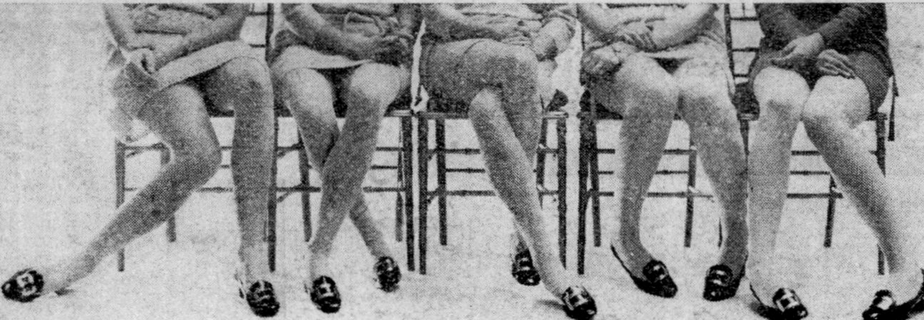

SOLUTION Choose tights. Any tights. Like the seamless mesh ones by Wolsey, 19s. 11d., above and right. Other possibilities: Mesh tights with seams, Berkshire, 16s. 11d. Micromesh tights, Pex, 21s. Sheer-legged skintights, Wolsey, 19s. 11d. Medium weight "light" tights, Bear Brand, 12s. 11d. Shoes by Lotus 5 gns.

Pictures: **DOREEN SPOONER**

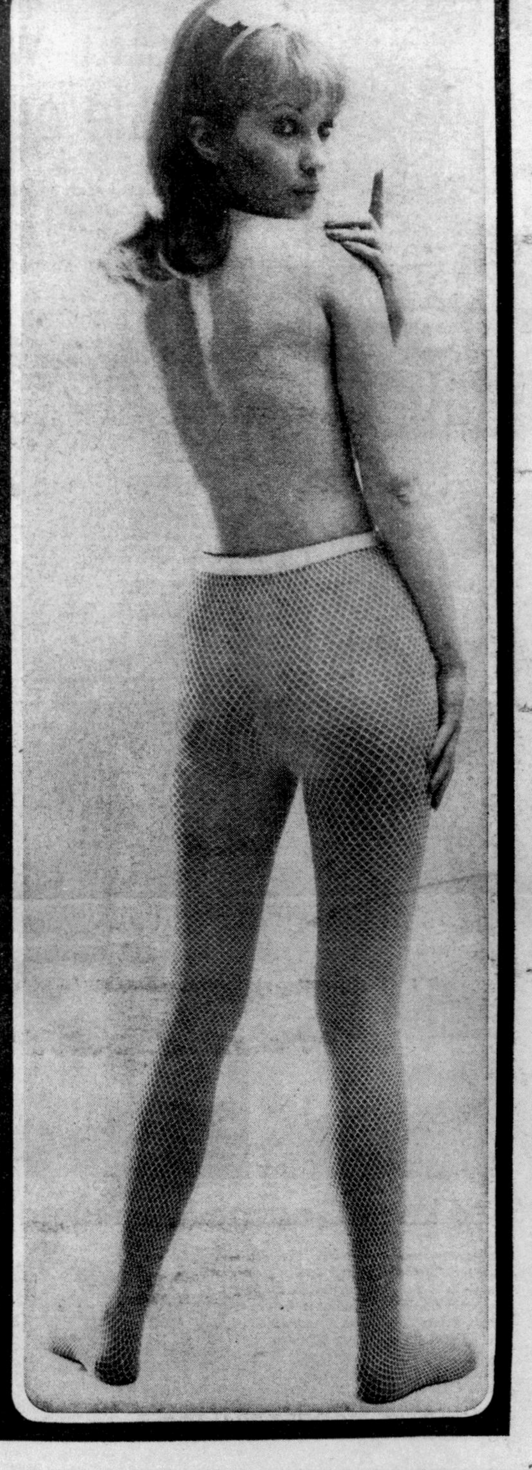

A new hazard faced the more modern girls in the Swinging '60s. The popular super-short skirts made the wearer of stockings risk indecency when she crossed her legs. This was a real problem that had to be overcome. However, thanks to a dramatic advance taking place in the hosiery business, a plan was revealed. A clever cross between fashion and technology had provided the solution and the hosiery industry was able to take a leap into the future – and the era of tights was revealed to the welcoming world of worried women. This combination of stockings plus knickers solved the decency or indecency problem forever. Sit down, cross your legs all you like and don't worry – all will not be revealed. Right, a happy marriage between '60s Op Art and the Minis: the Op Art mini-dress meets the Op Art mini motor. One of these minis had a longer life than the other.

Now—the matching mini!

HERE it is! The car for the Op Art girl who likes ALL her accessories to match.

But the mini does not come off the factory assembly line looking anything like this. It got the Op-Art treatment from an amateur with a pair of scissors, about a quarter of a mile of stick-on plastic and plenty of time and patience.

The car is for sale at a showroom in Thames Ditton, Surrey.

It costs £385—but that does not include the dress by Shubette, which costs 79s. 11d., or the sling-back shoes by Saxone at 59s. 11d.

26 MARCH 1966

FELICITY GREEN'S FASHION PAGE LOOKS AT THE AMERICAN SCENE

What isn't knacky is just darling

DARLING : CHRISTIE

KNACKY : STREISAND

TWO British hit films have given New York its latest "In" words. Now everything is either "Darling" or "Knacky."

And if you want to know what they mean, just think of Julie Christie and —heavens no, NOT Rita Tushingham! —Barbra Streisand.

The whole "Darling" bit started with Julie Christie's movie of that name and she is the No. 1 exponent of the look, from her wild blonde mane to her little-girl shoes.

Today on the New York scene anything that's frankly female, but not choc-boxy, is "Darling."

"Knacky" is farther out—boyish almost. Anyone with the Knack always has a Sassoon hairdo, wears strict shifts or T-shirt dresses. And boots. Or socks. And the shortest possible skirts to give her the "Kneeknack."

Naked flesh is Knacky and the all-knacky peep-holes and cutaways in current fashion are giving foundation firms ulcers. (Well, whatever DOES go under a dress with a target cut-out where a girl sits down?)

PANTS

Knickers are Knacky—but not the kind YOU know. Knickers is American for plus-fours, newest type of pants being worn here.

Darlings prefer floaty tent dresses in see-through voile (more sleepless nights for the bra and girdle makers!), high waists, lots of frills and flounces above bared "knack" knees. (It does get confusing, doesn't it?)

Giant sunspecs are Knacky, teensy gold-rimmed grannie types are Darling. Garish papier mache jewellery is Knacky, pearls in pierced ears are Darling.

Catherine Milinaire, the Duke of Bedford's step-daughter, is one of New York's favourite Darlings.

Singer Barbra Streisand has the Knack to the nth degree. And surprise, surprise—American newspapers say our own Prince Philip "has the Knack."

LATEST ARRIVALS on the madder-than-ever 1966 fashion scene are clothes that glow in the dark. Made of fabrics treated with a fluorescent finish, they are merely brightly coloured by day but shine after dark with all the sublety and brilliance of a neon sign. Wilder ideas in this newest rave (pictured, in the dark, above) are hipster skirts, pants, bras and see-through jackets with fluorescent trim. Prices of the threesome seen here are approximately £12, £17 and £14. And as you can see through the gloom above, it's not only clothes that are getting the fluorescent look—accessories like jewellery, hats and shoes have it, too. To say nothing of nail enamels, eye make-up and even lipstick. Unearthly, that's what it looks like. But guaranteed to add brightness.

Mattie Joy puts a new ZIP into jewellery

TAKE BACK your pearls, throw out your diamonds—that's the advice of New York jewellery designer Mattie Joy.

Mattie is currently doing very nicely with her realistic "gems" for people who want accessories as modern as themselves.

She saws up old zip-fasteners, dips them in gilt or silver, and sells them as brooches at one dollar a go. Wooden clothes-pegs get the same treatment.

She has done a roaring trade in ear-rings made from squeezed-out tooth-paste tubes — suitably gilded, of course.

She pulls and pushes pipe-cleaners into toe-rings—very popular with the beachniks. And, right now, Mattie is fond of brooches made out of biscuit cutters—"Great, because they are double duty."

"Traditional gems," she preaches, "are for diehards—and they are dead already as far as fashion goes."

HOLIDAYS ARE AHEAD, so how about joining the Maharajah of Jaipur on a tiger-shoot in India? Maybe you'd prefer the lazy Mediterranean life on the Onassis yacht?

Or a few days' sky-diving in Mexico, based at Merle Oberon's hacienda?

New York's latest travel agency, "Ports of Call," can fix snob vacations with all the In people.

One of its bosses is Lord "Derry" Moore, from Ireland, and New Yorkers LOVE collecting their jet tickets from a real milord. The privilege can cost from £750 to £18,000.

A LEADING men's wear manufacturer says male models look like "a bunch of self-conscious fashion plates, and stop people believing in our advertisements."

So he's showing all his spring styles on **GIRLS.**

Still, American men spent a billion dollars — about £357,000,000 — more on clothes in 1965 than they did in 1964. And it's all thanks to Britain's Mods.

"The publicity and news about the Mods got men interested in fashion again," say industry leaders.

AFTER POP ART and Op Art—Fur Art. Masterpieces made of real mink, or leopard and abstracts done in all the world's most expensive furs are being turned out by artist Ruth Richards.

She says they're for the "fur-tive" lover and calls them "Tactiles."

DAILY MIRROR, Wednesday, April 6, 1966 PAGE 15

From rags to rouges . .

Ten years later —little Miss Quant enters the paint and powder world

YESTERDAY little Miss Quant gave a party. To celebrate her entry into the world of lipstick, powder n' paint.

Thus Miss Quant has increased once again her area of activity which already includes dresses, suits, coats, sportswear, furs, handbags, rainwear and all sorts of undies.

The annual turnover of this erstwhile Kookie Kid from the Kings-road, Chelsea, is now up to £2,500,000, including exports to twenty-five countries, and her husband Alexander Plunkett Green estimates a nice £3,500,000 turnover for the current year.

Her cosmetics—she's holding a bunch of them up there on the left—have been produced in conjunction with the beauty firm of Gala.

They're starkly packaged in black and white and are in concept and appearance to most other beauty preparations what the first Quant clothes were to pre-Quant fashions.

"They are," says Mary, "a rationalisation of the model girl make-up that every girl wants."

Colour plays second place to shaping and the twenty-four products include a two-tone lipstick called Skitzo, a white block called a Face Lighter, a dark block called a Face Shaper, a nude foundation called Starkers.

Prices are "about average." Which means 7s. 6d. for a lipstick, block mascara or nail polish.

In a week's time the Quant daisy-trimmed containers will be on sale throughout the country at about 500 shops. "By June," said Mary, "we aim to have 2,000 stockists."

Are Mr. and Mrs. Alexander Plunkett Green millionaires by now? "Only in dollars," says Alexander modestly, "and only on paper."

FELICITY GREEN
picture by JOHN ADRIAAN

A CRATE FULL OF QUANT ON TOP, Mary herself, cosmetics in hand. Left, husband and business partner, Alexander Plunkett Green. Inside the crate, left to right: handbag by Bagcraft, bra and pantie girdle by Q Form Youthlines, stockings with built-in socks, trouser suit by Ginger Group, raincoat by Alligator, sweater and stockings from a pattern by Courtaulds, bra and briefs by Arnberg of Sweden, sleeveless dress, coat, culottes and shirt all by Ginger Group, fur by Debenhams.

On April 5, 1966 Mary Quant, seen here, top of the picture, launched her range of cosmetics. And they were as different from traditional beauty products as her mini-skirts were from traditional fashion. Quant, the world-famous innovator had done it again. The Quant colours were muted and subtle, the names were typically quirky – a two-tone lipstick called "Skitzo" and a nude foundation was "Starkers". By June, said the confident Miss Quant, we aim to have two thousand stockists.

HAVE SKIRTS NOW REACHED FAIL SAFE?

A young lady in Amersham, Bucks, was asked to leave a cafe last week because her three-inches-above-the-knee skirt offended the manageress.

If the manageress in question would care to take a quick flip round the more "in" establishments of so-called Swinging London, she would soon realise that what appears shocking in Amersham is modest in Mayfair.

Who are wearing these skirts?

Model girls, of course. But other girls, too. Shop assistants and office workers. Hairdressing assistants and factory hands. Comptometer operators and telephone operators.

Where do they wear them?

At discotheques, cinemas, coffee bars. At work, bosses permitting. And quite a few do.

Are these mini-skirts sexy?

Opinions vary. Some men, who after all are the ones who should know, say they're not.

"They may expose a lot of leg," said one moodily, "but some legs can't stand that much exposure."

"Boy!" said another, speaking with enthusiasm for that section of bird fancying British manhood who are leg men themselves.

What happens to hemlines?

Now that they have reached what the Strategic Air Command types would call Fail Safe, it's difficult to see how they can go any higher before the skirts disappear altogether.

Looking at the hemlines on this page you can see that in London at least, it isn't so much a question of above the knee as below the bottom—and only just, at that.

FELICITY GREEN on the eye-poppi case of the ever-rising hemline

RECEPTIONIST

Jenny Bird, 20:
I wear my skirts short for work, even shorter in the evening.

SHOP ASSISTANT

Jennifer Smith, 15:
I think short skirts are very flattering and feminine

SECRETARY

Carol Heber-Percy 19:
Daddy likes me in short skirts so I suppose they're here to stay.

LAW STUDENT

Lucia Han, 21:
Everybody takes short skirts for granted these days.

PICTURES BY ERIC HARLOW, KENT GAVI

DAILY MIRROR, Tuesday, April 19, 1966 Page 15

ECRETARY

cola Deck, 18:

Very short skirts are absolutely right when you are very young, but they also look good on older girls with nice long legs.

UR SIDEY

The question asked in April 1966, at the height of the Swinging '60s: Have skirts now reached fail safe? The answer in 2014 is no they hadn't. Year by year, inch (now centimetre) by inch they have continued to rise. And shine. Back then mini-skirts maintained a moderate degree of modesty, but today they have reached heights bordering on the indecent – and nobody seems to mind. A walk down London's Oxford Street exposes many a glimpse of an actual bottom or two peeping out from either a minimum mini-skirt or an even minier pair of the latest mini-shorts. Where will all this minimalism end? Who knows? I didn't then and I don't now.
For more thoughts on more '60s fashions turn to pages 116-123.

DAILY MIRROR, *Thursday, April 28, 1966* PAGE 15

ON THE FASHION SCENE

IMAGINE !

a pair of pliers to fix your bikini bra

Wearing the bikinis: Danish actress Maud Berthelsen. Gunnar Larsen took the pictures.

PACO RABANNE, a Paris fashion designer, who works with wire, sheets of plastic and a pair of pliers, decided six months ago that he wanted to be the most copied man in the fashion world.

M. Rabanne, I am happy to tell you your ambition has been realised.

Reasonable facsimiles of your king-size all-plastic earrings, sunglasses and jewellery—to say nothing of your swimsuits and shifts—have spread out over the international fashion scene like a rash in a case of measles.

No offence meant, but it does all clank a bit too much for my tastes.

In Paris at the moment, Monsieur Rabanne, who is nothing if not consistent, is just showing his latest collection of swimwear for summer, 1966.

It's all based—you guessed it !—on plastic discs clipped together with wire. If you drop a disc or two, a pair of pliers will repair the damage in a flash.

"My swim suits," said Monsieur Rabanne, reassuringly to anyone with the problem of rust on her mind, "are meant to swim in. They have been tested and stand up to water very well."

Monsieur Rabanne's shift dresses made, or should I say constructed, on the same all-discs-together principle, are being snapped up by Audrey Hepburn—hers is in silver with a short flared skirt—Catherine (Mrs. David Bailey) Deneuve and her sister, Francoise Dorleac.

"Plastic," said Monsieur Rabanne, "has only just begun to show its possibilities."

However, it does have obvious limitations.

The pants, you'll notice, are made of good old stretch jersey.

RABANNE: King of Plastic.

FELICITY GREEN on the fashion scene

THE SWEDES are noted for Stockholm, good modern taste, Ingmar Bergman films and the fact that they're the shortest-skirt-orderers in town right now.

Foreign buyers may be flocking to London to buy our swinging fashions, but when it's order-book time and the chips are down, so are the hemlines.

"They're lovely," they say in Italian, American, German or whatever. "We'll have a dozen in assorted colours, but we'd like them longer, of course."

"Of all the buyers who have ordered this season, only the Swedes are taking deliveries in the sample length," said John Bates, one of the prime espousers of the short skirt cult in England.

"All the other store buyers, except for a couple of boutiques, have asked us to add about four or five inches on the hemline, so that's what we do."

The truth about Swedish girls

Shapely

What's so special or so brave about Swedish girls?

Mrs. Birgit Hermansson, fashion buyer of Gulins, leading young fashion store in Stockholm, says it's because "Swedish girls are not only fashion-minded but pretty and brave, too.

"They're so well-shaped that they do not need to be afraid of wearing mini-skirts or any fashion."

I'd say that the overwhelming Swedish acceptance of the mini-skirt is more likely to be traced to the bravery of buyers like Mrs. Birgit Hermansson rather than any super-woman qualities of the undoubtedly pretty Swedish girls.

So on the one hand—or two legs—we have skirts going shorter than ever in Britain, and you have only to look around you to check that this is true. While on the other hand we have buyers still ordering in the same old knee-length.

No wonder the stores are doing a roaring trade in alterations.

Short

But then, as Aunt Edith used to say, it's better to be safe than sorry.

It's safe to have a great dollop of fabric available for turning up. And sorry if the skirt's so short to start with that there's nothing to let down for the less fashion-minded.

After all not *every* customer is a short-skirted swinging chick.

Except, it would seem, in Sweden.

● The dress in silver is from Jean Varon Autumn range designed by John Bates. It costs about 17½ gns., and will be available in July.

PETER MULLETT took the picture.

1 SAMPLE LENGTH (34")
Ordered by Sweden, 1 boutique in London and 1 in New York

2 DELIVERY LENGTH (38")
South Africa, Canada, Switzerland, Italy, Austria and New York plus London and provinces

3 MISERABLE LENGTH (39")
West Coast stores in America

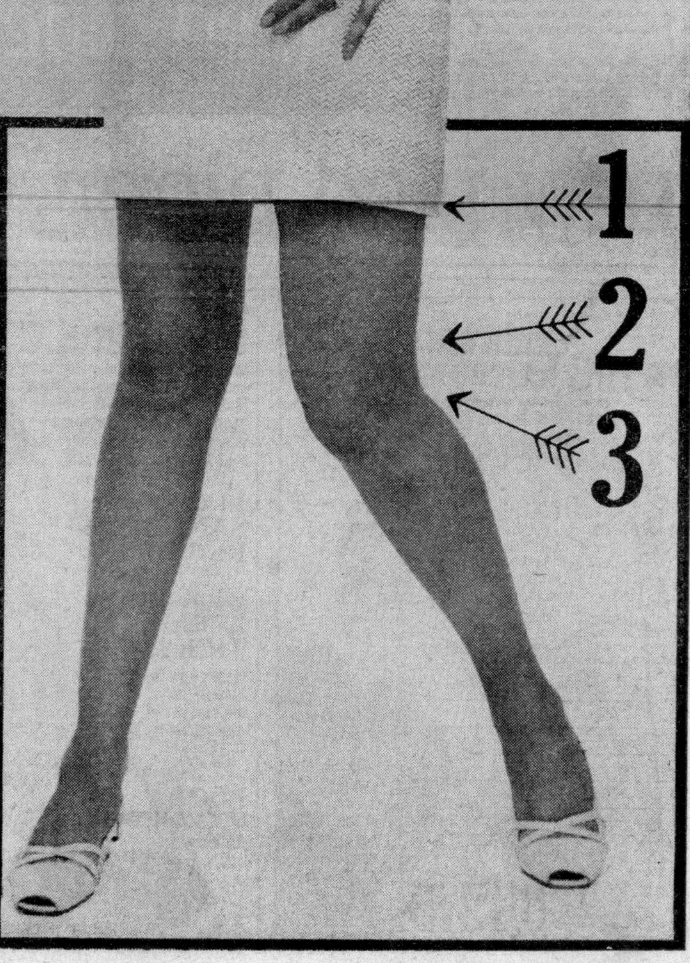

FELICITY GREEN on the fashion scene

Where's it all leading, this mania for sexy clothes?

THERE'S a lady in America called Helen Sisson who has just said she is working on the feminine hand as a new erogenous zone.

The hand—which she maintains is the most complex and expressive member of the whole body—is, she feels, sadly neglected in the world today.

"In India," says Mrs. Sisson, "there are more than 1,000 named movements of the hand. Here hands just don't have the importance they deserve."

It will come as no great surprise to learn that Mrs. Sisson is in the glove business. Having declared her interest, she continues thus:

"For autumn there will be a slipcover to wear over gloves. I've done a real shockeroo in silver vinyl—suggestive of Batman."

Fever

Mrs. Sisson is caught up in the erotomania—I *think* I made the word up, but you never know—that is sweeping the world at the moment.

From the emergence of the topless dress and ditto of the bosom in 1964, to the incident last week when a couple of models appeared in their undies in a Carnaby-street window, the pace of the shock-or-bust fashion stakes has hotted up to fever pitch.

Mary Quant, the original fashion rebel, is currently talking of unrestricted bosoms moving visibly inside light, skinny clothes.

The ultimate in undies? The body stocking.

Low

At London's swingingest nightspot last week, skirts rose yet another inch and one trouser suit was cut so low at the back that cleavage seemed imminent.

Where did it all start, this souped-up world of sexy fashion? Even more interesting, where's it going and how long will it take to get there—and what will happen on the way?

Will we be walking round starkers when the rising hemline finally meets the ever-growing cutaway armholes in the totally see-through dress?

The answer, which will cause mixed emotions, depending on the sex of the emoter, I can confidently predict is No. Starkers we will not be. For all sorts of reasons. Psychological, practical geographical and financial.

But apparently we have still quite a long way to go down the garden path of erotic trends.

My authority on the subject is Doris Langley-Moore, one of the greatest experts on fashion in the country.

Apart from being founder and adviser of the Museum of Costume in Bath, she predicted about ten years ago the advent of the boneless one-piece undie before it was even a gleam in the manufacturers' eye. (It later became the Body Stocking remember?)

Wild

Mrs. Langley-Moore sees fashion going even wilder and more way-out before the pendulum swings back—but swing, she insists, it will.

"I don't think we have reached the peak of eroticism yet," she said. "But what we have at the moment is a period of complete anarchy in fashion.

"There are no rules any more. Everyone does exactly what she or he wants. It's all very vulgar. But it's anarchy, all right.

"And after anarchy comes despotism. This is always true—in fashion as in politics. And after eroticism comes puritanism. Always.

"It happened soon after James I when the breasts were bared. This was a great time for eroticism and masquerade in fashion. Then came the Puritans.

Total

"The same swing happened after the Regency period with their transparent dresses and their 'fleshings'—these were the sort of tights they wore as undies.

"But gradually—and this kind of swing is always a gradual one—clothes became more and more voluminous. Look at the Victorian era when nothing showed at all.

"I'd say the girls of today who are going round in mini-skirts and transparent dresses will be the ones who will make sure that *THEIR* daughters are completely covered up. Total coverage, that's what we'll have, just like the Victorians."

Well that's what the lady says, and I can only recommend that the fuddy-duddies who go round muttering that they don't know what the world's coming to, should try to take a long-term view.

By 2066 they should be *MUCH* happier.

LOOK BEFORE YOU PAINT

THE PERILS of trying out new beauty products have taken an interesting turn. Colours are now so crazy that a lipstick might well be mistaken for an eyeshadow and foundation for floor polish.

This week a small bottle of pale grey liquid arrived on my desk. I couldn't wait to try it. So I didn't. I applied it liberally. In no time rigor mortis appeared to have attacked my eyelids. I read the label.

It wasn't eye shadow. It was nail varnish.

Gear for girls with mouths full of crunched almonds..

LET Mr. Ungaro, the Paris fashion designer, put it his own way. He says: "There is an evolution of women in the social framework which is very important. Clothes must no longer be looked down upon as ornaments or beautifiers. They must determine force in women, make them aggressive with a desire to work. I want to see them laugh with their mouths full of crunched almonds.

"With my clothes on, women feel something happens to them. When they put their old ones on again they say they feel 120 years old."

Yes, says Mr. Jeffrey Wallis, but if you cut out the guff, Ungaro makes some very wearable, nice clothes. We're doing him up big for summer. Great shapes and colour combinations.

With my mouth unfilled by crunched almonds I am able to say that these Ungaro adaptations will be available in the Marble Arch and Knightsbridge branches of Wallis Shops.

The combinations are purple and beige; red and green; orange and beige; green, navy and purple; navy and beige; yellow and brown. The material is a good looking cotton drill. Each coat and dress outfit costs 14 gns. complete. Sunspecs by Oliver Goldsmith.

Picture by JOHN ADRIAAN.

DAILY MIRROR, Friday, May 27, 1966 PAGE 7

✻ FELICITY GREEN on the fashion scene

THE ALMOST TOTAL LOOK

..well, shoes and stockings would have been a bit much

✻ THIS IS the dress that goes over the slip that matches the bra that teams with the pants that are made from the same material as the suspender belt.

And if it hadn't been felt that shoes and stockings would have been a bit much, these, too, would have been included in this summer's most total of Total Looks.

The idea of matching something to something else isn't, of course, new. ("What I want," the worst-dressed, least imaginative shopper used to say, "are matching navy shoes, hat, bag and gloves to go with my navy suit.")

Happy

The newness of today's Total Look is in the actual items themselves. And it's a happy, far cry from the days when you couldn't even get a bra to match a girdle, let alone a whole quintet from the birthday suit out.

This particular Total Look is a fivesome, specially designed for Daily Mirror readers and sold through branches of the Etam chain.

They'll be in stock next week. If you want to know the nearest branch to you, drop me a line and I'll let you know.

What's so important about carefully matching up things which the world at large can't even see?

It *feels* nice. Slightly wicked, in fact.

And if this sounds a bit on the whimsy side, then let's just say, with crushing practicality, they're cheap, washable and well-made.

Myself, I prefer the former reason. The latter's just a bonus.

STRIPE ME NAVY!

SHIFTY DRESS in navy and white cotton stripes, canvas belted in bright red. If you're size 36 to 40, it's yours for 49s. 11d. at branches of Etam.

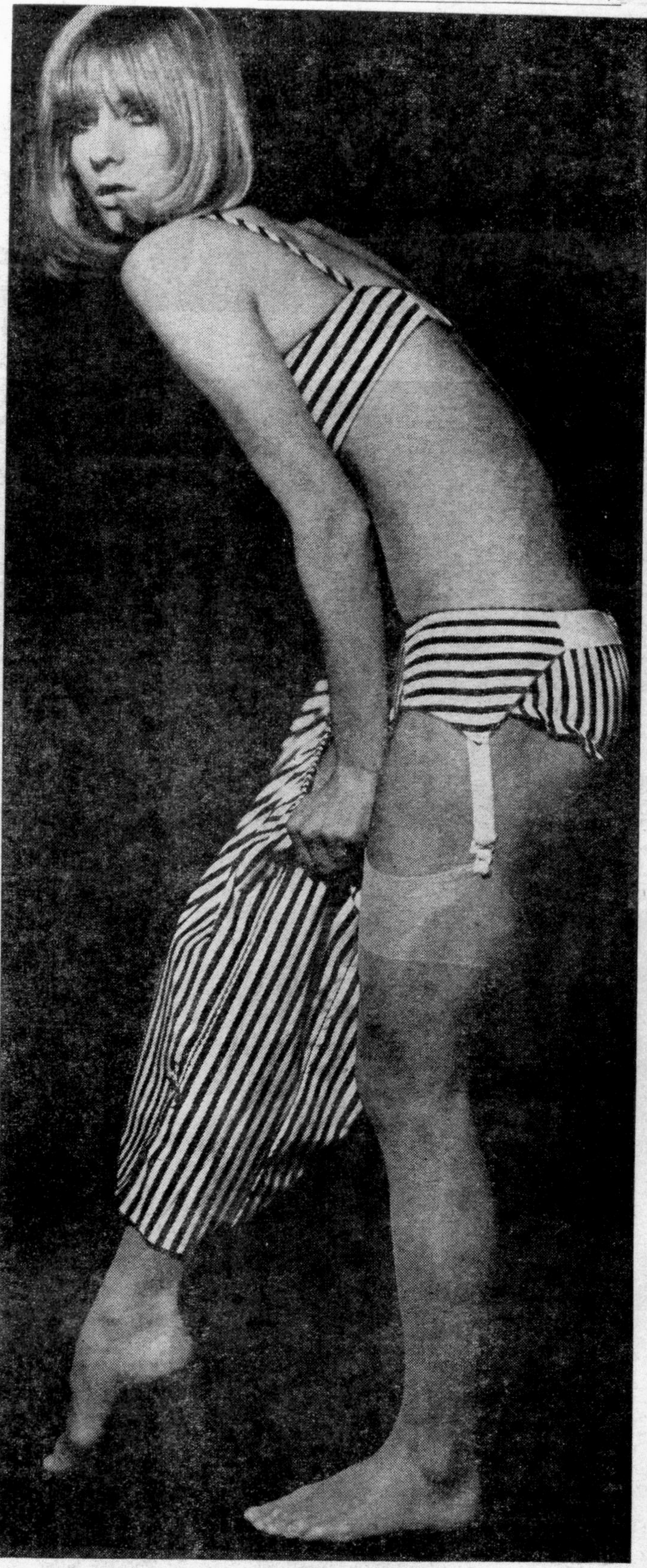

STRIPE ME ALL OVER!

TAKE OFF the dress to reveal in total the following matched undies, all in navy and white striped cotton. Half slip, 12s. 11d.; bra, 12s. 11d.; bikini pants, 5s. 11d.; suspender belt, 8s. 11d.

PICTURES: PETER MULLET

FELICITY GREEN on the fashion scene

WHY DO THEY STILL MAKE BRAS LIKE THIS

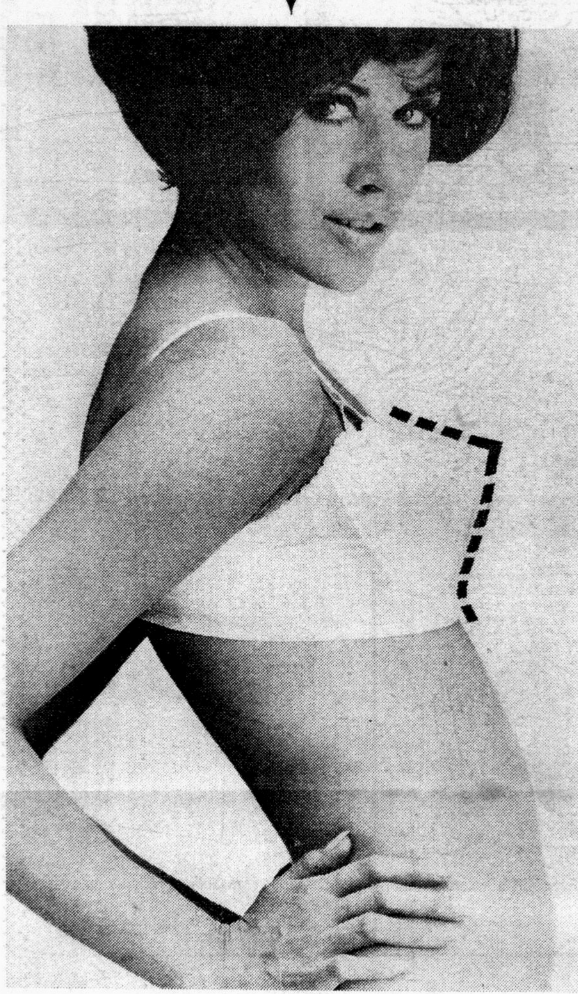

WHEN WE WANT A SHAPE LIKE THIS?

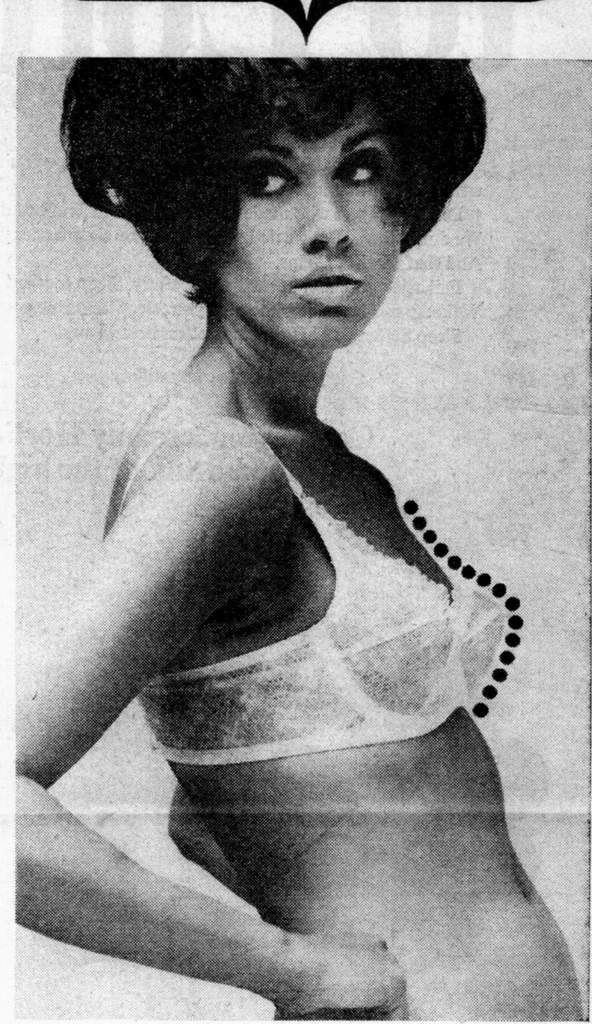

FACT: Bosoms are getting bigger. Size 34 is no longer top seller. (You'll have to bear with me while I battle with puns that will present themselves during the writing of this piece.)

Size 36 and even 38 are now coming to the forefront. (See what I mean?)

Some say this is because of The Pill.

Others say it's our improved standard of living.

To keep up with our more generous proportions, bra manufacturers are "sizing up." But, with certain notable exceptions, they are not STYLING up.

After shopping for bras this week I am prepared to stick my neck out—there I go again—and insist that too many bra manufacturers are still back in the Jane Russell days of maximum projection.

In fact, pointed bras like those in the picture on the left — the ones that look like cardboard boxes you keep eggs in—are still in the majority.

Despite the fact that they are as out of date as stiletto heels. (I know men like them, but that's beside the —er—point.)

Nobody is advocating FLAT bosoms. Well, nobody who matters, anyway.

But ever since the advent of the Topless dress, which frightened manufacturers into the realms of the no-bra bras, bosoms have become understated, to say the least.

And bosoms MUST be round to look pretty under today's close-fitting clothes.

NB. Girls with boyish bosoms may just want to extend themselves a fraction, in which case they should look for a soft "fibre-fill" shape which boosts only in the most restrained way.

And they don't run the risk of the pre-form bra wearer who leaned against her escort and dented her cups.

✻ SWEET TALK AND TALC TALK

SWEET-TOOTHED dieters take heart. There is yet time to indulge yourselves while getting down to bulge-free bikini proportions.

For a start there's Tab, the first suger-free drink from the Coca Cola Company.

Ordinary Cokes pack eighty calories in a 6oz. bottle.

Tab has just two calories in a 12oz. can.

If your sweet tooth craves chocolate bars, that cling-to-the-roof-of-your-mouth-type milk chocolate, you can now have your cake and eat it, so to speak.

Limmits, the people who sell slimming biscuits, have just produced a milk chocolate bar gooey enough to please the most insatiable sweet tooth.

One 2¼oz. sweetness-packed bar costs 2s. 6d. Expensive, but it's supposed to take the place of a meal.

It does. I ate one and felt I couldn't face food for a week

SALES PSYCHOLOGY is a high-falutin' name for figuring out why we buy one brand of something rather than another.

Johnsons, the baby beauty products firm, always seemed to me to have us women nicely figured out.

Their products may be for babies, but most women are happy to have Johnsons side by side with Arden and Rubinstein and all those other prestige pots of hope.

But Johnsons have just come a cropper as far as my dressing table is concerned.

Their new talc instead of being just discreetly cheap has a huge dotted line round the nicely designed tin which screams: "This much powder F-R-E-E."

Worse still, it has the price—2s. 3d.—embossed in red on the side.

I'll bet a man dreamed up that sales gimmick.

A bachelor.

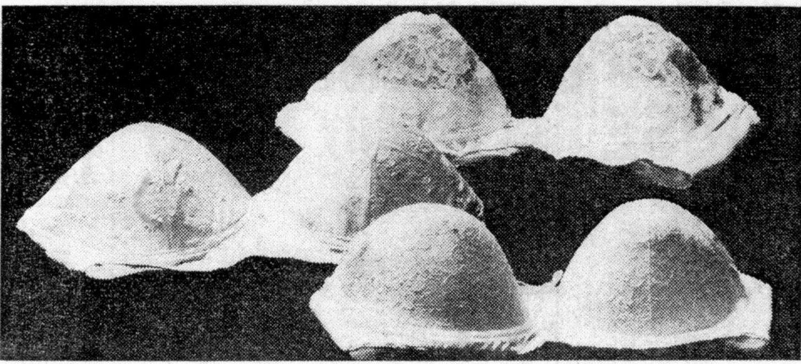

If your empty bra looks like this, it's out of date, and so's your silhouette

PICTURES BY GORDON CARTER

FELICITY GREEN looks at today's wildest designs

Way out in front

Golden breastplates on a golden mesh tunic

WHEN you've stopped laughing I'd like to explain that these are **NOT** fancy dress costumes.

It's true they're a bit fancy, but they were produced in all seriousness in Paris by a Vietnamese gentleman called Khanh who, with his first collection, has made a name for himself among the so-called way-out fashion designers as being the most way-out of all.

Khanh, first name Quasar, is married to a French girl called Emmanuelle who is reckoned by the experts to be one of the most talented ready-to-wear designers around today.

In her time Emmanuelle has produced some fairly wacky ideas, but they are as nothing compared with Quasar's offerings.

These bosom-conscious clothes were seen for the first time in Paris during the current crop of collections and the crowds were such that a gentleman at the door had to murmur dark threats about "entering at your own risk" and being trampled underfoot in the crush.

To the accompaniment of an unaccompanied opera singer, if you see what I mean, Quasar explained his preoccupation with precious metal and the two-piece suction bra, made and fitted individually for each client—and, if necessary, for each breast.

Women, he feels, have been held captive too long by their restricting clothing. Fabrics are old-hat and old-fashioned. The time has come for change, for a new concept of clothing, etc., etc.

Risk

Now whether wearing a hand-made copy of your bosom in solid gold appeals to you, is your affair.

For my part, I view this whole new fashion philosophy with a certain number of reservations.

For instance, there's a risk you may look as if you're wearing your falsies outside your frock.

But then again, just think what they must have been saying when the bustle was first invented.

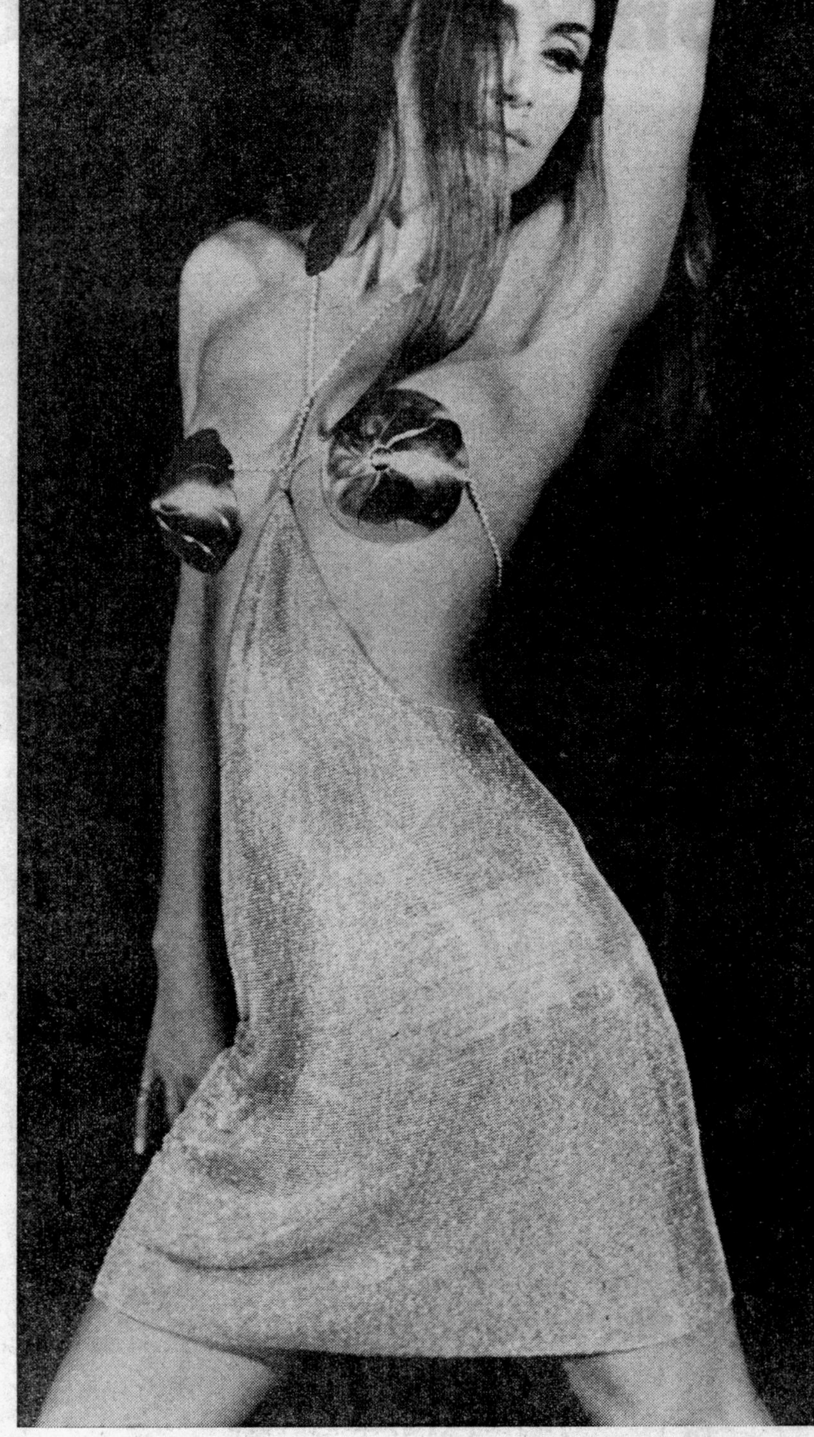

It's all done by suction . . . the Khanh bra dress in metal and mesh

Pictures by Gunnar Larsen

PAGE 12 DAILY MIRROR, Saturday, August 27, 1966

REVEALED TODAY: T

THERE'S no doubt about it. This season wil down in fashion history as the time that Paris v Pop. Instead of being out on an elegant limb their own, most of the top designers have gon for a look that just has to be described as Swinging, if downright Pop!

The biggest news is, of course, the long coat. Dior did it left) and so did other more minor members of the Big Lea

The long coat, please note, should be worn over the s skirt and with the high boot. No other combination is per sible unless you want to look as if you're tooling around in y dressing-gown. For faithful followers of the mini-skirt, th were knees galore revealed by Fer and Patou to n only a couple of Paris leg men.

Owners of big w and/or hippy hippy sh will view as manna heaven the comebac the Big Flare (see Patou outfit below for further reassuranc

Strip

Yves St. Laurent stu his audience with his Art numbers—shift sh decorated with co strip characters — those on the right. C St. Laurent ideas: brass-stud ton-up loo the knee-high boot left).

Pierre Cardin sh short-skirted pastel c shifts with black stoc and shoes. Very tarty. pretty. Very likely t very popular.

Tops

Brightest Paris new all—it will be the colourful winter Purple and red tie fo place.

Next choice is p and red together. O with vivid pink. Or and purple.

And so on through most vibrating com tions possible.

All in all, it was o the most lively P fashion scenes for age

But as most of th designers are now follo in the fashion footste the young-minded, r to-wear trade, this i exactly surprising.

NEW THE LONG COAT

The Czarina coat in red, worn, please note, with high boots and a short skirt. By Marc Bohan at Dior.

BUT STILL WITH US—THE

The Ton-up brass-studded suit. Boots again, you'll note. By Yves St. Laurent.

DAILY MIRROR, Saturday, August 27, 1966 PAGE 13

w looks for 1966/67

PARIS GOES POP!

FELICITY GREEN

The Big Flare. A scarlet coat-dress with hat, boots and stockings to match. Michel Goma at Jean Patou.

T SKIRT

Pow! Wham! And all that sort of thing. They're "The Body" and "The Face" dresses in jersey with Pop Art motifs on the front. By Yves St. Laurent.

PICTURES by GUNNAR LARSEN

A sort of mini-protest by
in mini-skirts

THE British used to be regarded as the most phlegmatic of races. Taking life very much as it came.

But nowadays, as you may have observed, they are ready to stage a protest march at the drop of a hat. Or, as happened yesterday, at the drop of a hemline.

The occasion which had them reaching for their placards was the showing in London of the autumn fashion collections which featured long, long coats that exposed very little leg indeed.

So along to the Christian Dior boutique went the demonstrators, describing themselves as the British Society for the Preservation of the Mini-skirt.

Inside the boutique the Dior people were showing coats all of five inches above the ankle. And outside were four girls, showing skirts all of four inches above the knee.

Actually the girls could have wished for a more impressive demonstration of faith in the short skirt. For they do say their society has 200 members already.

And Mr. Bill Scharf, 26, who calls himself their president, puts the figure even higher. Around 450, no less.

He is not leading the movement for any personal pleasure, you understand. "For the good of mankind" is how he puts it.

Mr. Scharf, an American who runs two male boutiques in London, confessed to being rather pleased with the placards the girls carried.

They bore legends, as you can see, like "Dior unfair to mini-skirts" and "Mini-skirts forever."

They are really general-purpose slogans. Knocked up originally for a show outside a television studi[...] a girl called Cathy McGowan [...] ened to appear in a long coat. [...] the names have been changed.

This seems a splendid thing t[...] Scharf and his disciples are [...] Preserving the most popular fas[...] have had since Dior last drop[...] hemline below the knee after t[...]

But this society need not f[...] the future of the mini-skirt. [...] as girls go on buying them, sh[...] go on selling them. Business [...] are like that. . . .

THE HEMLINE THEY DREAD

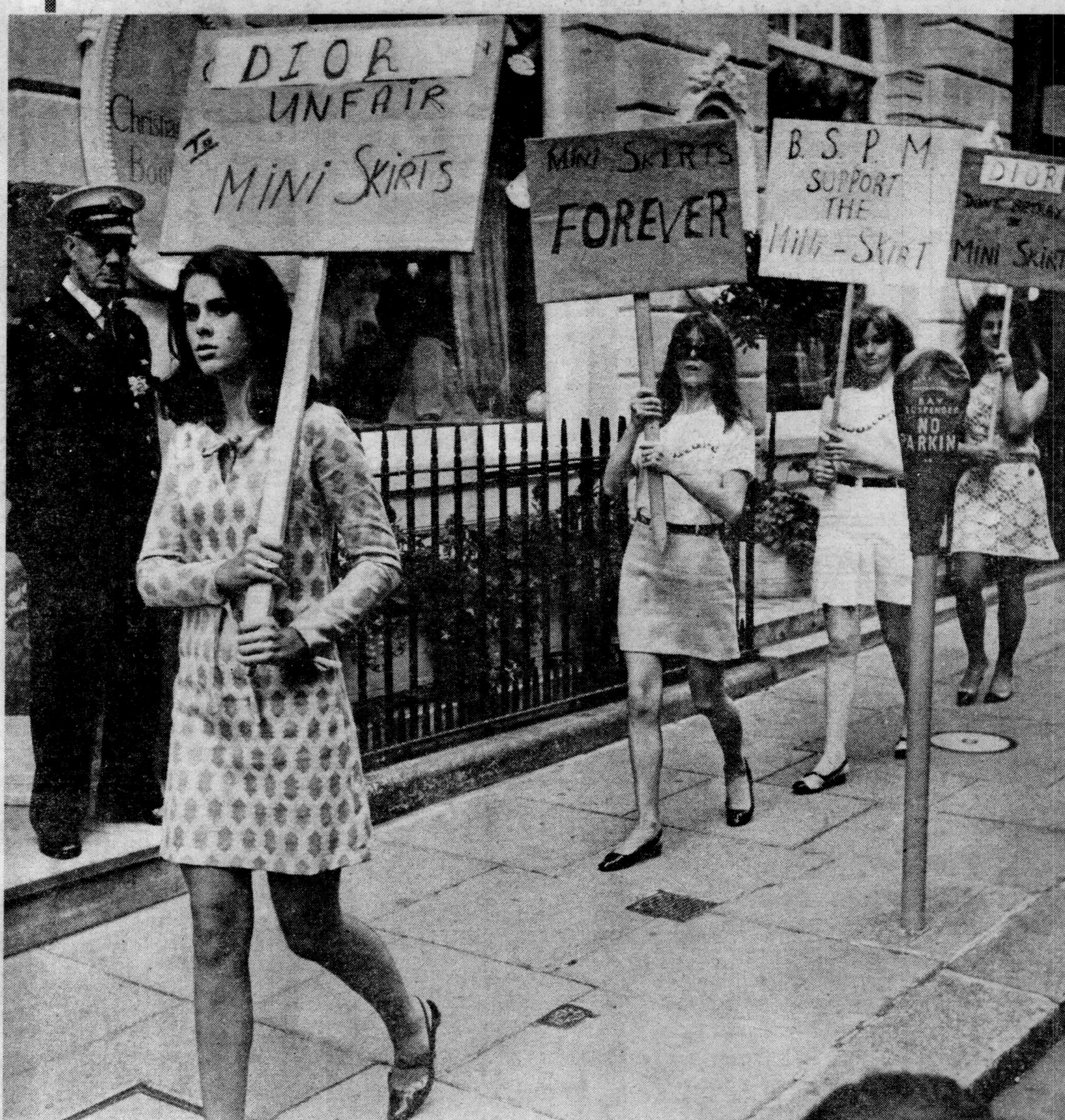

Mini-skirts and banners . . . for the protest girls demonstrating against the move towards a lower hemline.

Wednesday, September 7, 1966 PAGE 13

girls

his long ook, then, s strictly or coats

By FELICITY GREEN

IE hemline they're all worked up about . . . the mid-calf one designer Marc Bohan showed the Dior collection in Paris over a month ago and which shown in London yesterday.

lready a dozen different ver-s of the mid-calf coat are in' out all over the fashion e as the rag trade knock off r instant Paris adaptations.

Unnecessary

owever, the gloom and de-idency that has descended on i-skirt fans of both sexes—the s who wear them and the s who watch them — may be ecessary after all. Bohan him-has said not to panic. The , long coat is for wearing over short, short skirt, and the h of one new line does not n the death of another.

he mini-skirt will be with us, er fear, for many a long-legged son to come.

his particular coat (above) its white fox trim is not by . It comes from a London tique called the "Carrot on eels."

The mini may have taken a while to establish itself in the '60s, but once it took hold, the trend was well and truly here to stay. So, when in September 1966, at the height of the Swinging '60s, designer Marc Bohan at Dior decided to show the midi look, there was a distinct reluctance to embrace the new longer length. Despite Monsieur Bohan's reassurances that the arrival of the longer coat did not mean the disappearance of the shorter skirt, the London mini-enthusiasts were not convinced. While they were not exactly manning the barricades, the British Society for the Preservation of the Mini-skirt – or BSPM for short – nobly leapt into action. Well, four of them did. Future protesters please note: a smile might help your cause.

In September 1966, fashion photographer Gunnar Larsen set off for Moscow taking with him a suitcase full of the latest London Look – the world-famous mini-skirt. This fashion first, plus model girl Carole St John caused the crowds to gather. And this is how we introduced the mini to Moscow. Muscovites had never seen anything like it but, far from being excited, those stoic Russians eyed the latest fashion sensation with dour curiosity. Novelty or not, it would take more than a short skirt or two to get them aroused. There were masses of people but not a sound! In 1966, Moscow was a very quiet place. A year later in September 1967, *Daily Mirror* photographer Doreen Spooner and I set off for Moscow as part of the British Board of Trade Delegation, once again taking the British fashion to the Russians. This time the fashion shows took place in marbled halls but Doreen and I decided we wanted to meet the people in the street. Moscow was still a quiet place – even a bit quieter. The huge shops were still empty and there were long queues for bread. One shop we noticed had a long queue winding down the street. What were they selling? Heavyweight monster bras that looked like they were made of lino. But the buxom Muscovites weren't fussy about their bras. Apart from this there was nothing to tempt the fashion-conscious Muscovite. But just look at money-mad, fashion-fixated Moscow today!

On t

Captured—th

ПОЙМАН

when the mi

КОГДА МИНИ-

First meeting—the mini and the Muscovite man-in-the-street.

ashion scene with FELICITY GREEN

remarkable moment
ЗАМЕЧАТЕЛЬНЫЙ МОМЕНТ

-skirt first hit Moscow
ВПЕРВЫЕ ПОРАЗИЛА МОСКВУ

IT MAY be
commonplace
in Chelsea,
unremark-
able in Up-
er and acceptable
ccrington. But in
ow, the mini-skirt
first-ever appear-
did not, as you can
o unnoticed.

moment of impact
last week when
based photographer
r Larsen and model
role St. John took off
his particular symbol
rent Western culture
t out on the locals.

f they went as a couple
ppy-snapping holiday-

nowhere was anyone the
t bit put out by their
aphic carry-on in and
the Kremlin, the rail-
tions or Red Square at
our.

act," said Carole, "one
y came up and held
's hair out of his eyes
e was taking my picture.
I heard so much," she
ed, "about people being
and questioned by
r officials that we were
ervous.

Stolid

although we took pic-
f war posters, public
ents and soldiers, the
ne we were stopped by
eman it was for jay-
"

d large, it appears that
brothers are a stolid
n about mini-skirts.

certainly stopped when
v it. They looked long
rd. But they didn't
whistle.

man did shout some-
us when we were doing
ctures in the vegetable
' Carole reported.

sked Nona, our girl
ter, what it meant and
'He's saying the dress
ng and we should make
er.'

shouted something else
id Carole, "but Nona
tell me what it was."

ell, vegetable markets
ere are pretty fruity
or language.

TURES:
NAR
SEN

Crowd scene: Outside one of the state-owned department stores, the "yubka-mini" marches on.

Biba wasn't so much a shop in London in 1966, it was a way of life that was as well-known abroad as Carnaby Street or the King's Road. And on any Saturday afternoon Biba's sounded like the Swinging London branch of the Tower of Babel. Among the potted palms and Victorian hat stands at 19 Kensington Church Street an international band of dollies indulged their taste for Biba's highly-specialised form of self-adornment. With this under-sized over-populated interior, Biba changed the look of shops around the world. Shops even changed their name and the boutique was born. Simultaneously with this birth of the boutique, Biba branched out into mail order with 100,000 catalogues at the ready. In a way mail-order was nothing new for Biba – it was how this '60s fashion success story started. (See pages 78-79 for the famous pink gingham dress that launched the Biba mail-order boom). But there was no stopping Biba and in 1969 she moved to the vast vacant premises of carpet king Cyril Lord just up Kensington High Street. Here Biba, on its two vast floors, combined frocks and everything for the home. But the Biba story didn't end there and at the start of the '70s the vacant multi-storied Derry & Toms department store over the road in Kensington High Street came next – where Barbara Hulanicki's fantasy and fashion joined forces to take Biba into a whole new world of spectacular retailing.

Imagine! 0·5
square foot,
and Princess

SHOPKEEPERS EXTRAORDINARY

Barbara Hulanicki and her husband Stephen Fitzsimon.

by FELICITY GREEN

THE manageress is nineteen and wea
micro-skirt. There are twenty teer
assistants and each one gets a free f
every week, fifty-two weeks of the year.

There are twenty-nine hatstands and twenty p
palms. And there's a communal dressing-room t
a cross between Victoria Station at rush hour a
strip club at lunch time. In its 150 square feet
many a memo
occasion, up to ei
girls can be seen st
gling into and ou
£2 mini shifts—0.
a girl per square fo

I'm talking of c
about Biba's, the fa
Mecca of London's di
dollies, where Princess
popped in last week to
up on the very late
Swinging London gear

The Princess
actually buy anything
I'm not surprised sin
takes a couple of vis
get used to Biba's h
unusual approach to
keeping.

Noisy

For a start, it's as
as a discotheque, and
as noisy as the hi-fi g
out all the latest pop

The customers inva
look like the entire cas
film about Swinging
don.

At my last visit
were eight dogs ra
from a Borzoi to a
shund, and those
tomers who didn't
dogs had boy friends.
whom looked like
Jagger, and three of
were holding the baby
child-bride departed fo
dressing-room.

Biba's is like that.

Apart from Princess
other celebrated shopp
ones who actually b
there—include Mia Fa
Samantha Eggar,
Christie Susannah Y
Francoise Hardy, Ja
Mason, Brigitte B
(who bought four hat
a large handbag) and
McGowan (who has w

SALESGIRLS EXTRAORDINARY

Hatstands, hats and feather boas—and 15-year-old micro-skirted twins Nicole, left, and Michele.

half-undressed girls per hatstands, 20 potted palms nne just dropping in..

DRESSING-ROOM EXTRAORDINARY

Where no man treads. A peep behind the scenes into Biba's communal dressing room—some of the most swinging square footage on the London fashion scene.

3iba creation almost week on T V for the uple of years). terminding the whole llous mish-mash is herself, 28-year-old ion artist Barbara cki, and her 29-year-isband, ex-advertising ive Stephen Fitz-

Tidy

y given moment during ding week they're likely he oldest people in the

our assistants are in ens," said Fitz, "and it's lly difficult to get the pe. We've got two sets s at the moment. Our girls must have a special kind of look, and they have to learn three rules:

"Keep the place tidy, stop customers from swiping things —shoplifting's a curse and we're prosecuting people all the time —and they must never hound anyone. None of that 'Can I help you, madam?' stuff."

I can vouch for the success of the no-hounding rule.

If you spot something you'd like to buy at Biba's, there's quite a knack in telling the assistants from the customers as they're all apt to be wearing the same dresses.

"Our customers," said Fitz, "like to buy cheaply and often.

"In other shops people ask the price first and then say they'll buy it. Here they say they'll buy it first, and then ask the price."

Until recently Biba had dash, style and some of the worst-made clothes in town.

"That's true," she said, disarmingly, "and we were always terribly unhappy about it.

"But now we can afford to send things back to the factory if they're not up to standard. This winter we've got a real tailor doing our coats so we'll have lovely flat lapels and everything."

Kicky

Flapping lapels, waving hem-lines and rough old seams were indeed shortcomings. But to the 20,000 or so customers who pass through Biba's art nouveau portals each week, these faults were as nothing compared with the fact they could buy the kind of kicky clothes at prices that frankly the rag trade cannot match.

Everything in the place is designed or chosen by Biba.

Her stock at the moment, festooned over those ubiquitous hatstands and washstands she prefers to regulation dress rails and counters, includes a dozen different micro-length shifts, coats, trouser suits, undies, sweaters, stockings, shoes, feather boas, felt fedoras and enough baubles, bangles, beads, bags and chenille berets to make Aladdin's cave look like an understocked church bazaar.

Next week they start enlarging the premises.

"But we're not going to grow too fast," said Fitz, who claims modestly that he doesn't have much business sense but still has a bit more than Barbara. "We'll never let ourselves be taken over and we've already had quite a few offers."

Sorry

I'm not a bit surprised. Any-one who can spend five minutes in the frenetic atmosphere of 19-21, Kensington Church-street must surely know they're looking at the 1966 fashion equivalent of a gold strike.

But there's a sad side as well.

"I'm so sorry," said Barbara, "that I can't wear all these lovely short skirts. You see, I'm just not young enough."

You have that trouble too, Barbara?

PICTURES by DOREEN SPOONER

FELICITY GREEN ON THE FASHION SCENE

Cheap and exceedingly cheerful

Left: Striped dress in cotton Jersette in black, brown and beige. Etam, 39s. 11d. High-waisted double-breasted coat in tweed, Wallis Shops, 7 gns. Pictures by Gordon Carter.

SOME cheap clothes are just cheap. Others are cheap and nasty. And only here and there—beaming out from the dross like the darling little golden sunbeams that they are—are the ones that are worth more than what is written on their price tags.

Such are the styles shown on this page.

They are made from reasonable material, reasonably well put together with a minimum of fussy details that are the dead give-aways on so much bargain-basement fashion.

Their belts and buttons aren't fancy. They veer towards the classic, which is a better direction for cheap clothes than towards the showy gimmick which tends to look cheap even when it isn't.

All of these clothes look as if they cost rather more than they actually do, all come from stores or manufacturers with points of sale as far apart as Aberdeen and Plymouth.

If you fancy splurging out in a modest way on any one of them, I'll be happy to tell you where you can find it nearest to your home.

But let me know soon because they're the kind of fashions that don't linger around on the rails waiting for sale time.

"They walk out on their own, dear, just walk out," said the merchandise selector for one chain store stockist. "They're really the cheap and cheerful kind."

Well, that's what we all want nowadays, isn't it?

Something cheap we can be really cheerful about.

Left: Dice check coat, patent belted, C. and A., £6 19s. 6d. Right: Check shirt dress, Dorothy Perkins, 59s. 11d.

Left: Military topcoat, Richard Shops, £7 19s. 11d. Right: Chevron stripe jersey sweater dress. Etam, 59s. 11d.

FOR WHERE TO BUY WRITE TO FASHION PAGE: DAILY MIRROR, 33, HOLBORN, LONDON, E.C.1

HAPPENINGS

✻ THE MATERIAL cost 10s. 11d. a yard. The customer said she'd have half a yard.

"That will be 5s. 6d." said the assistant.

"No, it won't," said the customer, "it will be more like 5s. 5½d."

"We don't deal in halfpennies," said the assistant.

"In that case," said the customer, "it will be 5s. 5d."

"Oh no it won't," said the assistant, "it will be 5s. 6d."

"Oh no it won't," said the customer.

Eventually 5s. 5½d. it was, and if the stores computer had hiccups over it, that was fine, by her.

The store, a large one, in London, is adamant. It does NOT deal in halfpennies. And it always goes up, and not down, to the nearest penny.

Other stores in London and elsewhere are less cavalier in their treatment of small change.

The moral: Stick up for your rights as a shopper—but don't bring up the law.

The law, I'm sorry to tell you, isn't on your side.

Sad to say, you can't force a shopkeeper to sell you anything at the marked price. All you can do is walk out in a huff.

WHILE British model girls and other sensation-seekers are painting pale gold mock freckles all over their noses and cheekbones, in America they're going one better.

Their freckles are blue, green, violet, beige, slate, navy, sable, or purple patina white, whatever that is.

Made by Faberge at the dollar equivalent of 10s. a bottle, they help you to "face up to Fall's easy outdoorsy mood with a flattering fake freckling." Fancy!

IT'S a neurotic life we're leading. Even lipsticks are feeling nervous. The latest orange-pink shade by Orlane is called "High Tension" and is for "live wires in search of vivid lips."

A far cry from Rose Pink and Ruby Red and it costs 11s. 6d., which may make you even more tense.

SILVER, in case you've been down a pothole for the last few weeks, is today's biggest fashion craze.

One way to get a touch of silver—spray it on to shoes, bags, watch straps, earrings, etc., etc., with an aerosol actually produced with Christmas trees and Yuletide decorations in mind. It's by Swan and costs 5s.

Follow the instructions to avoid making a botch-up.

Crochet in the Twenties.

Like granny, like grand-daughter

WE'RE STILL HOOKED ON CROCHET

Crochet in the Sixties. By Judith Virginia.

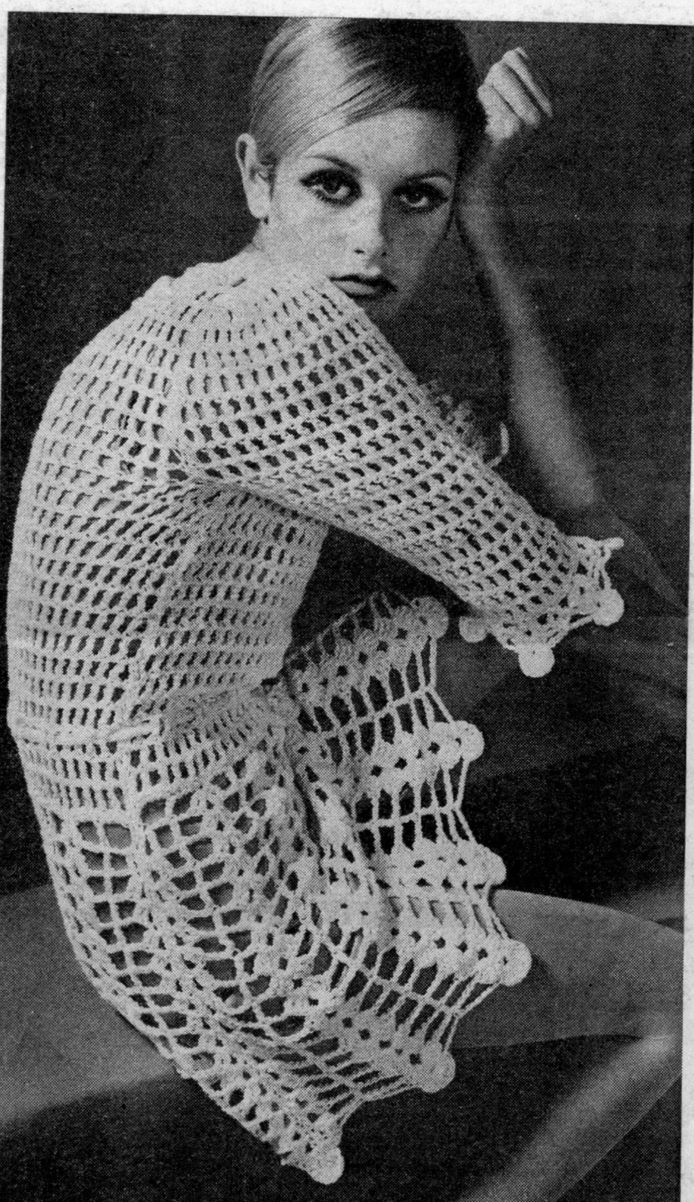

TWIGGY in crochet with the '66 look. By Lore, 13 gns.

Pictures by JOHN ADRIAAN

TWIGGY wears it. See left. Ladies of the Twenties wore it. See top left. Model girl Janni Goss wears it and looks super in it. See above.

(Actually, it's a copy of the Twenties version—had you noticed? And you can buy it for 15 guineas).

The subject under discussion is, of course, crochet—a sort of one-handed knitting that's done with one hook instead of a couple of needles and slipstitches and chain-stitches instead of the more familiar plain and purl.

I'm assured by experts that it's easy to do and it gives the fashionable see-through look with no trouble at all.

For those who want to have a go at do-it-yourself level, there's a helpful little book published by Coates for 2s.

Yarn

If you'd prefer your crochet off-the-peg rather than off-the-hook, there are umpteen pretty versions in the shops, including the white cotton one Twiggy is wearing on the left.

Other variations: Black to wear over a body-coloured slip or a body-stocking, silver or ice-cream coloured pastels.

Most of the current crochet styles are made of coarse yarn more usually associated with washing-up cloths, but that's the fashion business for you in 1966.

ANOTHER hazard with clothes made from these yarns is that they "grow" if you leave them on a hanger and this season's mini-skirt could well be next season's long evening gown.

Flat

So if you have caught the crochet bug, put the dress away flat in a drawer unless, of course, you actually need a new long evening gown.

To keep up with the demand for crochet fashions, cottage industries are booming all over the country.

At one busy centre—a tiny village in Essex—they're busily turning out swinging styles for swinging dollies which sell at about 12 guineas a go at the swinging boutiques.

Craze

And quite a few of the ladies who are frantically doing the loop-stitches, chain and double crochet don't even know what swinging means.

Last year British womanhood worked its way through a mind-boggling forty million lbs. of "knitting" yarns.

Unless I miss my guess it will be much much more in '67—thanks to the new craze for crochet.

DEIRDRE McSHARRY ON TWIGGY

Former Daily Express fashion editor who discovered Twiggy and named her The Face of '66

Leonard was my hairdresser for twenty years. One Friday in February 1966 he dropped some test shots of a new haircut on my lap. The snaps showed a fifteen-year-old, huge eyes, innocent face, hair cropped like a boy chorister. The eyes were a cherub on speed – false eyelashes and twigs of mascara painted beneath.

This was Lesley Hornby of Neasden, known as Twigs; those bendy long legs. Photographer Barry Lategan's snaps caught the gamine quality, Leonard fixed her iconoclastic style with that crop. Could she come into the office? Spreading the pictures on my desk I watched the fifteen-year-old drink tea from a mug in her shrunken sweater and skimpy skirt, giggling like the schoolgirl she still was, I knew this was the way fashion – style – was going. No one looked like Twigs back then. Chirpy, legs all over the place, shrunken sweater knitted by her Mum, little boy's shorts. The picture spread across two pages. (The *Daily Express* then sold four million copies a day.) I typed out: "Twiggy is the face of 1966..."

"Twiggy, totally unspoiled, rose like a meteorite to become one of the faces of the '60s"

FELICITY ON TWIGGY

The golden girl of the '60s beat me at Scrabble! Our book of reference was a huge American dictionary. The message in the front of this mighty tome read "To Felicity with love from Phyllis" – my former *Woman and Beauty* editor. "Oh," asked Scrabble demon Twiggy, "did she write this book?"

Twiggy was a natural, modest and funny with a winning way with words – describing a day out with mum and the family: "We were all packed into the car going somewhere for the day. Mum noticed we needed petrol so we stopped at one of them great big motorway places. I fancied some sweets so I slipped into one of them shops and when I came out they'd all gone! They'd forgotten all about me and it took 'em ever so long to notice!"

Twiggy, totally unspoiled, rose like a meteorite to become one of the faces of the '60s. Leaving school in January 1966 to pursue her career, this six-and-a half-stone, leggy waif with her blonde Leonard crop and catchy nickname took no time in getting straight to the top. Oh, Twiggy, how we loved your innocent combination of simple and smart, which today is less simple, but every bit as smart. A rare and winning combination.

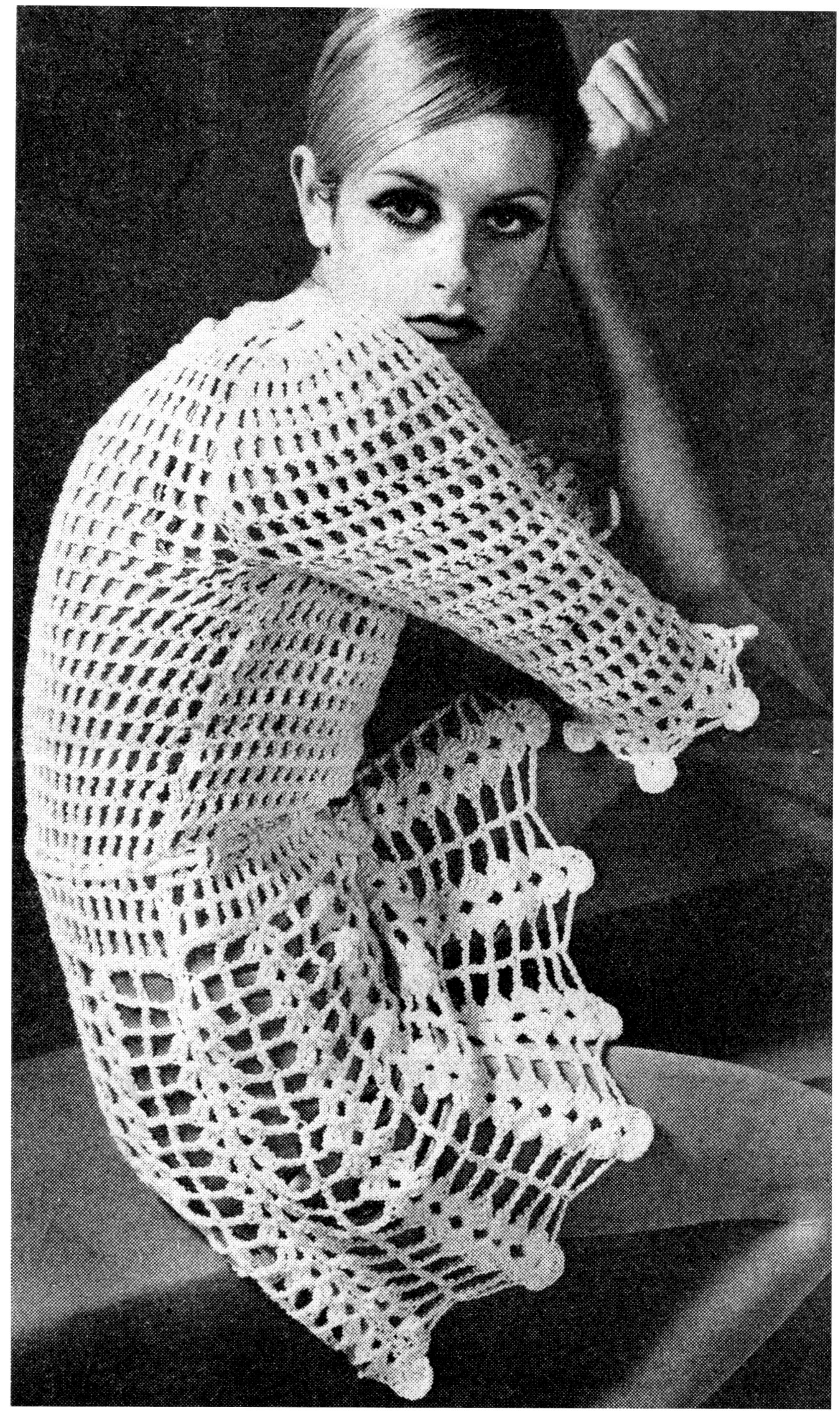

Winsome Twiggy '60s style: smooth sleeked-back hair, maxi eye make-up and machine-made crochet mini-dress designed to look like the real hand-made stuff

The sixteen shilling, eleven minute, do-it-yourself, silver, super, noisy Christmas dress!

Whichever way you look at it, this is a MOST unusual dress. It looks like the aluminium foil you wrap the cheese in but it's actually made of silver metallised plastic.

It weighs half an ounce and if it's too long you can snip off the hem with the kitchen scissors. It costs 16s., cut out ready to make up, and you stick it together with Sellotape, instead of sewing it.

It's so tough you can stamp on it, crunch it up in a clenched fist—I can't think why you would want to, but you never know—pull it apart at the Sellotaped seams and then stick it together again, unharmed.

If all this rough stuff leaves it with an interesting crackle finish you can iron it back to some of its former shining glory between a couple of sheets of newspaper.

I speak about all this with the voice of experience.

MILD

Using my desk as a dressmaker's table, I made a dress up yesterday in eleven minutes flat with only one false, but immediately rectifiable, move around the left armhole and a couple of mild expletives as one bit of Sellotape stuck to another bit of Sellotape.

This latest do-it-yourself dress is made by Incadinc (pronounced Inkadink) which has nothing to do with Schnozzle Durante and stands for Ideas Need Creative Art Direction Inc.

The brains behind this new venture—"We're not in the rag trade, we're in the business of selling good ideas"—belong to three young men—two in-work actors, Jonathan Burn, 26, and John Steiner, 24, in conjunction with one busy graphic designer, Paul Wood, who is 29.

I cannot vouch for any future Incadinc ideas—"It could be anything from advising Shell Oil on the lighting in their new building to inventing, say, a fully-automated electronic giraffe"—but unless I miss my guess, this dress will be a Christmas winner for those way-out dollies who inhabit the wilder shores of fashion.

MODES

Oh, and by the way, I am assured by Those Who Know that the newest essential for really In-type modes is noise. Lots of it. Decibels and decibels. Rustling, I'm told, is out.

Rattling is in, so this dress is very in indeed as the moment you move it sounds like a pop-crazy audience applauding the Beatles.

So for those who wish to rattle as well as shine this Yuletide, the dress will be on sale in shops and boutiques over the country in about two or three weeks.

If you're in more of a hurry than that, write to me for the address of the manufacturer who will send it to you in about 10 days, for 16s. plus a shilling for postage.

Happy rattling.

FELICITY GREEN

A dress to make a noise in. Picture: GORDON CARTER

✱ on the fashion scene by FELICITY GREEN

HIPS IN A TIGHT SPOT

I WOULD LIKE to address a word or two to the makers of stocking tights.

The boom they are undoubtedly enjoying in this mini-skirted age could be even boomier if they would remember one thing.

Ladies with size 8½ feet may have 34in. hips. Or they may not.

Feet sizes, please note, are not related in any way to hip sizes.

And it is dangerous to assume that the bigger the feet the bigger the hips.

Which is what they seem to be doing at the moment. (Size 8½ tights have 34in. hips, size 9½ have 37in. hips and 10½ measure a generous 42in.)

In fact, a very big-footed slim-hipped girl friend of mine has to walk with her knees together to keep her tights up.

This sizing and proportion business is obviously a headache for the hosiery boys, and is something that needs further thought.

After all, it took the dress business long enough to sort out their long size tens from their short size fourteens.

The tights people at the moment seem to be making everything from sheer nylon to black fishnet for that dratted, non-existent Mrs. Average.

And by the way, while I'm in a complaining mood, please can we have less reinforced top? It shows — and looks VERY unexotic. Defeats its object, you might say.

Dollies growing by the foot

FEET are getting bigger. Evidence —forty-year-old shoes found in the cellar of a Hampstead shop by a man whose father was a shoemaker.

All the shoes have thick heels, rounded toes and the high instep straps that today's dollies are mad about.

But Soukh, the Hampstead shop, which is selling them like crazy at 4 gns. a pair, has found difficulty with the sizes.

Nearly all the shoes are in sizes 2, 3 and 4. Feet today are nearly all 5, 6 and 7.

Must be all the milk and orange juice or something.

The Candys of England

DAVID BAILEY comparing English girls with French girls:

❝I think French women grow up far more quickly than English girls. If I walk through London I see the prettiest girls in the world —really unbelievable, but they're not women, they wouldn't know what a woman is—they're all Lolitas and Candys. I feel like a Dirty Old Man in London.❞

Mary Quant [in mini-knickers] practising what she preaches!

FASHION is a mini-knickered thing . . . Mary Quant at home in black satin. Shift 8½ gns., mini-knickers 3½ gns. Picture by Gordon Carter.

LET US be absolutely clear about it. There are mini-pants and mini-knickers. Mini-pants are a kind of Bermuda shorts garment that dribble down a strategic three to five inches below a mini-skirt.

They make a short dress look like a long tunic, and American designers are mad about them.

One designer called Mr. de la Renta reckons that, as the two things women are most mad about at the moment are short skirts and trouser suits, mini-pants give them the best of both worlds.

I disagree, but that's another story, and you may just be mad about Bermudas which I feel do less for a girl than halitosis does.

However, the point here is that mini-**knickers**, which Miss Quant is wearing on the left, are a different fashion proposition altogether.

"I wore my yellow satin shift with the matching knickers to a ball," said the mini-knickered Miss Quant this week, "and they were a riot.

Great

"In the beginning I felt a bit shy, but when the dancing started it was great. Pretty soon complete strangers were coming up and asking me all about them."

Since their debut at the ball, Miss Quant's mini-knickers go everywhere with her.

To work—in beige jersey.

To parties—in vivid satin.

Each mini-knicker has its matching mini-skirted dress and sitting down and showing an untoward expanse of anything that shouldn't be shown, becomes a hazard of the past.

They're **supposed** to show, which may remove some of the spice of life for bird-watchers, but there you are, aren't you?

"I got the idea for them," said Mary, "because I became fed up watching women on TV in short skirts forever tugging at their hemlines. Or fidgeting to get a knock-kneed pose so they'd look decent.

Drape

"It's a difficult business, sitting down nowadays. One of my friends used to practise for hours in front of the mirror draping her mini-skirts so that they fell correctly just between her thighs.

"But this is a bore, too contrived —and really rather ridiculous.

"Why do I call them 'knickers,' not mini-pants? Because it's a nice funny old word, and I like it.

"But the knickers I've designed are really a sort of boxer shorts— nothing like those old ladies' knickers with elastic at the knee.

"And for once," says Miss Quant happily, "I've found an idea I like personally that's also an instant success with the buyers."

MARY QUANT

The designer who made The London Look a worldwide success

Early on I knew that clothes would be the great interest of my life. I loved sewing and I was always tremendously interested in what people wore. For me, fashion is not frivolous; it's part of being alive.

I was acutely conscious that I had to break all the rules. I wanted to design a complete look from head to toe – clothes, make-up, hosiery, shoes, boots, underwear... everything! My aim was to create young modern fashion for women like me who wanted to get a kick out of what they were wearing. My style was daring and exciting, never dull.

There was a time when every girl under twenty yearned to look like an experienced, sophisticated thirty. Suddenly in the '60s this reversed with a vengeance – every girl with a hope of getting away with it wanted to look young and sexy.

This was The Quant Look, free and independent with a great sense of FUN – girls experimented with fashion and style, with colours and make-up. Quant-style meant cosmetics old style were out, as were all those structured foundation garments. Stockings weren't practical for mini-skirts so I designed embroidered and patterned tights.

While the ubiquitous mini-skirt crept ever higher, I experimented with traditional fabrics like flannel and new textures like PVC. Some of our other '60s successes: skinny sweaters, knee boots and black stockings, pinafore dresses, string tops, Breton berets, knickerbockers, shorts suits and hot pants. All these were labelled Quant gimmicks when they first appeared, but they struck a chord and became an integral part of the advance of '60s fashion, which was really all about Young London.

I felt we were moving towards exposure and body cosmetics, and certainly pubic hair – which we could now view in the cinema, and on the stage – would become a fashion emphasis, although not necessarily blatant. For instance, I revealed, I encouraged Alexander to trim my pubic hair into a heart-shape. This seemed to rivet both the people and the press. The *Daily Mirror*'s 16 October 1969 feature: Has Mary Quant Gone Too Far This Time? devoted a whole piece to this quote. It ricocheted everywhere. Strangers in pubs and restaurants bought me a drink on the strength of it. John Lennon adored it and started sending me various ideas of other shapes I could try. I had known him since he bought his black leather cap and lots of other things from our shop.

I plunged in to the whole London scene and broke all the rules. Revolution was the watchword of our generation – and what a generation!

"I was acutely conscious that I had to break all the rules"

FELICITY ON MARY

Mary Quant's middle name ought to be 'Legs'. Tiny Mary has the longest legs and she successfully exposed them to the eager '60s world with her Magic Minis.

But it was a different Quant erogenous zone that appeared in one of my *Mirror* pages in October 1969 that got me into trouble. In one of her interviews with me, Mary said that at her instigation her husband Alexander Plunkett-Greene had, in a lover's homage, shaved her pubic hair into a heart shape. I wrote all about this in the *Mirror*. The next day I was sent for by an obviously concerned editor. Both he and the company lawyer were waiting for me in his office. "You and the *Daily Mirror* have just been reported to the Press Council!" "What for?" I asked. "For running your story about Mary Quant's husband shaving her pubic hair into a heart shape." "But that's what she said!" Twenty-four hours later the sensible Press Council declared me innocent. Phew!

As the Quant global business was building up, Mary and business partner husband Alexander certainly led a colourful life in the Swinging '60s. Mary's shop, Bazaar in Chelsea's King's Road excited the in-crowd. Her way-out styling and mini-clad models in the window attracted so many onlookers fighting for a look-in, the police had to be called. And in the Bazaar basement, the Quant couple opened Alexander's, the famous '60s restaurant that became the most swinging place to eat and drink in the increasingly swinging King's Road. Some of the Quant methods and madnesses were nothing if not alternative. Gambling was still illegal so they set up gambling games in vans, and when business was booming they rushed round London making Quant deliveries in a pram.

If the '60s had a symbolic image it is certainly Mary's mini-skirt, still on the up and up, which changed the way women worldwide chose to look; and Mary's name remains justly famous around the world. This is Fashion Power indeed!

Mary saw the '60s revolution coming and designed the clothes for it. She was not only into mini-skirts, but also showed her famous legs in some pretty short shorts

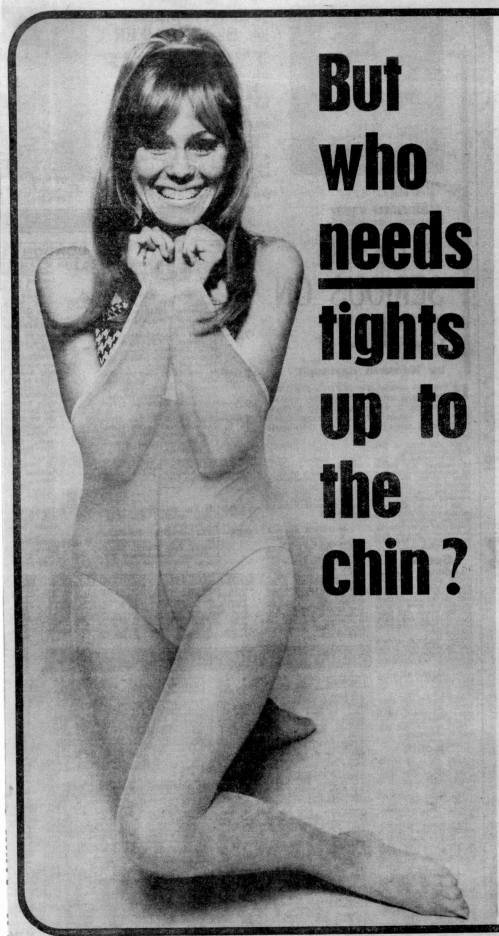

But who needs tights up to the chin?

FELICITY GREEN on the FASHION SCENE

BREATHES there a girl with soul so dead she never to herself has said: "What I need under my mini-skirt is a pair of well-fitting tights."

Well-fitting — ah, that's the problem.

There are now about a dozen different brands of tights selling in the shops, and having tried just about the lot I'm prepared to state that they vary in fit from the too-little to the too-much.

The too-little type look rather like a pair of stockings stitched together at the top and have as much staying-up power.

It's true that after they've been worn and washed a couple of times they stretch to hipster height—but they're a calculated risk in the meantime.

GROW

Others fit neatly to the waist when brand new, but like Topsy they just growed with each successive wash, and in a week would reach up to any respectably-placed armhole.

Take those on the left for a start. Six washes ago they fitted a treat and stopped where tights should stop.

Now, with no more than a gentle tug they're almost up to the chin.

"What I want," said a mini-skirted customer shopping alongside me at the jam-packed stocking counter last week, "is a pair of size 9 tights not measuring more than 5 inches up from the crotch."

The harassed assistant said something about not being rude and anyway she didn't know about that sort of thing and in her book size 9 tights were size 9 tights.

But, of course, she was wrong.

BAGGY

"We do best with our hipster styles," reports one hosiery buyer. "Most of the waist-length ones don't fit around the hips as snugly as they should."

When I complained to a chain store that their 10s. 6d. sheers had become baggy after a couple of washes, they immediately offered to take them back. And "to look into the question of fit."

I only hope they look quickly so that things improve while short skirts are still with us.

A fat lot of good well-fitting tights will be if we're all going back to wearing hobble skirts.

PICTURE: GORDON CARTER

DAILY MIRROR, *Thursday, January 5, 1967* PAGE 7

such a PHYSICAL QUALITY

WHAT, you may well wonder, are these leading men in British sport doing with Mrs. Emma Peel of T V and Avengers fame?

The answer, in current jargon, is they're projecting the same fashion image.

"As a series," said the fashion consultant for A B C-T V, "it has such a very *physical* quality, in addition to which it's so sexually elegant."

So, in order to show what Emma is going to be wearing when the new series starts next week, they invited along such very physical and sexually elegant people as boxer Billy Walker and Olympic weight-lifter George Manners.

Other than lending a hand in a more robust way than most male models could manage, these gentlemen are also, in a way, helping to boost Britain abroad, as The Avengers is now a highly successful export.

It sells to forty different countries and, for the first time, has been filmed in colour for America.

The Avenger fashions, as addicts will recall, have always run a close second to the plot.

This time, Emma's clothes—from action suits to underwear, from mini-knickers to thigh watches—have been specially designed for her by 25-year-old Welshman, Alun Hughes.

And from now on, Steed will be a sort of sartorial spectacular all on his own, with clothes by Pierre Cardin in Paris.

Should Avenger fashions, His or Hers, tickle your fancy of an evening, you can rush out and buy them the next morning as they will all be in the shops.

Which may help you to feel less deprived about not seeing Mrs. Peel and Mr. Steed in full and fashionable colour.

FELICITY GREEN

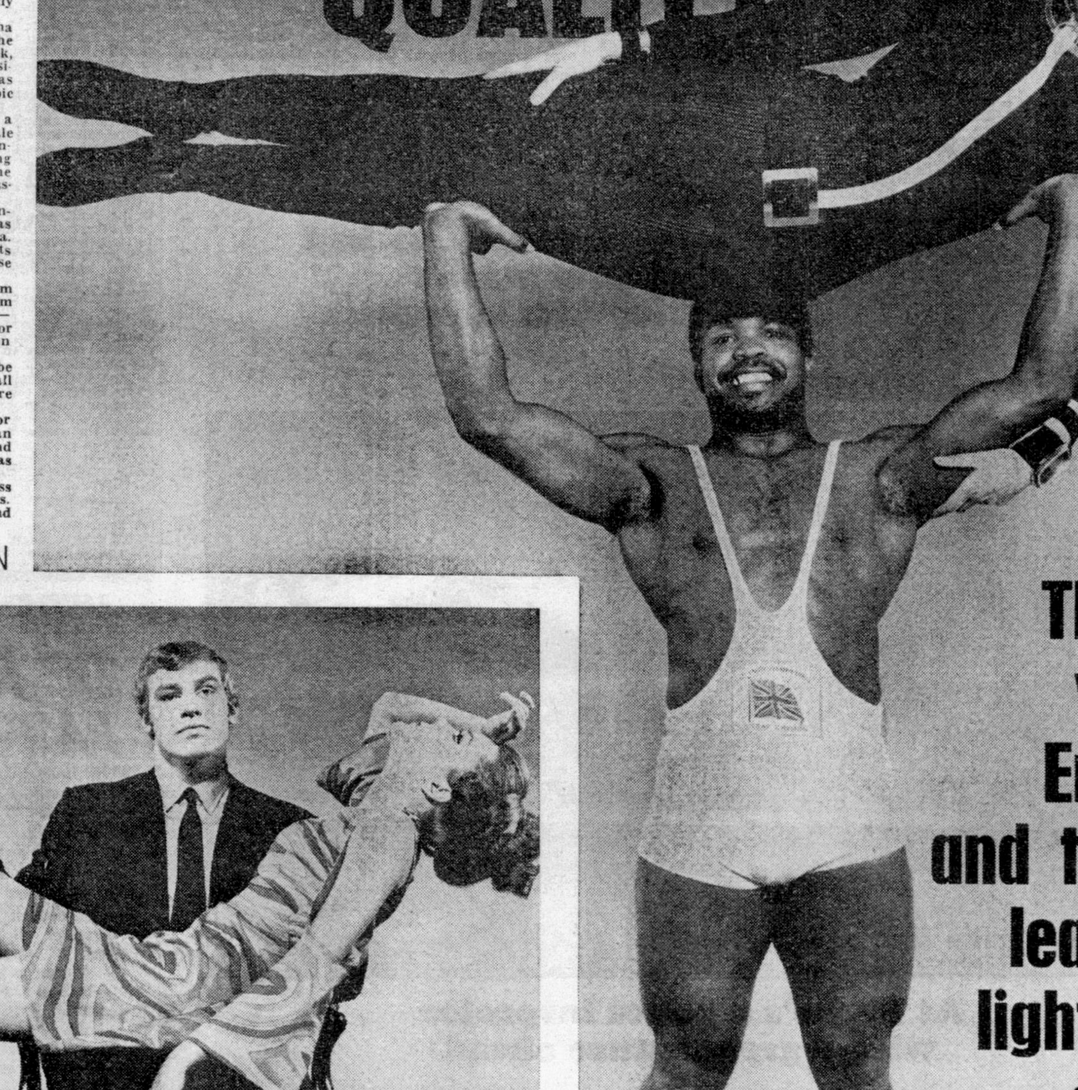

That's what Emma and these leading lights of sport have in common

All limp and relaxed on boxer Billy Walker's ample lap, Emma in an art nouveau print by Thocolette. Price 9 gns. Pictures: Terry O'Neill.

Emma on high in an "Emmapeeler" action suit. 8 gns. by Kashmoor. In sole support, George Manners.

FELICITY GREEN ON THE '67 F

The message from in a word, is KNICKERS

YOU COULD call them culottes. Or Bermudas. Or boxer shorts. Or bloomers. But whatever you call them, and nowadays knickers is *the* word, they prove that all Paris is on a knicker kick the like of which has not been seen outside the fourth form at gym practice.

As though some great bush whisper had swept the salons, the designers have unanimously decided 1967 shall be the year of the Great Divide. The year when every mini-skirt shall have its own underpinnings peeping provocatively out. When every suit has a sawn-off pair of pants in place of a skirt.

Will women wear them?

Some will, some won't. But this lack of unanimity is only to be expected in view of the fact that Paris now merely suggests and no longer dictates.

Other Paris suggestions for '67:

☐ The Jungly Look with African prints, safari hats and bush-jacket suits. We have, however, been wearing these for years, but it's always nice to have our ideas corroborated by Paris.

☐ The Tent Look, the great silhouette leveller, which swings out like a triangle from the shoulders, is easy to wear, and renders totally invisible any curve, bulge or jutting hip bone. But keep it short. More of a mini-tent than a marquee.

☐ And, above all, coloured legs. Leg-coloured legs are out.

The Knicker Look suit in navy and white wool. By Ungaro.

The Knicker Look goes on safari, A suit in white silk By Ricci.

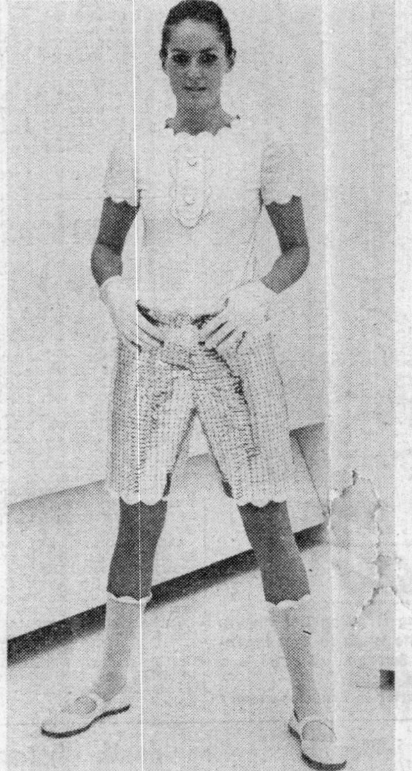

The Knicker Look goes festive. Sequin Bermudas. By Courreges.

PICTURES: GUNNAR LARSEN

DAILY MIRROR, Saturday, February 25, 1967 PAGE 15

ON SCENE

Paris,

…o much knickers—more like trousers. A touch of the old-time gangster's … in this natty chalk-stripe trouser suit. From Yves St. Laurent.

Paris in 1967 presented an unusually unified look among the top designers. Skirts were out and in their place came variations on the divided look. There were knickers peeping out from mini-skirts, there were short shorts and long shorts. And in place of the traditional Paris suit – with its matching skirt to accompany the impeccably tailored traditional jacket – this time the popular Paris suit had a very different look. This 1967 rule-breaker came, of course, from the revolutionary Yves Saint Laurent, who had been a rebel since his first love of black leather in his London-influenced 'Beat' collection back in 1960. The St Laurent trousers were as relaxed as dungarees. On top of the shirt came a gent's waistcoat and the jacket was as casual as a blazer. For those of us who preferred informality, we chanted 'Vive St Laurent!'

DAILY MIRROR, Monday, June 26, 1967 PAGE 11

AS ORDERED BY THE SHAH OF PERSIA, IN FLOWER-OF-SIN MARBLE, WITH ILLUMINATED BOTTOM (TO FIND THE SOAP) COST: £3,571-8-5. EMPTY

by FELICITY GREEN

IT MUST be transparently obvious to everyone concerned that the lady seen above is taking a bath.

And what a bath. . . . But then bathrooms with all the simplicity of the Throne Room at Buckingham Palace are the latest status symbols for those well-known People Who Have Everything.

Carpets, armchairs, telephones are all being connected up to the Hot and Cold, and furnishing a bathroom is now becoming a job for the interior decorator rather than for the plumber.

All this is joyous news to Monsieur Michel de Lacour, to whom bathrooms mean everything.

M. de Lacour lives, breathes and dreams of the luxurious ultimate in sanitary fittings.

He also sells them at his establishment—you just can't call that sort of place a "shop"—near the British Embassy in Paris.

One of M. de Lacour's previous efforts, a His and Hers model in pastel marble, cost £600; and at this very moment he has 84 satisfied couples splashing away in sub-aqua Togetherness.

But, points out M. de Lacour, that was last season's look. This season there is a new miracle of mod. con. that is just the thing for those who can afford £3,571 8s. 5d. in new French francs, give or take a sou.

You could call this new model a bath for people who have nothing to hide, among whom may be listed the Shah of Persia. He has already ordered one.

The main feature of the new De Lacour bath, in case you haven't noticed, is that it is see-through. Totally transparent.

As glass-sided as a fish tank or that Butlin's swimming pool at Clacton. Should you have your £3,571 8s. 5d. at the ready, but wish for further details, the sides are crystal, the fittings are bronze, the taps are dolphins' heads, and the bottom lights up to help you find the soap.

You can choose from pink, mauve, white, black, turquoise or green, and consideration will be given to any other colour a client may request.

However, this may be a problem as the material used for the top and the base is a very special marble, available only in limited supplies, and known as "Flower-of-Sin."

PICTURE by GUNNAR LARSEN

Novelty made the headlines in the Swinging '60s pages of the *Daily Mirror*. These pages were designed to amuse and attract readers of both sexes and the images are typical of the fascination with excess during the '60s. The picture above combined the saucy with the frankly unlikely: an all-glass bath with an illuminated bottom. Don't ask! And for something more mainstream: the pictures on the right demonstrate the late '60s fondness for psychedelic hippy fashion and Patti Boyd, the leggy model muse.

DAILY MIRROR, Tuesday, August 8, 1967 PAGE 7

Q Where did Patti get that gear?

PATTI . . . to Los Angeles Hippie style.

The Hippie cult, like it or loathe it, is here. Compared with its baubles, bangles, beads and bells, the Quant-type mini-skirts pale into Establishment respectability. Where does it all come from?

FELICITY GREEN

on the flower power fashion scene

IN CASE you have been kept awake o' nights wondering where on earth Patti Beatle Boyd Harrison got that get-up in which she flew off to Los Angeles, I can now reveal the secret fashion source.

It's a basement in London's Montague-square, where the founder members of the Hippie haute couture hang out.

Two girls, a man, and a business manager co-habit here among the paraphernalia of psychedelia, turning out those snappy little Hippie numbers for boys and girls that are being so enthusiastically received by the Pop elite.

You know the kind of stuff. The female versions look as if they're made of a patchwork quilt that has got too hot and melted. And the finished fully-accessorised effect is somewhere between Ophelia, Pocahontas and a sale of work.

Actually doing the designing are the two king-sized Dutch girls, seen right. They are Marijke Koger and Josje Leeger, both twenty-three.

Helping them along their beaded, baubled and braided path is Marijke's Dutch husband, Simon Posthuma, who is twenty-eight, has longer hair than either of the girls, and at the moment of our meeting wore a pendant, a purple velvet tunic, pale yellow peep-toe sandals and some extremely form-fitting pants in pink and lime satin stripes, bias-cut.

LOVE

The only un-Dutch member of this Hippie set-up is a Northern lad called Barry Finche, who goes in for rather self-conscious hand kissing, agrees with his Dutch chums that Love is All and was once a publicist for the Saville Theatre.

"We are now," said Simon, explaining their success in the dizzier reaches of Swinging London, "personal tailors to the Beatles."

"We also, of course, make Patti's clothes," said Josje pronounced Yoshy who claims to have had a "whole fashion scene going for her back in old Amsterdam."

Josje was wearing blue printed silk braid-bound pyjamas, a blouse in three multicoloured, unrelated prints, snakeskin thong sandals up to her knees, a jewelled breastplate and a bandeau and beads in her freak-out hairdo, so recently acclaimed by Paris.

Apart from designing clothes, Marijke—pigtails, purple thong sandals, beads, a string of hippie bells, and a multi-coloured mini-frock in the psychedelic manner — designs posters, while Simon concentrates on commercial art and painting.

His works include oils, water colours, a psychedelic surround for a fireplace for George Harrison and a psychedelic piano for John Lennon.

Immediate plans include writing a show suitable for all the family, opening a shop to sell Beautiful Things to Beautiful People and, most important of all, branching out into fashion mass production.

"Not just for women," shouted Marijke, over the Indian music on the hi-fi, "but for children too, and for men. Our things will be so beautiful that anyone who sees them won't be able to bear not having them."

Prices? They put forward some beautiful vague thoughts. "Oh, competitive," they said.

With what, I asked? They just smiled dreamily.

Well, how much, for instance, was Patti Boyd's dress?

"Expensive," said Josje.

How expensive?

"It's all pure silk and hand-done," said Marijke, counting her beads and bells.

With a deft change of the subject, Simon suggested that the whole world was not only ready but waiting impatiently for the Hippie way of life and fashion, and anyway, Carnaby-street was dead, finished, and full of cheap rubbish.

SQUARES

If it weren't for the Squares of the world, he said, there would be no problem. They wouldn't for a start have to repaint their front door.

Their landlord, it seems, would prefer something in basic black, to the electric blue with yellow stars, that now marks the portals of the headquarters of London's first Hippie hautes couturieres.

Leading the Hippie fashion parade—Josje (pronounced Yoshy) and Marijke. Picture by KENT GAVIN.

A The Hippie Hautes Couturieres

RELEASED TODAY—PARIS FASHIONS FOR 67/68 by F

SEX has reared its commercial head to such an extent on the Paris fashion scene that there are now almost as many ideas there for men as for girls. To perpetuate and encourage this jolly heterosexuality, today's Paris story is a His and Hers venture. Felicity Green concentrates on the fashion angle. Christopher Ward not only looks at the subject from the man's eye view—but, in the line of duty, actually tries out some of the men's-type gear himself.

GUNNAR LARSEN TOOK THE PICTURES

SEX SENSE AND NONSENS

THERE WERE proof girls, wrapped up in b presents, and dressed like Dra Who. Mellors th keeper, Bonnie Charlie and, fo mattered by t Uncle Tom C and all.

And from time there were gir were dressed lik

But that's th phrenic Paris collections for y sense, part n and nothing m between.

On the sen you've got the clothes that sen Loren in and ou like a yo-yo—fo

SEX AND NONSENSE Left, a white lace romper suit and stockings from Ungaro. Centre, Christopher Ward sweating it out in Paco Rabanne's metal jacket. Right, Bonnie Prince St. Laurent's knicker suit in suede.

SENSE Left, tweed dress and black cape by Patou. Centre, a varia on the earthbound cosmonaut kit, designed by Cardin. W by Ward. Right, the tunic or Alpine look in suede, by Yves St. Laur

y Green, joined today by Christopher Ward

Carlo Ponti, who the bill, deserves heartfelt sympathy. The nonsense cate- comes the sort of that would win a first prize at a -road fancy-dress

Bare

itably the ques- rises as to whether these outfits are ly *wearable*.

aro's bare-backed, highed man-stop- seen left, for in- . It was certainly xiest in Paris.

could a chap take rl to the flicks in Could she leap into it, wear it to the trot along Brigh- each in it or go a pothole in it?

her boy-friend d to get his own he could always st a roll in the hay at bullet - proof jacket by Paco ne. Paco has got to be joking, of course—only he isn't.

Neither is Cardin, with his multi-zippered Space suits; nor is Ruben Torres with his Batman capes.

From a man's-eye-view there is more sex paraded in Paris during fashion week than a strip-club attendant with a long-service medal crams into a lifetime's viewing.

But what were the *clothes* like? Like the man said—sexy, sensible and nonsensical.

The sex-in-Paris fashion tends to have sinister undertones.

Black velvet breeches for dining-out—and a whip would make a more suitable accessory than a handbag.

Bright

Lots of light and bright colours worn with black patent skin-tight boots rising up to new and invisible heights. Or party dresses in pastel crepes worn with black stockings in the best tarty tradition.

As for the Courreges number on the right, sex in fashion surely can go no further this side of nudity.

Sense, perhaps, came out best . . .

Tunics from St. Laurent, capes from almost everyone, lots of chain belts clanking away round suits, dresses and coats and if you don't own at least one, buy now.

Brown

Sensible colours — black and bitter chocolate brown. Why sensible? Because they don't get dirty so quickly. Winter white is a drag.

As for the nonsense, prizes should go to all rompers, plus fours and certain metal dresses that clank like a tank and weigh about as much.

NSE AND NONSENSE A bit of both, perhaps. Two of Cardin's colourful capers. a striped blanket cloth cape. Right, a dotty coat in white and pink.

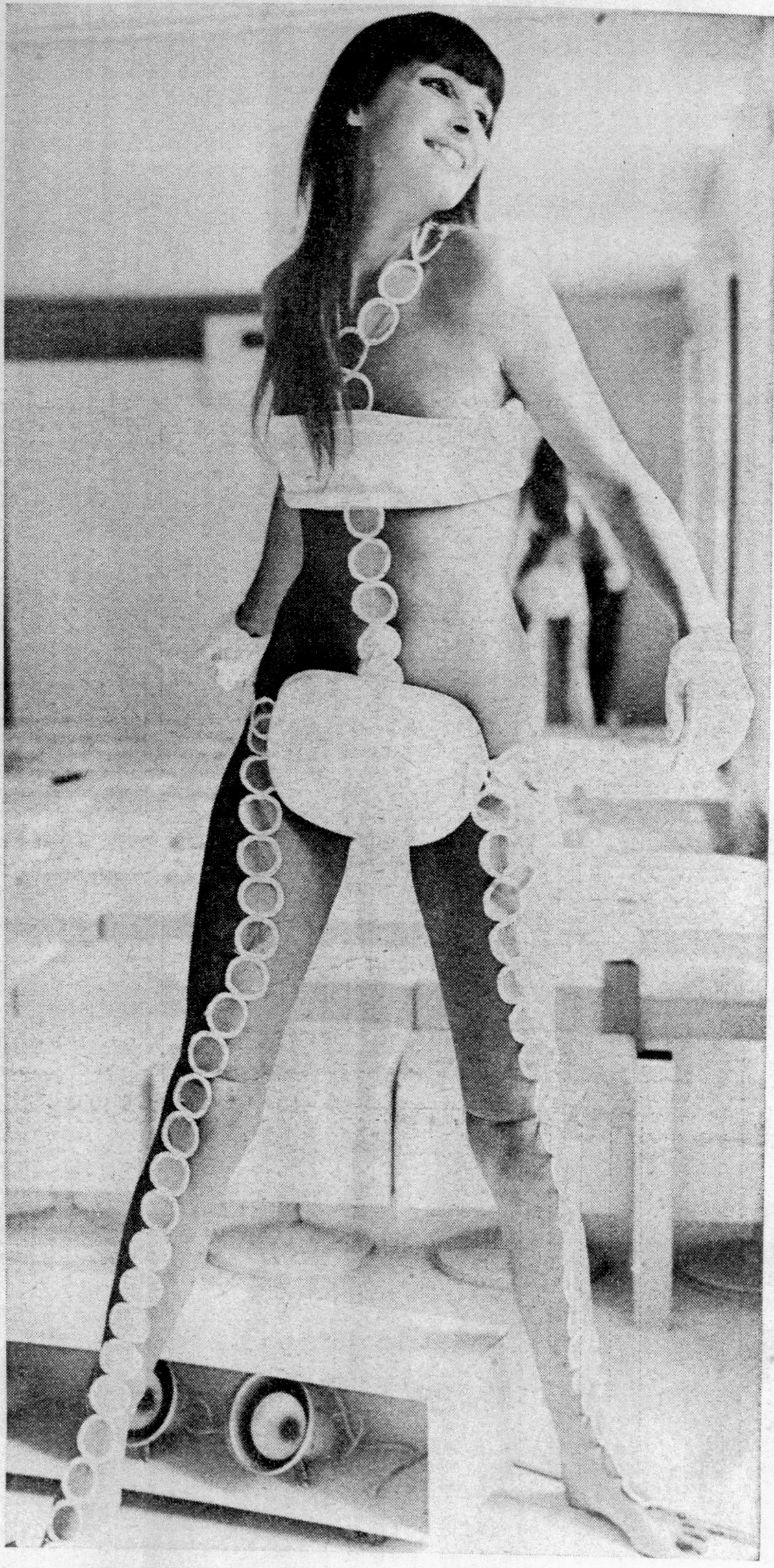

SEX PLUS A BIT OF NONSENSE A sort of two-piece. Or how a few plastic discs strung about the female form could come between a girl and her best friend. By Courreges. Of Course.

on the fashion scene with FELICITY GREEN

Flashback to plastic gear in April '66.

What a difference 503 days make!

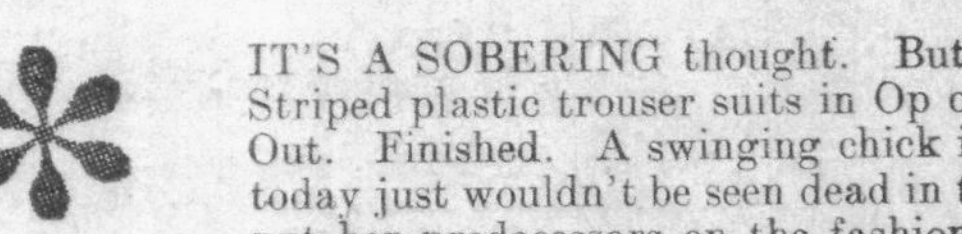

IT'S A SOBERING thought. But an undeniable one. Striped plastic trouser suits in Op or Pop are Old Hat. Out. Finished. A swinging chick in Swinging London today just wouldn't be seen dead in the kind of gear that put her predecessors on the fashion maps of the world such a short while ago.

To see just how much the scene has changed in just 503 dizzy days, see the pictures above and right. Then and now — and what a difference!

The legend of the brilliant British birds and their way-out plumage was born, as if everyone didn't know, when the U S magazine "Time" visited such Swinging London centres as Chelsea, Kensington and Carnaby-street in April, '66.

They were, as we all know, fair knocked out by what they saw.

Where, they and the rest of the world wondered, were all those British inhibitions? That famous reserve?

It was, praise be, sunk without trace under the kind of gear that has turned London into the young fashion capital of the world. A position it has now consolidated with very little opposition from the rest of the fashion world.

British birds, admit the connoisseurs, are still the best.

It's not so much that they follow fashion—they actually create it. And their rate of creativity is nothing short of breathtaking.

Kinky

In the fast-moving world of young fashion —is there any OTHER kind now?—last year's rave is this year's yawn and the passing fashion parade in London in mid-1967 bears little, if any, resemblance to last month's lot, let alone last year's.

The kookie kids of '66 have been replaced by the flower girls of '67. Swinging London is awash with Hippie fashions.

Kinky plastic boots have given way to Roman sandals with overtones of slavery.

Short sharp hairdos are now freaked out in a riot of fuzz or curls and the air is filled with the rattle of beads and the jingle of bells.

And if anyone doubts the continuing influence of the place let them just remember that the Hippies were just a way-out sect in California before London turned them, for better or for worse, into the newest fashion rave.

AND IT'S STILL VIVA BIBA!

ON THE RIGHT is a brand new fashion thought from Biba's boutique in Kensington where the Swinging London atmosphere is so thick on the ground that I'm surprised no-one has bottled it for export.

Biba—fashion artist Barbara Hulanicki —and Mary Quant were two of the fashion names being bandied about in '66 as typical of the new London scene.

Both designers, unlike some, are still with us and going stronger than ever.

Mary's fashion venture is now an empire with world-wide ramifications.

Biba has just received a South American fashion award as it was reckoned that she — along with American Rudi "Topless" Gernreich, and Paco Rabanne of Paris—is one of the three most significant designers in the world today.

Biba's husband and partner, Stephen Fitz-Simon, says he thinks "significant is a lousy word" but they're thrilled to bits with the honours heaped upon them down South America way.

In fact they have just received 1lb. 12oz. of lyrical Press cuttings to prove how wild the locals were about Biba's Swinging London Look in such far-flung places as Brazil and the Argentine.

"I think they preferred us to the other two because our skirts were shorter," said Biba modestly.

She may just have a point. Legmen are everywhere.

Flower power gear in August '67—a new Hippie fashion from Biba, 4 gns.

Picture: MONTY COLES

DAILY MIRROR, Thursday, December 14, 1967 PAGE 13

TWIGGY by JUSTIN

By FELICITY GREEN

YOU could call it the ever-changing face of Twiggy. Or, perhaps, Twiggy Mark IV.

After Twiggy the Teenage Wonder, Twiggy the Rag Trade Tycoon, and Twiggy the Twenties Flapper, we are now in for Twiggy the Dramatic.

"I'm tired of people getting Twiggy all wrong," says that latter-day Svengali known as Mr. Justin de Villeneuve.

Justin, as followers of the model girl phenomenon of the age must surely know, is the boy-friend and manager of this 18-year-old half-pint-sized waif, who has adorned more covers in her time than all the rest of her illustrious predecessors put together.

To get the Twiggy image as he feels it should be, he has added another occupation to his already profitable portfolio.

With one click of the shutter, he has now placed himself in the same bracket as Lord Snowdon, David Bailey and Cecil Beaton.

While Twiggy poses in front of the camera, Justin is now behind it.

Seen here are his first-ever attempts with the magic box.

Above, Twiggy the Dramatic with her wide-screen hairdo. Left, Twiggy the Dramatic in a dramatic dress—designed by Twiggy.

He insists, however, that photography is only a passing phase.

What he is much more interested in at the moment is getting lush and luxurious art books all about Twiggy at 6 guineas a time on to the best coffee tables around the world.

To achieve this aim, Justin is currently working with Erte, the famous international fashion artist, who plans to design a series of costumes for the first "Twiggy through the Ages" book.

Said Erte, talking to me in London yesterday: "The Lady of the Camellias, a Ziegfeld Follies girl, a Twenties Flapper . . . She has such a lovely romantic face."

We are obviously in for a veritable torrent of different Twiggies in 1968.

Justin . . . He took the pictures.

All the other photographers have got her wrong, he explains as he finally takes up the camera himself

Far left, Swinging London's fashion scene in 1966 was setting the fashion world on fire – all monochrome Op Art and plastic. And then just 500 days later, London changes direction – though still Swinging, it goes all soft and psychedelic. Variety is surely the spice of London fashion life and, left, Barbara Hulanicki's Biba is right there, out in front. Above, Introducing one of the Big Romances of the Swinging '60s and yet another New Face of Twiggy. The gamine, crop-haired girl from Neasden has metamorphosed into the film star glamour girl of Garbo mystique. The photographer who has captured the new Twiggy is her manager, boyfriend svengali Justin de Villeneuve, who says all the previous famous photographers haven't captured the inner Twiggy. No comment.

JUSTIN DE VILLENEUVE

'60s entrepreneur who made Twiggy a worldwide superstar

For me the '60s are 1966 – 1972! Lady Luck was looking down on me when I was given a job in the mid-'50s with the extraordinary Vidal Sassoon, who had just opened his first salon in New Bond Street. So from the poverty of East London to the glamorous West End, I was ready for the '60s. Indeed, dear Mr Sassoon was to become one of the heroes of the Swinging '60s.

Of course, like many Jack the Lads, I had my ups and downs, but once again Lady Luck looked down on me when I met the amazing Miss Lesley Hornby. Things took off in 1966 when a national newspaper printed a front page story about the new young model and her entrepreneurial boyfriend. I quickly jumped on the carousel, became my girlfriend's manager, immediately creating the very first of the so-called 'super models'.

The '60s were a very different kettle of fish from nowadays. Everything became possible and of course money wasn't so hard to obtain for entrepreneurial activities. I really don't think I could have achieved what I did then if I were a young man starting out now. One great thing about the '60s was that a lot of my heroes from a previous era were still tap dancing. For instance, Twigs and I became good friends with Noël Coward. We visited him both in Jamaica, as well as at his house in Chelsea, and there were lots of meetings at the Savoy. In Los Angeles I often had lunch with Myrna Loy or Ava Gardner! The glamour, the glamour! I don't see much of that nowadays! I don't think I'll be influenced by the dispiriting sartorial *je ne sais quoi* of Mr Bieber. My heart doesn't flutter glimpsing Lady Gaga.

"Lady Luck looked down on me when I met the amazing Lesley Hornby"

London in the '60s was amazing. The Beatles had really started it off by conquering America, followed by The Stones and The Kinks, to name just a few. The fashion world had also taken off in tandem with the music scene. There was the great designer Barbara Hulanicki who created Biba, the first famous Kensington boutique where young girls – and boys – flocked in their droves. There was the fabulous Mary Quant, there was Billy Gibb, and Ossie Clark – these were just some of the Fashion Stars of the Swinging '60s.

There were also dramatic changes in the fashion magazine world. The Glossies were for the Upper Classes, featuring older models and ladies who went on to marry Lords. The mass market magazines catered for a more 'mumsy' readership. Then along came Twigs and everything changed. Fortunately there were journalists like Felicity Green on the *Mirror* who understood the new market and their fashion pages reflected this new excitement. It couldn't have happened in the decade before.

The important thing to remember is that – like The Beatles who had made it big in America – the newly arrived 'Swinging London' as the Americans called it, had become in the '60s the centre of the world for music and fashion.

FELICITY ON JUSTIN

Justin was a character – he was common, he was clever, he was extremely engaging and deeply impressive... and I liked him. Never one for modesty, Justin lists his previous occupations – which are pretty comprehensive – as : hairdresser, villain, PR, manager, interior decorator, boxer, poet.

Justin was also somewhat of a fancy dresser. With his long hair, Tommy Nutter suits, big knotted tie, eighteenth-century gold watch and fob dangling from a mannered waistcoat, he looked like the young Oscar Wilde. I could see this comparison pleased him, and he confided disarmingly, "It's all part of the image." And as Twiggy's manager/agent/promoter and boyfriend, Justin appreciated the importance of image. He and Twiggy went together like bread and jam. Justin and Twiggy made the perfect '60s double act. Like Bailey and The Shrimp, Justin and Twiggy complemented each other in a typically '60s way.

Justin was enterprising, indefatigable and he got on with it whatever it was. Twiggy was quiet, seemingly gentle and knockout stunning. Together, Justin and Twiggy made '60s magic happen.

Glamour, '60s style: Twiggy, formerly Miss Lesley Hornby, photographed looking like a film star by Justin de Villeneuve, formerly Nigel Davies

DAILY MIRROR, Thursday, March 21, 1968 PAGE 15

TWO OF THE WORLD'S TOP PHOTOGRAPHERS PICTURE THE FACE THAT'S ABOUT TO BECOME A CULT.

Penelope Tree by RICHARD AVEDON

Penelope Tree by DAVID BAILEY

The Magical Miss-Tree-Tour

MISS PENELOPE TREE, in case her name is not yet familiar to you, is the girl who is causing a great deal of excitement in those areas where Jean Shrimpton and Twiggy have, in their time, reigned supreme.

Seen here are just two faces of this 5ft. 10in. 18-year-old, who will undoubtedly be the prototype for a whole host of other teenage faces when her full impact is felt.

Helping to launch this half-British, half-American waif—her American mother was U S representative to the United Nations Trusteeship Council and her British father a multi-millionaire banker in New York—is our own David Bailey.

Bailey, whose interest did Miss Shrimpton's career no harm, says he knew the instant he met Miss Tree in New York a year ago that they'd "be sure to hit it off."

They have been hitting it off ever since and, undoubtedly, the result of this new affinity between photographer and model is some of the most interesting fashion pictures around at the moment.

Body

Waxing, for him, quite lyrical about "The Magical Miss-Tree-Tour," Bailey names Penelope as his Girl of the Future.

"It's in her face," he says, "in her body with those incredibly long legs, in her attitudes. In this sense, Penelope is to modelling now what Jean Shrimpton was in the very beginning.

"She's a very intelligent, sensitive girl, who has some really wild, way-out ideas. She doesn't take modelling all that seriously and, in a way, that's what enables her to be so good at it."

Richard Avedon—reputed to be the world's highest-paid fashion photographer—is also a Tree fan.

"She's a delight," he said, after taking 14 pages of pictures of her for American Vogue. "Every moment she's posing, she invents a new little role for herself which she plays with devastating humour."

The main difference between Penelope and say, Twiggy or Jean Shrimpton, according to Tom Wolsey, creative director of the London advertising agency which chose Miss Tree to model for the picture seen above left, as used in the current Quant cosmetics advertisement, is her intelligence. So much more articulate, as he puts it, than the shy Shrimp and the untalkative Twiggy.

Face

"I think self-consciousness is just another form of egotism," says the articulate Miss Tree, who in her time has studied anthropology, psychology and semantics.

How does the subject of all this adulation react to the familiar eulogies that greet every new face on this highly inconstant scene?

She says right away that she doesn't think fashion is all that serious a business, doesn't want to go on modelling for any length of time. Badly wants, she says, to become a wife, a mother and a writer.

One of the main reasons for planning to come to London is that she's turning her hand to a spot of fashion designing, basing her styles on the American Indian Look. A way-out dresser herself, she feels London's atmosphere is more daring and inventive.

"Anyway," she said, "most of my friends are there and I feel more relaxed."

She'll be arriving in about two weeks' time and we shall be hearing a lot more about the magical Miss Tree from now on.

FELICITY GREEN

It's 1968 and the two most famous photographers of the day both photograph the same model. The photographers: Richard Avedon and David Bailey; the model: socialite Penelope Tree. And what a contrast between Mr Avedon and Mr Bailey. Avedon, the leading fashion photographer in America, sees Miss Tree with her outsize halo of backcombed hair as a glamorous example of artistically posed glossy magazine fantasy styling. Bailey, on the other hand, sees his model – and latest love – as a wistful flower power child. And the difference is delightful. Opposite, Bailey photographs hairdresser *extraordinaire*, Vidal Sassoon, certainly looking *extraordinaire* in the pirate outfit he wore to celebrate his move into the mail order business. Why a pirate? Who knows? In the Swinging '60s anything goes. Near right, the first of the '60s multi-coloured hairstyles arrived – Space Age style – from Leonard, an early Sassoon-trained talent. Leonard, whose inspired crop cut helped launch Twiggy's career, here predicts exotically-coloured hair streaks are the future – they remain fashionable today.

DAILY MIRROR, Tuesday, May 14, 1968 PAGE 11

FELICITY GREEN on the hirsute scene

HAIR-1 ..or Vidal practising what he preaches and how!

* THIS IS Vidal Sassoon as his fans have never, ever seen him.

Gone, if only momentarily, is the serious crimper with a film star wife and a diamond-bright reputation on both sides of the Atlantic.

In his place we have Vidal as a kind of Fifth Musketeer by courtesy of Douglas Fairbanks, Snr., celebrating his first-ever entry into the Sassoonery-by-mail-order business.

Accepting the premise that it would undoubtedly look better on a girl, Vidal is actually wearing one of the hairpieces that he reckons to send plopping through a thousand letter boxes in the next few weeks.

It will cost 9 guineas a go and is made from first-quality Asian hair (the kind they're mad about in America but can't import as it may well come from Red China).

I've handled the stuff and can vouch for the fact that it's the kind men long to run their fingers through.

Sleek to handle and as soft as the most expensive falsenesses around, the Sassoon-cut hairpiece measures 16-18 inches from the hand-made front to the slightly curled ends.

Those who do agree about its looking better on a girl, should send a cutting of hair together with a postal order or cheque for 9 guineas (plus 2s. 6d. for postage) to Vidal Sassoon, Dept. 9, 171, New Bond-street, London, W.1.

The Musketeer outfit, which looks better on a man, came from Bermans, the theatrical outfitters.

A dash of Douglas Fairbanks Snr., a touch of the Musketeer. It's a ne looking Sassoon celebrating his move into the mail order busine

PICTURES by DAVID BAILE

HAIR-2 ..or the 2001 Multi-coloured Set

Colour it all shades of red from crimson to orange

* MEANWHILE, round at Leonard's, another top flight hair-styling establishment, the multi-coloured hairdo is the big new story. But not colour as we have come to know and love it.

Seen above is one of the first ever multi-colour jobs in which—you must take my word for it—there are as many shades of red as there are colours in the rainbow. More, in fact. Everything from crimson to pale orange. All shaded and mottled like marble.

Mr. Leonard reckons that the multi-coloured head is here to stay and will soon take over from all the short and curly cuts which are now out as far as he is concerned. Because he feels that it's the hairdo of the future, Leonard calls it his "2001 Space Cut."

"All my clients are mad about it," says Leonard, who is the stylist responsible for such famous heads as Twiggy and Patti Boyd. "We're already doing shades of plum, shades of red — even lavender mixed with green. Or white on white."

It really does sound like Space Age stuff, but Leonard is convinced it's the coming thing. "In a few years," he prophesies, "women will be wearing these exotic hair colours all the time."

If you bump into a lady with lavender, green and plum-coloured hair, you'll know she believes him already.

TERRY O'NEILL

World famous photographer whose pictures combine Style and Sexuality

As the '60s started I had this feeling that something special was happening in London and I'd decided I wanted to be the one to record it. For us working class lads it was amazing. Suddenly boys like Michael Caine, Terry Stamp, David Bailey, even me, were supercool. Terry Stamp got Oscar-nominated for *Billy Budd*, his first film. Michael Caine was making *Zulu*, his breakout film . I photographed them all and their soon-to-be-famous girlfriends.

In music, in fashion, in culture, films, writers, artists – we could be what we wanted to be. Nobody questioned or challenged it or asked for qualifications – they just let you do it.

With my camera I was trying to record this amazing change as a news story. There was a buzz, we didn't know what it was and we didn't think it would last – but we wanted a piece of it all and we wanted to do it our way, in our own style, so we made it happen.

Felicity Green was instrumental in all our careers – Mary Quant's, Vidal Sassoon's, Barbara Hulanicki's too. Felicity had joined the *Daily Mirror* in 1960. The *Mirror* in those days was a very important and influential paper, selling five million copies a day.

Felicity's instinct was to use young photographers like me, Bailey, Donovan, and Duffy because we took the type of pictures she wanted, sexy, but acceptable, never an inch beyond good taste, exciting with beautiful girls, reflecting the times and the mood of young people. She was the journalist who first put '60s fashions in newspapers. Felicity recognized our scene and its potential to influence and change fashion and she put us all together, the models, the photographers with the clothes and hairstyles we all wanted to wear, everything we paraded in when we went dancing or clubbing – and Felicity made it news.

"We took the type of pictures Felicity wanted, sexy, but acceptable, never an inch beyond good taste"

FELICITY ON TERRY

Terry O'Neill was a man about town – irresistible, charming, good-looking, naughty and a genius with his camera. Model girls, usually preoccupied with fashion, fancied him and he fancied them. The result – brilliant, unique photographs that forcefully combined fashion with high-voltage sexuality.

Terry's '60s fashion pictures stood out from the crowd. His casual style, his use of outdoor locations turned fashion model girls into film stars and famous film stars into models. (He married one of them. Remember that glamorous, sexy pic of Faye Dunaway by that Hollywood pool, an iconic image if ever there were one – pure Terry.)

Terry also did for sports stars what he did for model girls – see page 167 for bare-chested World Cup footballer Bobby Moore and pages 156-157 to see how Terry glamorised international tennis star Virginia Wade and champion athlete Mary Rand – and changed their images forever. Terry's pictures look immediate and casual, but the skill involved is immense. Terry is not only a brilliant photographer, he was, and still is, a dream to work with – and always FUN!

The perfect Terry O'Neill combination – sexuality and sensuality – and muscles. The model is typical of the challenging almost aggressive attitude of the '60s

DAILY MIRROR, Tuesday, June 25, 1968 PAGE 13

FELICITY GREEN looks at the changing face (and shape) of women

The 1968 girl—Marilyn Rickards

Pin-ups 1958: June Wilkinson

..and Sabrina

BUT, DADDY, WHAT IS A PIN-UP?

PIN-UPS have been with us, one way or another, ever since Mafeking was relieved, and they probably had something to do with that event, too.

But pin-ups, like everything else, are subject to change, and today's model has as much in common with her goo-ey lipped, thrusting-busted predecessor as a morning coat has with Mick Jagger.

Although the basic raw material may be the same, my word, the dishing up is different.

Just ten years ago the busty blonde was queen of the pin-up scene with Sabrina (41-18-36) above right, leading the field by what you might call a short head, until she was overtaken by June Wilkinson (43-22-37), above left, who began a promising career as Miss Plastic Hardware of 1958.

In those days, vital statistics were all, and no barrack room, bar room or factory floor was without its scantily-clad pouter-pigeon pin-up with the popular peanut shape.

For all I know she may still be there, but among the modern-minded of us she is a relic of the past, and another type of pin-up is knocking her off the trendier walls. (For example, see left.)

The coyness has been replaced by an aggressive, if not downright threatening, honesty.

In place of the glow of make-up, there's the gleam of sweat. Actually, it's glycerine, but I'm not supposed to tell you.

She wears more of a muss-up than a hairdo, and there's an obvious and total absence of underwear.

The change over ten years from what you might call the come-hither to the come-and-get-me look took place gradually, and while bosoms haven't exactly disappeared—I mean, where would they go?—interest has been diverted.

Fusing fashion pictures and pin-up pictures in a way never before attempted, photographer David Bailey produced what has been referred to as The Crotch Age. Bailey's birds had no breasts worthy of mention, but their legs, it was rumoured, went up to their eye-brows.

One of today's most successful photographers of the kind of girl who feels more at home slopping around in the King's-road than lounging around on a pink satin sofa is Terry O'Neill, who pictured Marilyn Rickards, seen left.

How near, I asked him, is a real-life photo session to the studio romp portrayed in the Antonioni film "Blow Up"?

You may remember the scene where Mr. David Hemmings is taking pictures while sitting astride a temporarily floored top model girl.

Mr. O'Neill hedged like a happily married man should.

"There has to be *something* going between you," he admitted, "or you'll never get the one fantastic shot you want. You've got to work the woman up gradually—music helps her but not me—I'm too busy trying to change the film quickly so she won't even notice.

"A job can take two hours and I'll shoot over 140 pictures. But I know I won't get the one great picture until the last roll—or maybe the one before the last."

Marilyn, a typical 1968 girl, is part model, part actress.

Her biggest break so far is one of the four leading roles in a film called "The Touchables" and no one, I imagine, is wondering why

By the way, if any male reader feels he would be more at home with the 1958 pin-ups above, don't write to me.

This is perfectly in order all right since no girl can be all things to all men.

Picture by TERRY O'NEILL

Pin-ups in the '50s used to be curvy to the point of buxom. Scarlet lips pouted full-on, bosoms overflowed and bottoms competed for prominence. Then in the '60s everything changed. Pin-ups became part of the fashion scene and models had a whole new image. Muscles vied with curves, aggression was sexy and even a splash of sweat was allowed!

Opposite: Mary Quant says when it comes to hemlines anything goes and aren't we lucky! To prove the point she shows her followers their choices for autumn 1968 – minis with and without pants, the split-to-the thigh maxi and the rather boring midi. And on the slight and svelte and model-shaped Miss Quant they all look good.

FELICITY GREEN on the hemline scene

MARY, MARY SO CONTRARY

Exclusive preview of Miss Quant modelling her autumn predictions

Skinny mini plus pants. 15 gns.

Micro mini minus matching pants.

Slinky maxi showing a leg. 11 gns.

Midi for the more modest. 10 gns.

AMERICA has declared the mini isn't fini. Paris decrees the mid-knee hemline. The maxi is still a threat on the horizon. It's enough to make any dedicated follower of fashion dizzy with indecision. With the autumn clothes arriving on the rails in just a few weeks, where's a puzzled girl to go for guidance?

Off hand, it would be difficult to think of a better oracle than Miss Quant who practically invented the mini, has toyed with the maxi, flirted with the midi and is now giving a whole new look to hemlines. These pictures show Miss Quant practising what she preaches. For the Quant theory read on:

"Designers all over the world are searching for a new look. They're looking for a hemline that will make all previous hemlines look dated.

But there's no such thing as a brand new hemline any more.

Of course, there will be maxi's and midi's again this autumn. But I predict the great new thing will be micro-skirted dresses with matching Indian-style trousers—like the white crepe mini dress I'm wearing here—or tunic dresses over bell-bottom pants.

I've always thought that skirts as such will ultimately disappear.

But for the present —and immediate future—skirts are like sleeves. They can be any length or simply none at all.

Personally, I want mini's to stay. And with the new trousers they will."

This, then, is the latest pronouncement from the high priestess of the short-skirt cult.

From the designer who prophesied that when clothes have disappeared altogether, women will be painting themselves.

Until then, however, we're in for crepe or warm jersey trousers that match mini-skirted dresses.

Obviously the most sensible things when you come to think about wearing mini-skirts next winter.

JEAN DOBSON

Pictures by JOHN ADRIAAN

PAGE 14 DAILY MIRROR, Friday, September 27, 1968

For tennis fans, athletics far

VIRGINIA WADE

Left, concentrating on the business of winning.

Right, a different Virginia. And vive la difference! Harold Leighton did her hair. Eylure put on the false lashes. Echo made the catsuit. As the man said—anyone for tennis?

This is a memorable 1968 *Daily Mirror* spread: two world famous British sportswomen – each with a brand new surprising image – present their amazing New Looks. Right, Virginia Wade, the first British tennis girl for thirty-eight years to win the US Open Championship. Then Virginia met this man. On the far right, the running jumping Mary Rand, owner of one gold, one silver and one bronze Olympic medals. And then she too met the same man. The man of course was the photographer Terry O'Neill, famous for making famous film stars even more glamorous. So thanks to the hairdressers, the make-up artists and some sexy fashions, Virginia Wade and Mary Rand were transformed into veritable pin-ups. As one who was present in the studio during this transformation scene, I have to report that a good time was had by all. Specially the Two New Top Models.

...nd followers of female form

Vive le Sport!

MARY RAND, on the run.

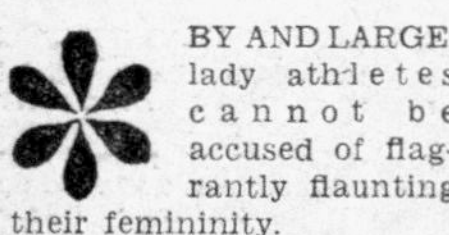

BY AND LARGE, lady athletes cannot be accused of flagrantly flaunting their femininity.

In fact, femininity in the sporting world is such a rare quality that it can take the combined knowledge of a gynaecologist, a somatologist and a radiographer to establish whether the competitor in question should be running in the women's 100 metres or throwing a discus in the men's decathlon.

There are, however, some happy exceptions to this confusing state of affairs and I submit that no such tests are necessary in the case of either Mary Rand, or Virginia Wade.

The running, jumping Mary Rand, blue-eyed and long-legged, with the Mia Farrow haircut, has been described as Britain's most successful woman athlete. She has one gold, one silver and one bronze Olympic medal to prove the point.

Now out of active athletics due to an ankle injury, she will be commentating on the Mexican Olympics for the BBC.

Above, right, the business-like Mary Rand as she is best known—concentrating on the business of winning. Right, a brand new Mary Rand, who could give that other famous sporting girl, Miss Brigitte Bardot, a fair old run for her money.

Above, left, Virginia Wade, the first British tennis girl for thirty-eight years with enough drive to win the US Open Championship.

Left, a new style Virginia Wade that the Centre Court spectators didn't even suspect existed.

Moral: when it comes to the absorbing business of clothes and hairdos, make-up and false eyelashes, sportsgirls and other girls are sisters under the black mesh cat suit or the black lacy negligee.

In fact, if Mary Rand and Virginia Wade were competing for the title of the World's most Sizzling Sportsgirl, it would be the photo-finish of the year.

report:
FELICITY GREEN
pictures:
TERRY O'NEILL

MARY RAND the standing still girl—all wrapped up in femininity and a frilly black lace negligee by Weiss.

FELICITY GREEN on the Fashion Scene

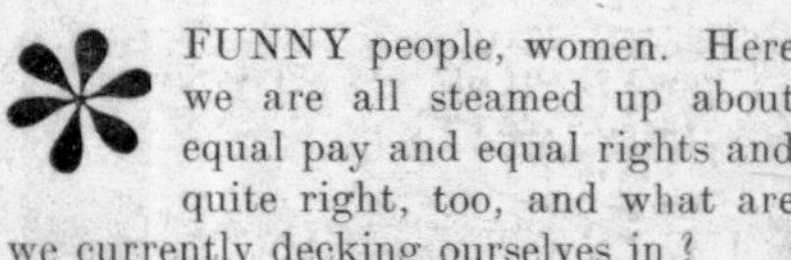

FUNNY people, women. Here we are all steamed up about equal pay and equal rights and quite right, too, and what are we currently decking ourselves in ?

That's right, all the symbolic trappings of sexual slavery.

Emancipated and freedom-loving as we are, we're choosing to wear chains galore clanking away like crazy, likewise broad bracelets of bondage in studded leather and the kind of anklets that used to belong only in a harem—and we all know what kind of slavery went on there.

In fact, the fettered look has taken over the accessory scene to such an extraordinary extent that any time now the ball-and-chain could make a great fashion comeback.

Seen here are three typical symbols of slavery with which today's emancipated girls can confuse their image:

Chain-mail belt (right) that could double as a necklace, by Paul Stephens, 5 gns. Above it, wide brocade belt with overtones of bondage by Swordtex, about 4½ gns.

Bangles of bondage (below, left). Left arms: Spanish leather by Randee Heller. Right arms: English version by Neufeld, from £1 to 25s.

Anklets for ankles and rings for your toes (below, right): Paste snake, 8 gns., gilt snake, 27s. 6d. by Adrien Mann; gilt tassel by Vendome, £6 16s. 6d.; toe rings by Corocraft from 12s. 6d.

All belted up for bondage PICTURES: JOHN ADRIAAN

Symbols of slavery, clank clank . .

Coupled up for complete captivity

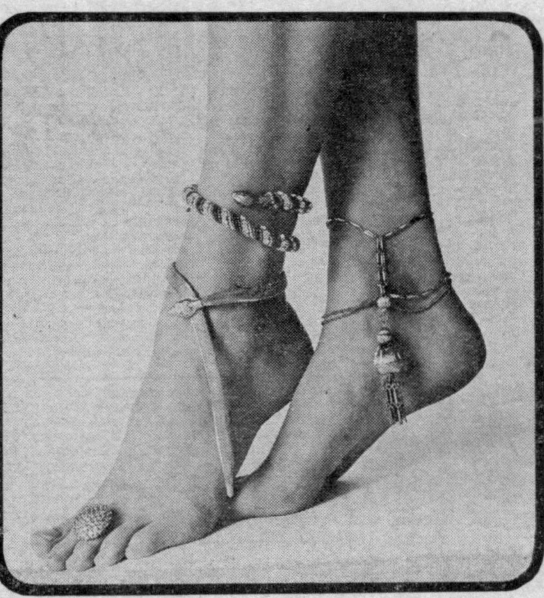

The fettered look for feet

HOW'S YOUR OPHIOPHOBIA THESE DAYS?

SNAKES, it is well known, have always had a kind of repulsive fascination for ladies. We won't go into why. Suffice it to say that snakes—alive or dead—are making fashion news.

A live one — about three inches round and eighteen inches long, as far as I could tell from a most respectable distance — was worn round the neck of a swinging chicklet at a party in London the week before last. It was, said the wearer, very warm.

For less enthusiastic snake fanciers there are umpteen pretty snake rings, antique-inspired, at Cornucopia, the shop run by fashion artist Gerry Richards at 12, Tachbrook-street, London, S.W.1.

Prices start at £4 10s. for single-strand silver snakes to £12 for three-strand gold ones. Some at £6 10s. have a turquoise in the head. Others are the real McCoy, Victoriana at £4 10s. There are snake bracelets, too, at £6 10s. for a single strand. Treble-strand gold ones cost £9 10s. Barbra Streisand, should you care, has just been pictured by David Bailey wearing a multiplicity of snake rings, one per finger.

CAN'T cope with individual lashes? Eylure now make the long spiky kind on an invisible strip. For under the eyes, of course. 12s. 6d. a pair. Your tiny hand is frozen on account of you can't buy false nails? Eylure have just introduced a special mini-kit of eighteen nails at 13s. for the standard pack and 17s. 6d. for the self-adhesive kind.

UNISEX is here to stay, says Women's Wear Daily, the American fashion trade paper. No, not another Kinsey report. Merely the tale of the trouser trend, which shows that girls and boys are now buying the same style in the same shape. I wonder whatever happened to Vive la difference?

HAVE you noticed how, when you've just lost a lot of highly dispensable weight, it's only your fat friends who tell you you're too thin?

GIRLS, it has been said, have developed chill-proof, fatter thighs since the advent of the mini-skirt. Cattle may follow suit though not exactly in mini-skirts. In France they're experimenting to see if farm animals can be induced to develop more generous curves by shaving what are called "the appropriate areas." Tell me, do sheep have thighs?

TINY tights for subteens are now on sale at Woolworth. In 20-denier crepe nylon they cost 5s. 11d. Made for seven to twelve-year-olds they fit a certain slim 5ft. 2in. grandma I know down to her size 4 shoes.

DAILY MIRROR, *Wednesday, January 1, 1969* PAGE 9

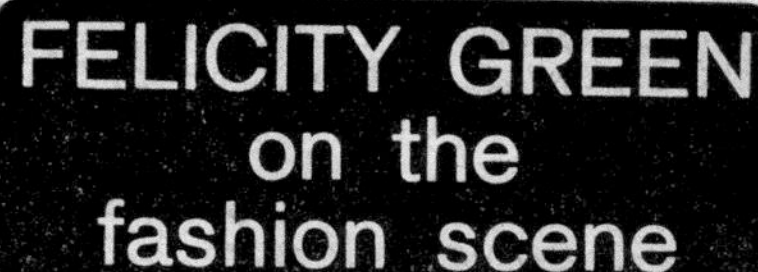
FELICITY GREEN
on the
fashion scene

A little bit of leather. By McDouglas of Paris.

It's going to be tough on the beaches in 1969

Laced-up frontage. By Rudi Gernreich of New York.

Leather again. By McDouglas.

THERE are, according to my ready - reckoner, just 174 days to Midsummer Eve.

Between now and then, as I feel confident to predict, we shall be having snow, slush, frost, delayed trains, no trains, bus queues, leaky boots, dampened spirits and all the other eleventh-hour lovelinesses that an English winter manages to keep up its New Year sleeve.

One tried and tested way to minimise the gloom is to read the current holiday chat that speaks of golden sand and even more golden bodies, and to ponder what you yourself might fancy for two weeks in Scunthorpe or, perhaps, Sardinia.

For those with the requisite imagination to project themselves far enough ahead in time, shown here are the latest swimsuits with which to drive the local lads wild.

As you can see, 1969 is going to be a tough year on the beaches. Especially for those who favour femininity. Bikinis in Bardot-type gingham with frills and ruffles, may make you feel all girlie, young and tender inside.

Outside, alas, you'll merely look like you're wearing last year's suit. Or even the year before that.

The tough look has more than something to do with the fact that 1968 was the year that leather became fashion fabric No. 1.

In 1969, leather is also for swimming in. In France, there are already leather bikinis, sometimes punched with brogue holes, sometimes studded in real "rocker" manner.

Another "toughie"—clear plastic—is also making its bid for popularity on the beach.

The bikini, bottom right, is in black jersey strapped about in clear plastic, fastened with metal pop studs. This device anchors the back of the pants to the front, and a time-and-motion-study expert of my acquaintance reckons it can be ripped off in one-tenth of a second.

However, perhaps the most stunning 1969 suit of all is the lace-up job, top right, designed by American Rudi Gernreich, of Topless fame.

Gernreich is so sold on the tough look, he says that good, contemporary fashion comprises just trousers, shirts, jackets and what each woman can do with those items together with her own scarves, chains and belts.

Having spake, Gernreich is taking off on his own holiday scene. He plans to make it a twelve-month Sabbatical in order to refresh himself for further creative efforts. His plans include visits to Morocco, North Africa and Turkey, and I just hope he doesn't come face to face—or face to bare front—with too many of his own designs.

Thought for today: with all this 1969 tough-looking beach gear, you'll look very silly indeed if you can't even swim.

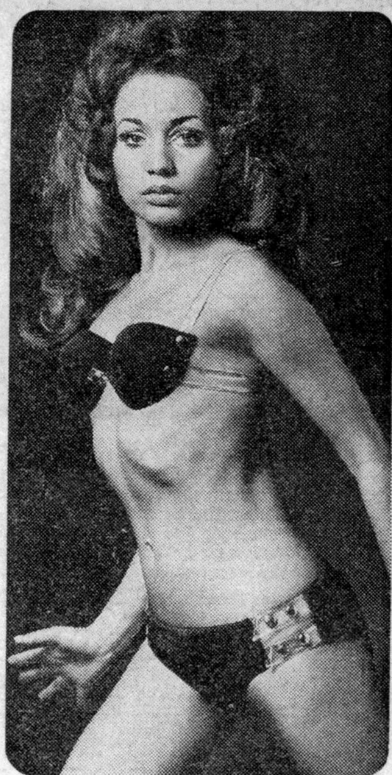

Plastic straps and studs. Jaeger.

BARBARA HULANICKI

'60s design rebel whose Biba boutiques broke all the records

Savour some of the fun and the fast pace we all lived in! The '60s was a giddy time, fuelled by energy generated by the release of new ideas and freedom of thought after the depressing, stifling post-war years. Biba burst from this background as a rebellious free spirit. I'm always asked: Who did the marketing? It was all Fitz, my husband Stephen Fitz-Simon. He picked it up and ran with it. He used to call me the golden goose. Business life was spontaneous, lived from day-to-day, untouched by corporate rules. Everyone in Biba worked hard. There were no passengers. Drones were wholeheartedly rejected by the girls in the shop. Biba was the first feminist company. Only Fitz could keep up with the disciplined energy generated by women working together. No need for fancy offices, boardrooms or endless meetings producing no results. There was no time for that. The shop up front was the show, the beautiful shop girls who worked the front becoming more gorgeous by the hour. At the back of the house was the hard grind to produce new product, colours and décor to satisfy the hungry customers. It was always a strong family team that moved the whole business forward, with Fitz at the helm.

"She turned shops into boutiques. She turned dressing rooms into unisex hangouts for boys and girls"

FELICITY ON BARBARA

Barbara Hulanicki first came into my *Daily Mirror* life when she was a freelance fashion illustrator. The drawings she did were delightful and her female figures were a mirror image of Barbara herself: neat, and trim with swinging bobbed hair. Very trendy, very '60s. After several visits impressing me more each time by her understated, but very definite sense of style, I wanted to find a way to offer this look to the *Mirror* readers. So I had this idea. I asked Barbara to design a dress that looked like her. Barbara designed that gingham dress of utter simplicity that I thought would appeal to the *Mirror* readers. I decided the dress, photographed by John French on Paulene Stone, one of the top models of the time, should be offered to the *Mirror* readers by mail order, for twenty-five shillings. And thus the famous gingham dress was born. I dramatically underestimated its appeal – it sold more than 17,000 and Britain ran out of pink gingham. It not only made history in the fashion world, but also made a big name for Barbara's '60s Biba.

But there's more to Barbara Hulanicki than just one gingham dress. Her Biba history may have started there, but her fashion invention and ingenuity continues to flourish and today Barbara remains an international fashion name. She turned shops into boutiques. She turned dressing rooms for ladies into unisex hangouts for boys and girls who just wanted to try on her clothes and didn't care if they were showing their knickers or taking off their trousers. Barbara's Biba broke every fashion rule in the book. She made fashion more exciting than it had ever been before, and, I am prepared to say, more exciting than it has been ever since.

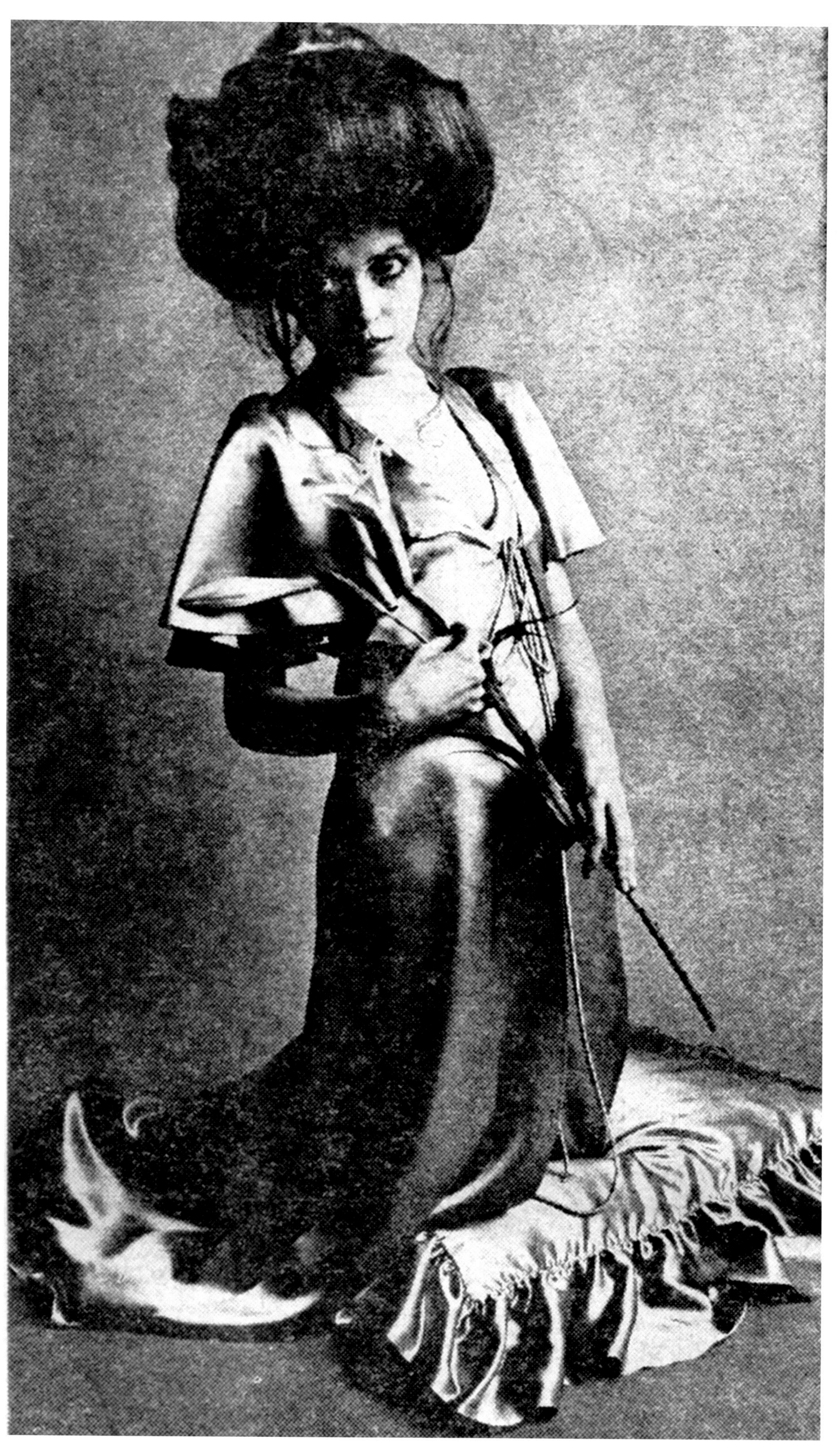

There's more than one Biba look. This is the '60s Biba Geisha Girl with her flowing robes, holding an exotic lily and wearing a cross between a hair style and a balloon

FELICITY GREEN on the fashion scene

PROTOTYPES FOR SPRING '69

Stephanie Farrow in the Madame Butterfly look

FACT: What Biba does today, a great deal of the rag trade does tomorrow.

Knock-offs—immoral if not actually illegal—copies of Biba's best-sellers, are as common in the High Street shops today as were replicas of Whistler's Mother.

There is, however, nothing that can be done about this piracy since copyright in the fashion business is non-existent. Therefore protection of a good idea is virtually impossible.

Some stout hearts have tried it, all have failed.

Liberty, the store in Regent Street, once had the temerity to put a ban on one of their best customers who happened also to be in the dress business.

One week they were selling her a Dior adaptation for £45. The next week she was adapting it herself and rushing out copies by the dozen for a fraction of the price.

In Bond Street recently, I stood window gazing at the modish goodies in Fenwicks, when an Oriental gent whipped out his camera and started snapping away.

Merely an enthusiastic sightseer capturing local colour? Or someone who's kinky for window dummies?

I doubt it. More likely, he was a branch of the Far Eastern rag trade who knows a good thing when he snaps it.

For copyists in search of new inspiration next week promises some prime pickings.

This is when the third Biba mail order catalogue gets itself posted off to 300,000 swinging customers situated the length and breadth of Britain—and a happy January postal revenue to you, Mr. Stonehouse.

As much like a mail order catalogue as "Hair" is like "The Sound of Music," this atmospheric little publication will launch a dozen intriguing ways to look in 1969.

Two of the best — and most contradictory — are worn here by Mia Farrow's sister, Stephanie.

Right, the last of the rough, tough, trouser tribe. This lot is in cotton jersey The jacket costs 4 gns., the pants £3 15s. 6d. The shirt is £3 15s. 6d. The hat costs £1 19s. 6d.

Above left, another Biba-ism which is a sort of Madame Butterfly out of Isadora, as the serious studiers of form might say. This satin nightie and negligee—you can't call such a period piece a housecoat, now can you?—is in flesh pink or pale turquoise. They cost £3 15s. 6d. and £4 10s. each.

The pillow-case, if you fancy going the whole dressed-up—or undressed—hog, is £3 19s. 6d. You provide your own lily.

● MORE NEWS from Biba—alongside Biba's main mail-order business comes a pilot scheme of five made-to-measure outfits from 60-120 gns.

Made up to your own vital statistics from a special canvas pattern you fit at home, this gives mail-order its first high fashion couture rating.

The male-order look

..and the hairstyle likely to succeed

I'M NOT prepared to guess which of the new outfits on this page will be the No. 1 choice this year. But I am prepared to put my money on the hairstyle, which is bound to win friends and influence other hairdressers.

It's casual looking, if not downright untidy. It's new and it's fun and only one female in a thousand would look good in it.

Modelled here by Stephanie Farrow, sister of Mia, it was created by Cheveux. Barbara Hulanicki, the genius behind the Biba set-up, suggested it and Valerie Russell actually built it up over a "rat" of false hair from Woolworths, stuffed into a stocking. (Ah, grandmother, how well you remember the feeling!)

Cheveux, one of the lesser known of the London ladies' barbers, is what you might call a family affair. There are three Russell hairdressing sisters: Annette, 26; Valerie, 24; and Frances, 19. Another sister, Gina, 22, is part-time receptionist.

Mother does the coffees and the lunches and on Saturday 11-year-old sister Maxine comes in to help Mum. In fact, a veritable hot-bed of femininity, if that's not too unfortunate a way to phrase it.

Butterfly hair-do

DAILY MIRROR, *Thursday, February 6, 1969* PAGE 13

Like Sandie was saying as she sat on her husband's head: 'As underwear it's marvellous for a midnight swim'

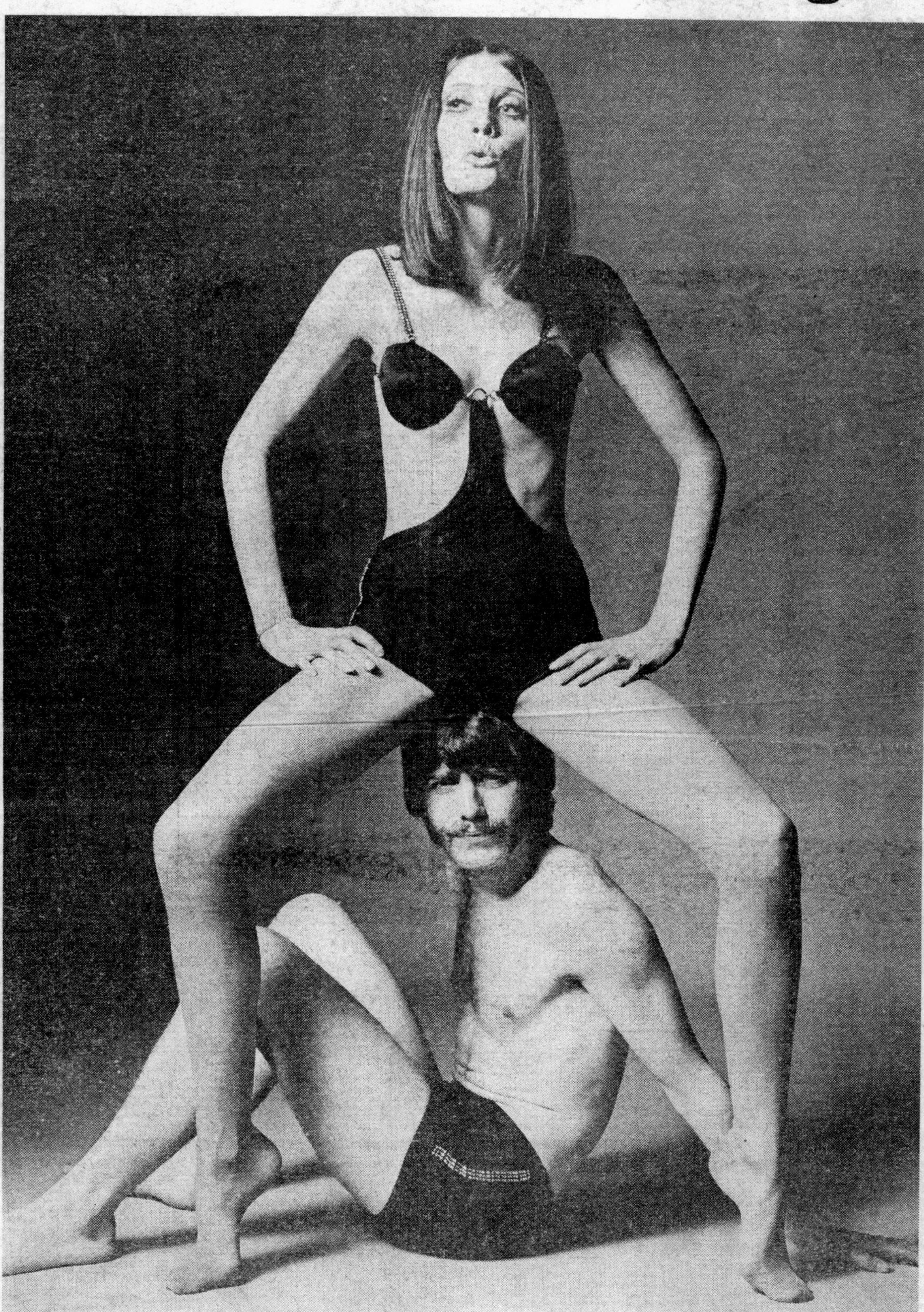

Togetherness undies, for Mr & Mrs Jeff Banks PICTURE: TERRY O'NEILL

THEY may look like swimsuits to you. They may look like swimsuits to me. But to the designer, a certain Mr. Ruben Torres, who lives and works in Paris, they look like the last word in undies.

In fact, Mr. Torres has high hopes that these His and Hers scanties (or not-so-scanties) will be top of the pops at the French Corsetry and Lingerie Show which opens in Paris tomorrow.

They are made in a synthetic fabric called Lycra which is well known for its figure-controlling properties. Presumably so He and She can get into shape together.

Certainly they made a deep impression on singer Sandie Shaw and her husband, fashion designer Jeff Banks (left) who demonstrate here a new angle on Togetherness.

For those who feel that undies are not what they used to be, it should be pointed out that Ruben Torres is one of the leaders in the great fashion gender-merger called Unisex.

(The principle of Unisex, of course, is that girls and their fellas look as one in identical outfits.)

However, the biological fact remains that we're not all brothers under those matching zip-up boiler suits.

Happily, this has not escaped the notice of Mr. Torres who at least feels that in the undie world there's still a case for *vive la difference* !

Sandie, who stars (fully-clothed) at London's Talk of the Town next week, has reservations about the new undies. "They'd be marvellous for midnight bathing parties," she said. "Otherwise, who'd know ? "

JEFF BANKS

Entrepreneur designer whose shop, Clobber was a trailblazing boutique of the '60s

Someone said of the '60s if you can remember it you weren't there. I was there and true to form can remember only bits. What made this era so unique? A galactic collision of time and events.

At the beginning of the decade the Second World War had been over for fifteen years and young people who had either suffered or had been born during the war started to flex their muscles. No longer were class constraints acceptable. Differences of skin colour were still a barrier in parts of the planet, but not in Swinging London. Economic restraints that had plagued their parents were not a consideration. Harold Macmillan told us we had never had it so good and we took him at his word. A tidal wave of creativity swept the country and ended up on the shores of the King's Road and Carnaby Street. Traditional barriers that had existed for centuries were washed away in an instant in the force of the storm.

Pink and white striped trousers, velvet jackets and floral shirts in the 1960s could have been a great new wardrobe for women. Oh, no! This was Carnaby Street, this was John Stephen's boutique, this was for MEN. Brian Jones and bandmate Mick Jagger would fight harder over a shirt than who got the publishing rights to 'Jumpin' Jack Flash'. Further up the street, Lennon and McCartney would leave the confines of Abbey Road Studios and wrestle over ex-army bandsmens' jackets for the *Sergeant Pepper* album cover at trendy men's boutique, I Was Lord Kitchener's Valet.

Carnaby Street, this little three-block strip at the back of Regent Street, London W1 changed the way men dressed forever.

"Miss Sandie Shaw sportingly sat on her then husband's head"

FELICITY ON JEFF

Those Swinging '60s young fashion designers needed just a fragment of Jeff Banks's business acumen and they'd all have been a lot richer. Even millionaires!

Jeff, the lad from Ebbw Vale, South Wales started to make a profit as a schoolboy, when he bought cans of paraffin at the bottom of the nearby hill, carried them to the top and sold them for a penny more.

Jeff had another equally keen interest – the fashion bug had bitten him, so in 1964, straight out of art school he opened his first shop, the trendy Clobber boutique in Blackheath – not exactly the heart of London's Swinging '60s boomtime, but Clobber was an early and important style outpost that certainly got noticed. First came the it-crowd opening: John Lennon and George Harrison of The Beatles, supermodel Jean Shrimpton and actor Terence Stamp. Then came the customers and then came the press and Jeff became a fashion sensation. His clothes were stylish and sharp – rather like Jeff.

He began by selling the big designer names and they all sold so quickly he couldn't keep stock in the boutique, so he started to design his own styles and sold these alongside until, in 1969, he launched his own label.

Jeff was not only Big in Fashion, because of his energy and personal style, he became one of the '60s 'names' and his marriage to the famous barefoot pop singer, Sandie Shaw, made front page news. To please the persuasive top photographer of the time, Terry O'Neill, Miss Shaw sportingly sat on her then husband's head and I'm hoping that this picture had nothing to do with the subsequent marriage breakup.

Jeff's career has been on the up and up since the early '60s and today his business booms in umpteen countries. Jeff is a hard worker and a constant smiler. Like all my favourite fashion people, he is FUN.

In 2009, Jeff was awarded a CBE, which is a bit of a feat when you remember Jeff's business career started selling paraffin up a Welsh hill.

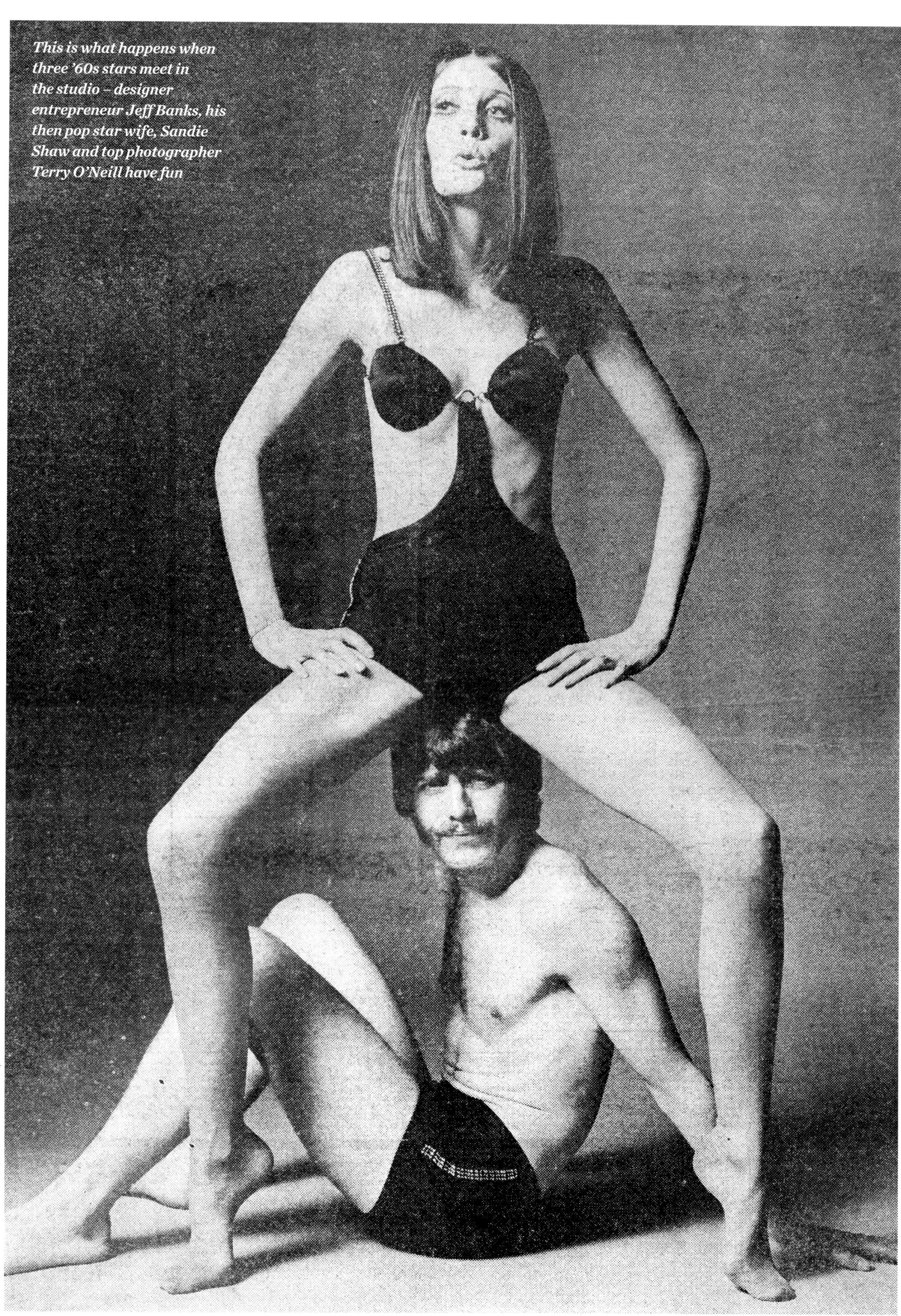

This is what happens when three '60s stars meet in the studio – designer entrepreneur Jeff Banks, his then pop star wife, Sandie Shaw and top photographer Terry O'Neill have fun

DAILY MIRROR, *Thursday, February 27, 1969* PAGE 15

These romantic singers, you know, are ordinary tough guys underneath

By CHRISTOPHER WARD

NORMALLY Engelbert Humperdinck appears before his army of female fans wearing a tuxedo.

He's a tuxedo sort of singer, you see. Romantic. Heart-throbby. Smoochy. More at home in a night club than burning it up along the M1.

So what in Heaven's name is he doing here looking like a Hell's Angel?

Well, like so many other singers who have reached the top of the pop tree, Engelbert is thinking of branching out into films.

Frilly

And he thought it was time he showed the world the other side of his nature – the ton-up, leather-jacket Wild One hiding under the frilly lace shirt.

"This is how I really see myself," Engelbert said last night. "Tough, but still romantic. That's how I would like to be thought of.

"Of course, the fans may not approve of it . . but I hope they like me enough to understand."

Engelbert, who starts a tour of Britain next week, has already had several film offers

Demand

One was playing the part of Dick Turpin. Another was a Western. Parts, you could say, that demand a good rider—but not a motor-bike rider.

"We haven't made any decisions yet," Engelbert added, "but we hope to have something lined up in Hollywood by the end of this year."

After this picture was taken, by the way, something really did stir down in the forest—the engine of Engelbert's powerful Harley-Davidson motor-bike. He went for a spin on it

Change

As Engelbert said: "It was too much to resist. I rode a motor-bike as a dispatch rider in the Army and I got the call again."

At £1,800, the Harley Davidson is the Rolls Royce of motor-bikes Even so, it did make a change from his real Rolls. Apart from any thing else, you could actually hear the engine.

Picture by
TERRY O'NEILL

It's 1969 and vanity, thy name is man. The peacock revolution is here to stay. Terry O'Neill, the famous photographer who makes beautiful girls look even more beautiful, decides to do the same for some high-profile men. Above, singer Engelbert Humperdinck goes Beat, helped by his leathers and a high-performance Harley Davidson bike. Right, captain of the World-Cup-winning England football team Bobby Moore OBE, poses nude while star footballer George Best and singer Tom Jones bare almost all – famous men become sexy pin-ups in the '60s.

DAILY MIRROR, *Tuesday, March 11, 1969* PAGE 11

Bobby Moore OBE, Captain of England and West Ham joins the pin-up team

WHY THE PEACOCK MALE IS BARING HIS BREAST

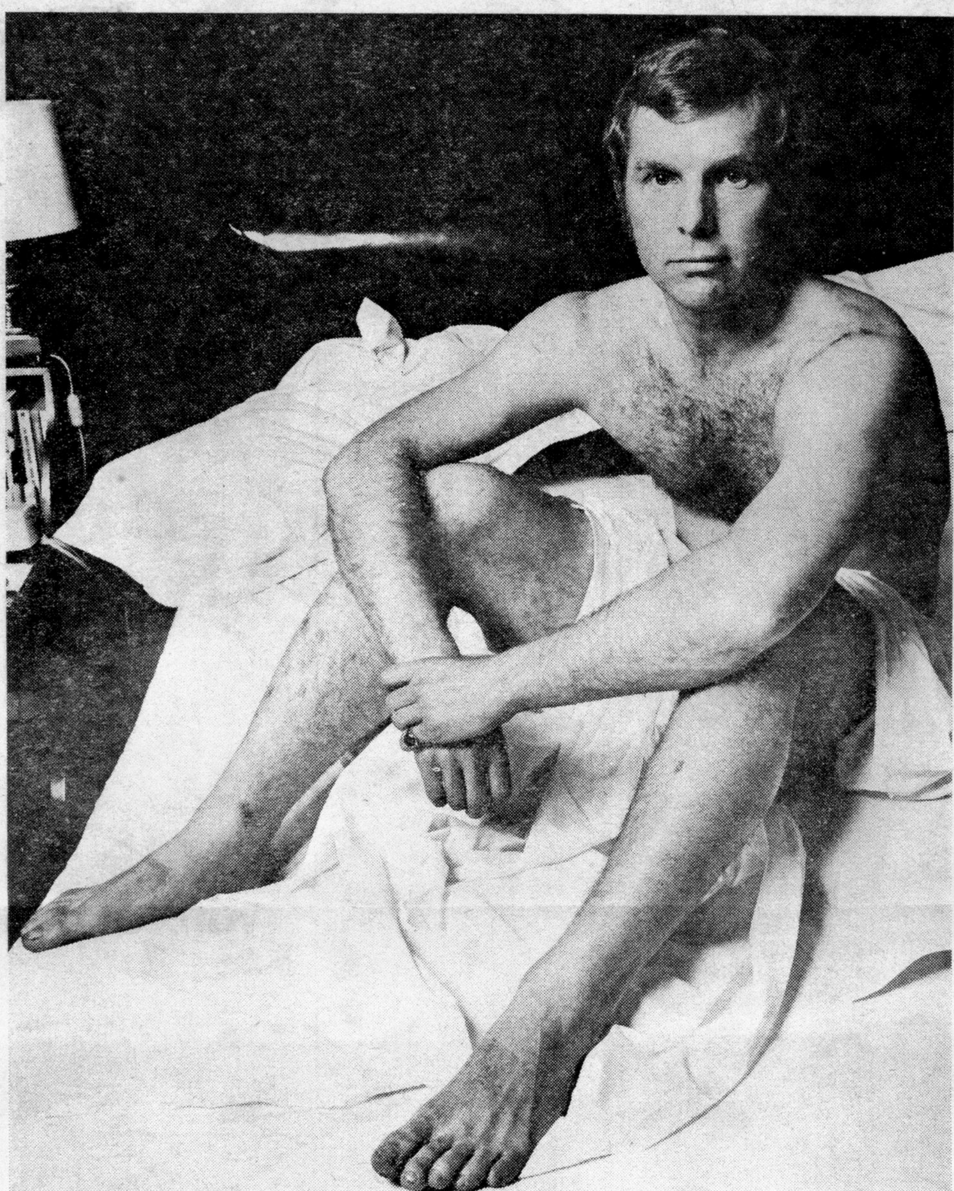

BOBBY MOORE, OBE (41-31-39). Picture by Terry O'Neill

THE GENERAL term is, of course, the pin-up. But the female of the species is often referred to as cheesecake and no disrespect intended.

Famous females who in the past have added stature and lustre to the cheesecake business were Miss Lana Turner in her sweater, Miss Jane Russell more or less in her blouse, Miss M. Monroe face downwards on a rug wearing just her Chanel No. 5, and you can take it from there.

Drawing-pinned or stuck on to walls and cupboard doors around the world, these were the first of the great pin-ups who helped the war effort, or boosted production, or merely served to keep the British workman's mind off his work.

In those days, when the lads wore their hair short and the girls wore their skirts long, a pin-up, it was taken for granted, was a female.

True, Prince Philip, who was once voted the most popular man in Britain, got himself pinned up from time to time along with Frankie Vaughan and The Beatles. But their appeal was always emotional rather than physical.

The male pin-up, until now, has always tended to keep his clothes on.

The only exceptions were those torsos belonging to Mr. Universe types. And if there's a less sexy sight to a woman than a muscle-bound gentleman with what appears to be a skinful of grapefruit, all tensed up and prepared to slip a discus, I for one cannot name it.

Today, however, the male pin-up is coming into his own and beefcake looks like rivalling cheesecake.

Obliged

While some men may chunter "Disgusting" or "It would never have happened in W. G. Grace's day," the stripped-off, or at least stripped-down male is baring his chest for posterity and the camera.

Georgie Best (37-31-38) bared his chest in Woman's Own recently, and Bobby Moore, O B E, Captain of England and West Ham (41-31-39) follows suit here. Singer Tom Jones (40-30-39) also obliged.

What is causing the British Male to be so uninhibited about undressing?

A Harley-street psychiatrist thinks it all stems from their well-known peacock urge.

"With the interest in men's clothes," he says, "the male has been allowed to become what he wants to be—a peacock. It's just male exhibitionism coming out after years of suppression in conservative clothes.

"This current trend may be due to the fact that there is beginning to be a surplus of men, so they have to compete to get girls, and the emphasis is on their appearance."

But the Editor of Woman says her readers are not yet ready for the Cover Boy. They are more interested in a man's personality and beliefs than just his pretty face.

She also says it would be too difficult to choose the right male since, when it comes to men, one woman's "Ah!" is another woman's "Ugh!"

The Editor of Woman's Own, who is a man, says they've already had Prince Charles, Michael Caine, David Nixon and Tom Jones on *their* covers. All fully clothed, of course.

"But on the whole," he said, "men don't look as beautiful as girls."

Oh, I don't know. Some do, and some don't—to us girls.

But it will be a funny day indeed when the Playmate of the Month is called Fred.

Felicity Green

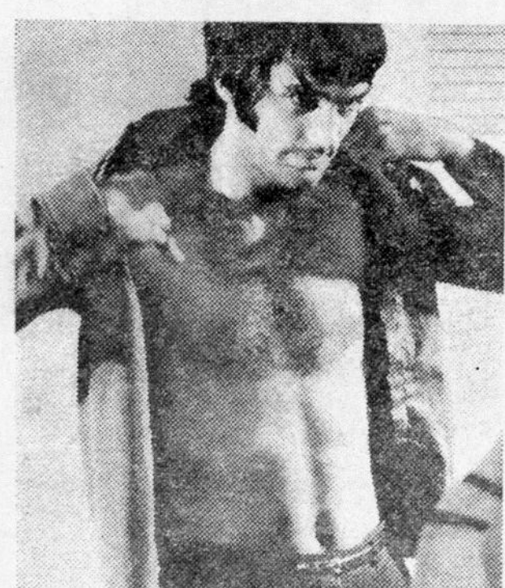

Two other members of the team showing the great new undressed look for men. Right, singer Tom Jones, (40-30-39). Left, footballer Georgie Best (37-31-38).

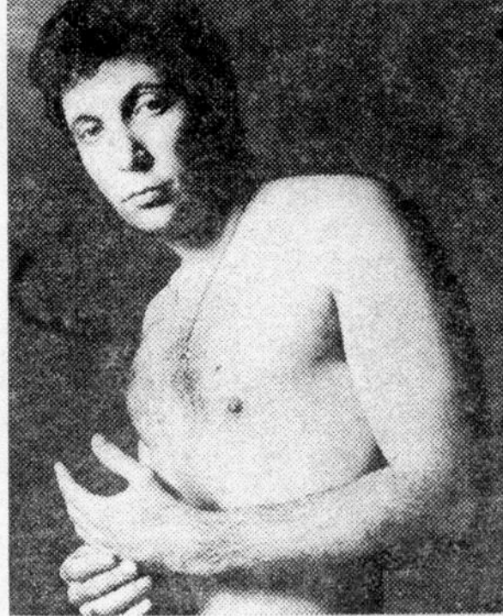

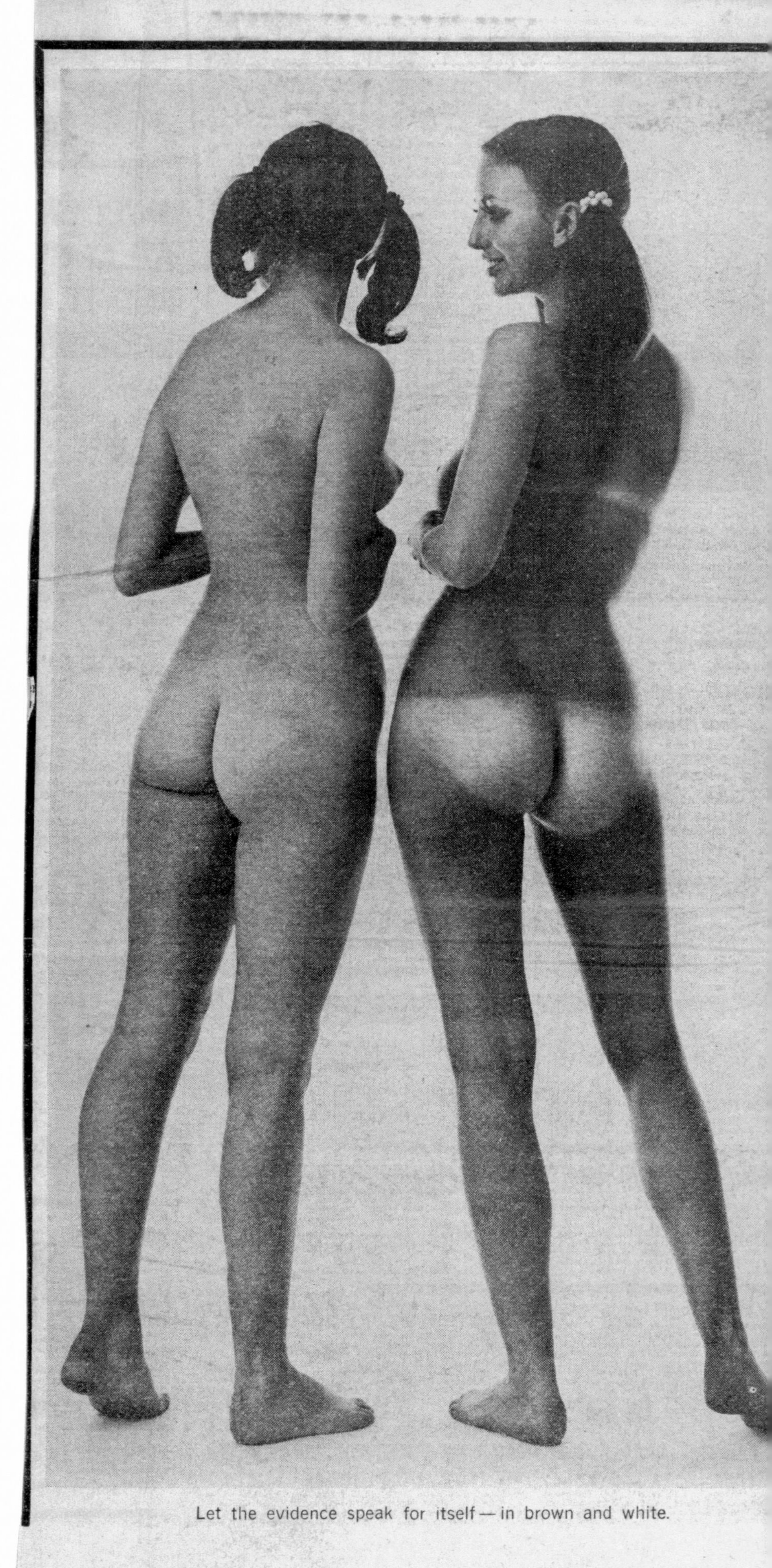

Let the evidence speak for itself — in brown and white.

DAILY MIRROR, Wednesday, May 14, 1969 PAGE 19

WHICH TWIN WORE THE BIKINI THAT LETS THE SUN SHINE THROUGH?

* THAT'S RIGHT, it's the one on the far left. The one with the suntanned bottom. Actually, the two game ls who exposed their all in the me of truth and science are sley Russ and Mary Lou Hayden.

Each girl had a series of sessions der one of those artificial sun ıps that are nowadays called on give a pre-holiday boost to a ter-than-white skin.

Their great strip-off was to test accuracy of the claim that a new ini made in a specially treated ton fabric lets you tan all over— n the bits where the bikini gets ween you and the ultra-violet rays.

eeing has to be believing and no , I think, would doubt that Lesley, wore the bikini with the built-in " factor, has fewer of those tell- white marks about her person.

'he shine-through bikini is a scrap quite ordinary-looking, fairly sy, floral printed cotton selling the shops at under 6 gns. and nade by the Continental firm of Buin.

s you can see for yourself, it did eed let the sun shine through — an unsuspecting onlooker might think Lesley had found a nice e beach on which to do her tan- . Look, no white patches!

Mary Lou, on the other hand, not mention the other bottom, is vn only in parts as any bikini-clad might be.

his latest boon to sun-worship- womankind was invented by a nese Doctor of Science who got idea a couple of years ago and been working on it ever since.

or content with just telling the ing world of their discovery, the Buin people, with typical Austrian ication, called in the law to ess their claim.

his week I received a letter which me that the shine-through bikini tested "on several models at St. ez under the strict supervision of eminent French barrister, who d a legal statement, authentic- g the complete efficacity of all ns made by the manufacturers, that the Piz Buin bikini enables wearer to obtain a suntan through fabric, thereby achieving an ver tan."

me legal eagles get the nicest

rting thought: but do you really an all-over tan?

e, I think there's something in- ely satisfying, to say nothing of in those little white triangular hes. I'd be sorry to be without . They're among my favourite ay souvenirs. Sentiment apart, ver, they're also the only way easuring exactly how brown you y did manage to get.

ORY:
LICITY GREEN
TURES:
HN ADRIAAN

Bikini-clad for the experiment.

This 1969 *Mirror* spread had two interesting results. First, it won me an award, as Woman's Page Journalist of the Year, 1969. But this didn't happen without a fight. The judges disagreed. Against: the national press journalists objected on the (ridiculous) grounds that it was only a photograph and not proper journalism. Fools! Rushing to my defence came the celebrated journalist, Sir Tom Hopkinson, whose illustrious career included his editorship from 1940 to 1950 of *Picture Post*, the ground-breaking news magazine, celebrated for its photojournalism featuring the work of the leading photographers of the age. It was an immensely important publication, its pictures not only captured, but made headline stories around the world. Sir Tom, knighted by the Queen for Services to Journalism, argued that, of course, photographs were journalism and he carried the day. So, yes, I got my award for this page with its photograph by John Adriaan, and the second result was that it confirmed that henceforth photographs must be accepted as journalism! The story was the arrival of a new French fabric that "lets the sun shine through." The girl on the left, a sensible, moderate sun worshipper shows no difference between the exposed parts and the covered-up ones. No tell-tale difference. The girl on the right, a dedicated sun worshipper who didn't care a fig for the tell-tale difference. Me, I didn't really know whose side I was on. In fact, I found it quite nice to see how really tanned I managed to get in those days when we hadn't been warned about dangerous overkill sun worshipping.

DAILY MIRROR, *Friday, May 30, 1969* PAGE 9

High under the arms, nice and tight . . Justin and Twiggy side by side in their machine-knits.

TWIGGY . . ON KNITTING THOSE JUMPERS FOR JUSTIN

Twiggy working at the loom.

by FELICITY GREEN

WE ARE, as everyone must surely know by now, a nation of knitters.

Mention two plain, two purl and the man with the statistics pops up to tell us that if all the yarn we annually knit into sweaters, dresses, socks, etc., were laid end-to-end it would reach from here to there provided the points were 12,000,000 miles apart.

Doing her best to improve upon this already heady total is Miss Lesley Hornby, who to date has knitted four jumpers for Justin, three jumpers plus a dress for herself, a sweater for her sister, a sweater for pop star Jackie Lomax, a sweater for Patti Beatle Harrison and a suit for her mum.

From all of which it is easy to see that Miss Hornby, better known as Twiggy, has become a dab hand at the knitting game.

However, as befits a child of the age of the technological revolution, she has spurned altogether the hand-held needles.

She is strictly a machine-minded purl-and-plainer and on her recently acquired Knitmaster she reckons to turn out the back of a sweater in an hour and a half, the front, ditto, on the next day, and the sleeves the day after.

She reckons the purple V-necked Lurex number which is her current favourite took her about six hours altogether.

"I *could* do it all in one go," she assured me, "but what's the 'urry ?"

What indeed ?

Her urge to create started, as the knitter herself puts it, "as I was looking through all them French magazines with all them lovely skinny sweaters which you can't get over 'ere. So I said to meself, I said, aha, why don't I do it meself ?

"I decided I'd get a machine—I never did like 'and knitting. It don't grow quick enough.

"You 'ave to 'ave lessons though. I 'ad about four hours. It was all free and once I'd learned 'ow it worked I only 'ad to ring up a couple of times and say 'elp what 'appens now ?

"The girl who taught me was ever so lovely. She never minded and she was always able to sort me out on the phone."

Getting patterns small enough is Twiggy's main problem.

To get the look their new young customer wanted the knitting machine firm delved back into their archives and came up with an acceptable style, circa 1950.

"It 'ad a girl looking ever so funny, like Grace Kelly, on the front," said Twiggy. "It was quite nice, though, because they wore their sweaters tight in them days."

For her second effort, based on a more up-to-date pattern, she chose a size 28 bust, but it was too big so she gave it to her sister.

"They 'aven't got their sizes worked out right for today," she said. "I mean Justin measures 42 inches and size 36 was too big."

She gave her barn-owl imitation which, as her fans and friends know, is the Twiggy high-decibel laugh.

"Now I can make up me own patterns. It's quite easy really. Mind you, you gotta concentrate, I mean you can't do it while you're watching the telly or anything.

"I do all the sewing-up bit by 'and. After all, I used to make all me own clothes when I was at school and when I first met Justin I used to make all his trousers. Didn't I Justin ?"

And to think there are those who still believe the girl is just a pretty face.

PICTURES by CHRIS KILLIP

DAILY MIRROR, Monday, June 9, 1969 PAGE 9

FELICITY GREEN on the fashion scene

THE IMPORTANCE OF BEING OSSIE . .

TODAY Ossie Clark is twenty-seven. So Happy Birthday, Ossie. Your friends and fans wish you continued success.

Since a list of Ossie's friends and fans includes such names as Julie Christie, Julie Driscoll, Britt Ekland, Patti Boyd Harrison, Emmanuelle Khanh, Brigitte Bardot and Twiggy, it's easy to see that Ossie moves in swinging circles.

Ossie, in case anyone should still be wondering, is a fashion designer. Some say *the* fashion designer

Highly individualistic and about as aggressive as a startled fawn, Ossie is to the world of Establishment fashion today what Mary Quant was ten years ago. And, as in the case of Quant, not everybody loves the wayward one.

A criticism of Ossie's latest collection indicated that he was "totally undisciplined," that he made "tortured creations," that he "should call a halt to his quest for sensationalism."

Ossie says he doesn't believe everything he reads or hears about himself, which is just as well for someone so sensitive. Though the praise outweighs the blame by a nice healthy majority.

There are those among us who might feel that while Ossie's talent is undoubted, it could also be said to be a teeny-weeny bit uncommercial.

Sold

However, one wholesale dress firm called Radley has sufficient faith in Ossie's ability to appeal to a wider audience than the polar extremities of the King's Road, that they decided to get him on their designing side.

His first wholesale range has sold "like a bomb," they admit, with happily raised eyebrows and profits.

As one perhaps slightly over - enthusiastic store buyer put it: "He's *real* fashion. He's one of the few originals. He's a genius!"

He is also extremely temperamental and admits to going off and getting lost if things don't go his way.

Sometimes he goes home to Bradford to see his mother whom he loves "very, very much." The rest of his family include "lots of brothers and sisters who are just ordinary people."

Extraordinary Ossie started life in Bradford, was evacuated to Oswaldtwistle where his name came from, then went to school in Manchester where he thought he might be an architect, and then, having won a coveted fashion scholarship, arrived at the Royal College of Art in London.

One of his more alarming contributions to an end-of-term fashion spectacular in 1965, his last year, included an outfit trimmed in electric light bulbs. His first professional job was designing some clothes for a little boutique in Chelsea called Quorum and, at that time, run by his current friend and partner Alice Pollock in conjunction with a "load of hooray girls"—which is Clark-talk for debs.

The hooray girls fell by the fashion wayside, but Alice and Ossie — born, they discovered, on the same day of the same year—stayed together.

They both design, they both compete for the fashion honours, "but I lead," says Ossie.

Those who have followed his lead wear the kind of clothes that couldn't have been designed anywhere else in the world at any other point in time.

"I don't think I'm the greatest designer," says Ossie with a rare flash of unassuming and communicative modesty. "I just think I make the kind of clothes certain people want to wear. They look great in them and they're my best advertisement.

"Like Bardot. She came in and scooped up £250-worth. We sent them over to her hotel and the receptionist wrote out a cheque for the lot."

Ossie, who is more Twiggy-shaped than Twiggy and measures a mere 33-25-33, is also a dab hand at the practical side of tailoring. "If I want to I can cut it and sew it all myself," he said. "I always make my own trousers, but I get my jackets and waistcoats from a tailor I know in Croydon."

Keeping Ossie busy at the moment is a specially designed wardrobe for Mick Jagger's forthcoming TV spectacular.

One of the most interesting numbers promises to be a pale blue snakeskin suit, which makes one seriously consider hiring a colour TV specially for the event.

Patti : A favourite client

ONE of the people who like the kind of clothes that Ossie makes is model girl Patti Boyd Harrison, who has been a client from way back when. Although she now models only rarely, she's always prepared to oblige her chum Ossie. Here she wears a typical satin outfit in one of the exclusive prints designed by Celia Birtwell. If you think the print looks familiar it's because it has been knocked off, as they say in the Rag Trade, or copied as they say elsewhere, by a dozen different beady-eyed fabric people. This tunic and pants will be on sale at Quorum stockists as well as at Ossie's new shop in the King's Road from the end of next month. It will cost £27 5s. 6d. That's Ossie on the right.

Picture by JUSTIN de VILLENEUVE

If Ossie Clark had either a business brain, or a business partner, I reckon he would still be up there with the top '60s designer names. But he had neither and he flew a bit too close to the Swinging '60s sun. Showbusiness stars loved his sexy designs and model and Beatle-wife Patti Boyd Harrison was among his famous customers – and friends. He made jumpsuits for Mick Jagger, clothes for The Beatles, Bianca Jagger and Marianne Faithfull. Ossie became a bit more grounded when he teamed up with fabric designer Celia Birtwell and made his famous creations from her delicate printed chiffons. These have become a '60s classic and today are precious souvenirs of the time. I had two of these classics and wish I still had them, but they were too fragile to last – a little like Ossie perhaps.

Did you know Miss Lesley Hornby was an accomplished knitter? Back in the '60s when the picture on the left was taken, she had already knitted trendy skinny sweaters for her boyfriend and manager and for model Patti Boyd Harrison, a sweater and dress for herself and a suit for her mum. No clickety click of the needles for Twiggy – it's all done by machine.

ONCE UPON A TIME..

IT WAS ALL TWEEDY AND DOWDY. THEN IN CAME THE DOLLIES AND PEACOCKS AND THE TILL RANG OUT £84 MILLION

♀ COSMETICS £17,500,000

♂ TIES £1,000,000

♂ SHIRTS £2,000,000

♀ UNDIES including stockings & tights £5,000,000

♂ CLOTHING £16,200,000

♀ CLOTHING £26,000,000

⚥ SHOES £25,800,000

♂ : HIS ♀ : HERS ⚥ : THEIRS

Picture: John Adriaan

BRITISH FASHION used to be nothing but twin-sets, tartans, tweeds, raincoats and sensible shoes.

The world went to Paris for design, cloth, colour and taste. They looked for the "Made In Britain" label only for clothes that were practical and classic—a polite way of saying dowdy and uninspired.

In 1947, when Britain's fashion exports were a meagre £11,000,000 a year, a schoolgirl awoke crying on her thirteenth birthday: "The horror of being a woman is getting closer."

The girl was Mary Quant, who even then dreamed of dressing the world her way.

"Women didn't have nipples, they had great appendages of bosom. They didn't have bottoms, they had seats. The young dressed exactly the same as the old, from corsets upwards," she said.

Her ideas set the imagination of the world alight and gave Britain that first Swinging image.

The new wave of designers inspired by Quant have, in their turn, influenced the international fashion scene.

Today, London challenges the world as the No. 1 fashion centre and Britain is the biggest clothing exporter in Europe.

Fashion—not including many types of specialised and industrial clothing—is an export business worth £84,000,000 a year for Britain, and still rising fast.

And funnily enough, among the big money spinners are those twin-sets, tartans, tweeds and other frightfully British classics.

DAILY MIRROR, *Thursday, November 6, 1969* PAGE 11

CONJECTURE:

THE MAXI MEANS BACK TO SUSPENDERS AND STOCKINGS

TIGHTS were invented, as any disgruntled man will tell you, to bridge that gap between stocking top and skirt bottom. Or, come to think of it, between stocking top and girl bottom. In the era of the mini, the gap had to go and the suspender was seen no more in the land.

From a shaky and expensive start in 1964, tights now account for about three-quarters of all hosiery sales in this country.

In 1964 they cost 16s. 11d. a pair. You can get them today for about 6s. 11d. which must surely be a sunshine point in someone's cost-of-living chart.

Now, however, the suggestion is being made that the maxi will oust tights from the scene. After all, with no gap to bridge, who needs them and the stocking-and-suspender syndrome will, therefore, be with us once again.

A nice thought, no doubt, for some—like stocking manufacturers, suspender manufacturers, girdle manufacturers and cónnoisseurs of the girlier type of girlie pictures.

But the rest of us?

The answer comes through loud and clear. It's a big unanimous NO.

Today's girls are too used to the feeling of freedom they get from tights and if to members of the opposite sex this sounds like a contradiction in terms you must just take our illogical feminine word for it.

Tights mean goodbye to those bumpy suspender bulges. To pulling down our girdles. To putting on four garments instead of one and I hope you've finished counting by now.

At the moment sales of tights go something like this:

Girls aged from 15 to 24 buy 30 per cent. tights to 4 per cent. stockings. At age 25 to 34, it's 34 per cent. tights to 10 per cent. stockings. From 35 to 44, 20 per cent. buy tights to 18 per cent. who buy stockings. From 45 and over, it's only 16 per cent. tights to 68 per cent. stockings.

Do the manufacturers of all the aforementioned tights feel the maxi is a threat to their booming sales?

They do not.

At Pretty Polly, sales director Robin Wright says happily: "We don't expect ever to go back to stockings as the great sellers. Firstly, we optimistically believe that the maxi will never be more than a relatively fringe fashion element. The only advantage, as I see it, that stockings have over tights is that if one leg goes you don't have to throw the whole pair away."

At Marks and Spencer, that bastion of cautious comment, they admit that they are currently selling 75 per cent. of tights against 25 per cent. stockings.

"We have no comment to make on the possibility of skirts swooping down in length"—they say in the we-are-just-good-friends vein—"and for the moment, it isn't in our plans to anticipate a swing back to stockings."

Since it's the wilder birds of fashion who are the most maxi-minded, are they going to be first to forsake their tights in favour of the stocking top?

There is certainly no sign of same in their King's Road habitat.

Out of a dozen of the more bizarre bazaars, not one sold stockings.

"Stockings?" said one teenage salesgirl blankly. "You mean proper old-fashioned stockings? Oh, no, we don't sell *them*."

At The Drug Store the girl even made so bold as to say "What a funny thing to ask for!"

The Girl in the Street — actually about twenty of them—said well, no, not really. Who wants *suspenders*? Emphatically, no! No, *thank* you! Maybe hold-ups sometimes, just for fun. But suspenders—I mean, they're not sexy or anything, are they?

Well, that's what they said and who am I—or you—to argue?

For all these girls, stockings are strictly out. And I wouldn't be surprised if they meant it. At least for a month or two.

Black stockings by Aristoc, 6s 11d., suspender belt, Weiss, £1 12s. 6d., no-bra bra by Twilfit, £1 7s. 6d. Sheer black tights by Echo, 8s. a pair.

Pictures by JOHN KELLY

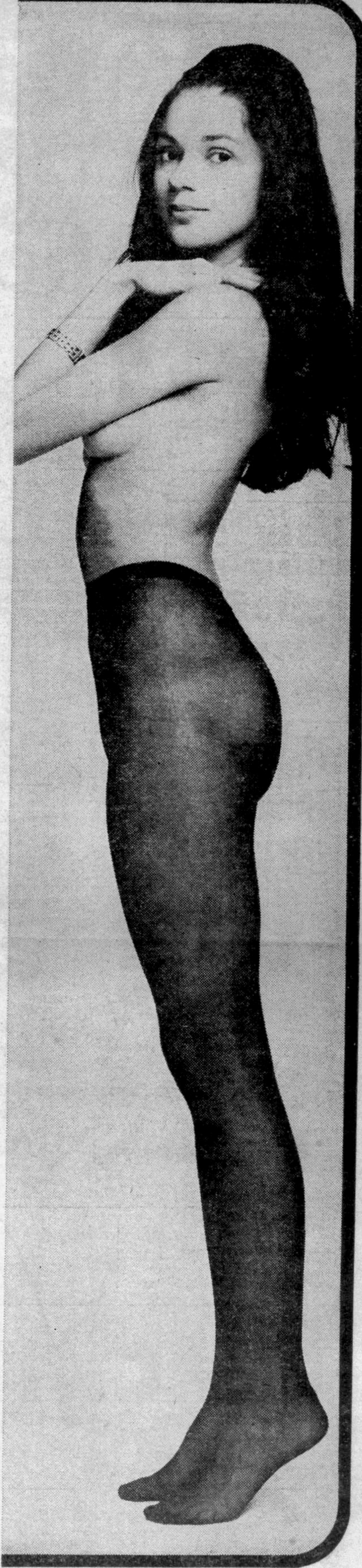

CONCLUSION:

NOT ON YOUR NELLY IT DOESN'T

CONFRONTATION !

The Body meets the men whose passion is fashion

The Body meets Mr Fashion: Raquel and St Laurent. She wears his Rive Gauche Edwardian Can-Can dress

Raquel in Pierre Cardin swirling, w
skirt in red wool. Worn over black

It's the Raquel and Yves and Card

DAILY MIRROR, *Tuesday, January 27, 1970* PAGE 15

FELICITY GREEN in Paris

PARIS fashion has a reputation for having nothing much to do with Real Women. ers tend to be inspired el girls, and model girls, l known, tend to have where others have

ugh the sight of a spare sn't actually resulted in te couturier having y, flesh and blood aren't red to be among their e things.

vell-stacked Miss Welch, 22-35, is as different our actual Paris model an hour glass from a neter.

fared well, if not even Face to face and equally in touch on other levels she conquered three of the top men in fashion—Pierre Cardin, Andre Courreges and Yves St. Laurent.

In Paris to choose a wardrobe for her forthcoming TV colour spectacular, the luscious Raquel endeared herself, curves and all, to these aesthetically-inclined men whose main passion is fashion.

They lent her their top secret styles in advance of their collections. They even agreed to come along and cuddle up for the camera.

"She's a dazzler," said Courreges.

["He's so manly," said Raquel, "and his clothes are built for action."]

"She is a very modern type," said Cardin, "and looks perfect in my clothes."

["He makes me feel like a lunar ballerina," said Raquel.]

"She has such a lovely waist," said St. Laurent.

["He has more sense of the female body than any other designer," said Raquel, "and what's more his leather neck-bands are erotic and his full skirts turn me on."]

See below for a most unusual fusion of high fashion and the Body Beautiful.

Confrontation with Courreges: Raquel Welch wears a breast baring Vinyl jumpsuit in pink and black

and Courreges Show

PICTURES by TERRY O'NEILL

This spread of photographs is typical of the way the *Mirror* combined fashion with glamour. Our fashion pages ignored the boring bits about the latest looks in traditional rainwear and were lively and fun, and designed to appeal to all our millions of readers – men as well as women, old (or mature!) as well as the new with-it young who, like me, were film fans. These are the fashion photographs that only Terry O'Neill could have taken. Models, Film Stars, Paris Couturiers, they were all the same to Terry. Here, he has super-sexy superstar Raquel Welch making unlikely but flirtatious twosomes with three of the most famous leaders of Paris couture fashion: Yves St Laurent, Pierre Cardin, Andre Courrèges. Truly fashion pictures with that truly Terry O'Neill extra something!

BAILEY

As The Beatles are to pop music so Bailey is to fashion photography. Bailey invented model Jean Shrimpton in 1961 and married French film actress Catherine Deneuve in 1965 – the leggy look has become his signature tune

"The first words I ever heard Bailey speak were: I doan' eat flesh!"

DAVID BAILEY, *Daily Mirror*, 1965

I wasn't really ambitious when I began, I just wanted to be John French's assistant, and then it all sort of happened. But I never felt about fashion as I feel now about going into films. I think the cinema is the greatest thing today. Who do I think is the greatest photographer in the world? Richard Avedon. In England? Me... But I can't even talk about fashion any more. All those women in the business getting excited about some new dress. And they're always retouching my pictures. Taking out the knickers. When I photograph a girl in a chair all curled up and her knickers are showing they're always lengthening her skirt. I don't know why. If that's the way she sits, it don't worry me. But I'm not giving fashion up altogether. I've just signed another two-year contract with *Vogue*... I'm opening a boutique next week. It's called the Carrot on Wheels. It doesn't mean anything it's just a name. Pat Knight – she's a model is a partner in it with me. Then I'm gonna open an antique shop in the spring. That's what I'm really keen on. Antiques.

DAVID BAILEY, *Daily Mirror*, 1967

I'd like to be remembered as a lover, and then maybe as a fighter. And, perhaps, after that, as a photographer.

DAVID BAILEY, *Daily Mirror*, 1971

I've always had a thing about legs. That's what's wrong with the French girls. They've got no legs. Haven't you noticed? They've just got long ankles and low-slung behinds. All the ones over 5'8" with the good legs were killed off in the Napoleonic Wars. I don't think it matters about breasts.

FELICITY ON BAILEY

Bailey was one of John French's assistants, and when John felt a meeting with me and the mighty *Daily Mirror* would provide Bailey with a suitable newspaper launching pad for his talents, a lunch at The Ivy restaurant was deemed ideal. So there we were, we three, menus in hand. John chose, then I chose, and Bailey, silent and shy, scanned up and down the foot-long menu. Seeing his dilemma, John, always gentle and kind and helpful, offered some advice. "The steaks, dear boy, are excellent, particularly the Steak Diane – very thin and tender and quite delicious." Pause. Long pause. Then Bailey spoke. "I doan' eat flesh!" They were the first words I ever heard Bailey speak.

Bailey developed year by year into one of the world's great international photographers. The first pictures Bailey took for the *Mirror* in 1961 were of model Tania Mallett in the new stretch fabrics, which meant Maximum Movement.

And then David Bailey met Jean Shrimpton and everything changed. His love affair with The Shrimp captured the world's imagination. Their success on both sides of the Atlantic was due to this gifted, pixie-faced elf of a man about whom a friend wrote the jingle that began: David Bailey makes love daily. When the Bailey/Shrimp relationship ended the world wept. At least I did. It had been such a Swinging '60s fairytale.

But the Bailey fairytale continued with a long list of beautiful models – and as Bailey himself admitted, "I only went into photography for the girls" – then he married French film star Catherine Deneuve! Full of surprises – that's Bailey, then and now.

This Bailey image is a bit of a cheat because it's from the still swinging '70s, but it remains one of my favourites – testament to Bailey's constant grip on glamour

PAGE 14 DAILY MIRROR, *Wednesday, September 30, 1970*

HEMLINE

FOUR years ago, a London dress designer named Barbara Hulanicki (Biba to the initiated) created a dress in which the hemline billowed ten inches off the ground.

The lady didn't claim any originality for it. She merely produced a sophisticated version of the handed-down long dresses then being worn by a handful of trail-blazing young Chelsea birds feverishly doing their own thing.

Well, female Britain paused momentarily in its permissive long-legged stride, looked critically, then went str
on cultivating even min
minis.

But this first down-to
calf prototype went c
become a fashion wave c
the midi and another
bending exercise in comm
persuasion is under way.

IS THE MIN ON ITS LAST LEGS?

The first midi —designed by Biba (circa 1966)

MEN, outraged as they usually are by fashion changes, have rarely been so hotly opposed to a new line. Fashion writers, in general, have raved about it.

And women in general?

Mirrorscope set out to find the answer by talking to the men who have to measure female fashion. Two things became obvious from the outset.

1 If a fashion is going well, manufacturers and wholesalers will not release figures "because it would help our competitors."

2 If a fashion is going badly they will remain tight-lipped about the details in case women get the idea that it's a flop.

To begin at the spinning: Britain's textile manufacturers are not going to make a fortune out of the midi. Not yet, anyway.

None

The British wool industry supplied the world with 286,000,000 square yards of cloth last year and can spot an upsurge in their output before it happens. They report no rise in demand at all this year.

Courtaulds, our biggest makers of artificial textiles, also record no dramatic rise.

Both make the same point, in all fairness: one yard of 58-inch material makes three miniskirts but only one-and-a half midis. Since the midi uses more material and must be tailored, it costs more. So, women are unlikely to buy as many midis as minis. Therefore there will be no leap in demand for material.

The most inquisitive people in the textile industry are the market researchers at ICI Fibres.

Their chief, Scott Doble says: "We have found no dramatic move to long skirts but our people have had a look at all the ranges being produced by the big manufacturers and there will probably be a move downwards.

"A typical range will have more minis than midis but there are lots of dresses reaching the knees. However, women are still not convinced about the midi and they are even now still waiting to see."

Winner

On average, British women buy only 2.8 dresses a year, but in the 17-20 age group that figure doubles.

According to a Courtaulds executive: "We have found from observation and inquiries in the trade that some young girls have been buying as many as one mini-dress a week.

"The midi is a different proposition, though. In the same multiple store, a mini will cost 29s. 11d. and a midi £4. The only clear indication of the midi's success will come in Spring — if girls don't go back to minis."

So far, one of the country's major dress manufacturers, Alfred Young, Ltd. (Richard Shops, Paige Shops and half a dozen other labels), have notched up what looks like a winner.

Their style Number 790 (brushed acetate printed top with plain Orlon buttoned midi skirt and belt) is selling as fast as Young's can make them.

At the High Street end of the game, Marks and Spencer have added the midi to their range. Their figures, they say, are a trade secret but "there has been an appreciable trend" towards the longer skirts, largely in the West End of London.

On the other hand, they have found no falling-off in mini sales.

One thing is clear. There is more female resistance to this swoop below the knee than most fashion changes. The National Economic Development Office had the Tavistock Institute prepare a report on consumer habits, and made this conclusion:

"Consumers tend to feel exploited and almost insulted by being pressurised by fashion changes into excessive expenditure on clothes."

AS ever, the persuasive tactics in America are rather less than subtle and the mini-to-midi change has had some chaotic repercussions.

"Eighteen manufacturers have closed or gone into bankruptcy," said Mildred Sullivan, director of the New York Couture Business Council.

"The sudden push for the midi has taken the industry to the brink of financial ruin."

The garment industry is New York's largest and the second largest industry in the United States.

In a country which lives on lightning statistics, the midi sales figures are strangely "unavailable." Garment industry sources believe that when the publicly-owned manufacturing companies issue their annual reports they will show a tremendous loss.

Along Seventh-avenue they all agree on one thing. Women will have to start wearing the new length soon —because there will be no other types of dresses in the shops.

In every major retail store in large cities across America the racks are bowing beneath the weight of midis, and in the garment industry morale is lower than the hemlines.

Says Monte-Sano: "It's no good saying the wome
got to buy midis—
they'll just go out and
well make their own r
there are none in the

A SPOKESMA
Marcel Bouss
leading French te
manufacturer, said:

"Textile manufactur
a setback earlier this
when the midi came in
as usual the average
was resisting a cha
fashion. That always
pens when a style cha

"Now we are pulling
that area and as far
are concerned the r
dead in Paris.

"We are now produc
lighter materials suita
the flowing silhouette
longer garments.

"There is no doubt t
maxi and midi lengths
suit the flowing line w
great success this autu
winter and we expect t
up for our low sales
beginning of the year

The waiting g

FLUID fabrics, daring silhouettes, dramatic accessories — that's what the new long look is all about.

Manufacturers who are making the same old sensible suits with ten inches added on to the same old skirt are the only ones who are going out of business.

The firms
delighted wi
given to flag

There is no
the whole c
midi overnig
three years t
long skirts a
their life-spa

They are s
among the s

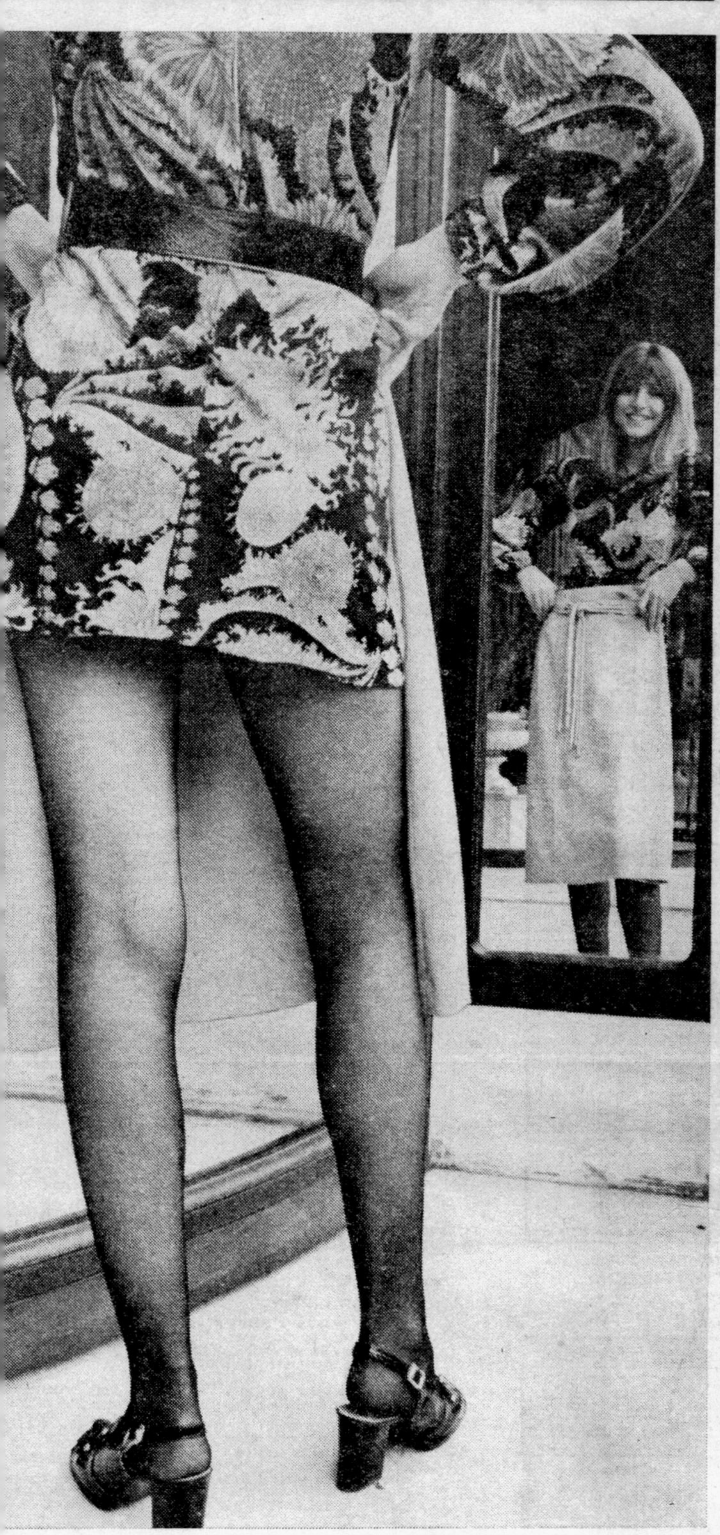

or midi? Moment of decision at Biba boutique.

—by Felicity Green

ght are
nidi has

er, that
enly go
two to
end and
nning of

moment
ecialised

departments which cater for the young or more way out customers.

Large department stores who try to cater for everyone — young and old, fashion-conscious or not — must obviously play it very much safer.

Buyers from most stores, therefore, are in an extremely tricky position at present. They have to anticipate how many of their customers will become midi-minded as the winter wears on.

But budgets have to be laid down in advance.

The state of the nation, fashionwise, is truly one of flux and the clever buyer this season has to play it all by ear.

By the way, yes, I do think there will be a lot of minis around next summer. Old ones from last year mostly, but at least the thought will help to get many a male through a long winter.

Q. Is the Mini on its last legs?

A. Very definitely No – it wasn't then in 1970 and it isn't now. It's been living happily ever after ever since Mary Quant first introduced it in the early '60s. It has survived challenges from midis and maxis and trousers and shorts. But today all these fashion challenges live happily together since we live in the fashion age of Anything Goes – and aren't we lucky. But as far as the fashion eye can see, I reckon the world-famous mini is certain to be with us for as long as girls want to show off their legs and this is likely to be a very long time indeed. The mini survived being hidden under the long-line fashionable maxi coats. So long live the omnipotent mini! It brought a lot of fun and flavour to the '60s and is still a fashion favourite, and even shorter, fifty years later. A real fashion legacy if ever there were one.

WOMEN IN A MAN'S WORLD

The writers and the photographer... and what a brave lot we were. I decided to people my office with talented young women. Any initial male journalist antagonism soon disappeared. Well almost

DOREEN SPOONER

Doreen Spooner was the first female staff photographer in Fleet Street. She studied photography in London and then worked at the famous Keystone picture agency. She then moved to Mirror Features agency before being offered a staff job at the Daily Mirror in 1948, thus becoming the only woman photographer in a team of thirteen. Doreen married and moved to Paris where she worked for the celebrated Magnum agency. She returned to London and the Daily Mirror in 1962 and stayed until she retired in 1988.

When I joined the *Daily Mirror* in 1962, I was lucky enough to meet Felicity Green. Felicity was producing lots of wonderful feature pages for women with lots of fashion pages. I was a staff photographer not a fashion photographer, but it was suggested that I should work with Felicity on some of her ideas. We got on really well and started to make some great pages.

The youth at this time were loving the fashions from Mary Quant and Biba – our readers were influenced by anything new and modern. The mini-skirt was all the rage and there was a new freedom for the young. Felicity covered all the fashion shows in London, Paris and Rome. I went to all the London fashion show photocalls and we started to produce lots of innovative work together.

The *Mirror* was at this time using regular pictures under the title Gorgeous Girls. I was doing quite a lot of these pictures and tended to present them as happy, smiling and in poses that flattered their figures and the clothes were never vulgar. The fashion pictures that I shot I treated the same way and tried to make them glamorous and lively. The following four pictures are particularly memorable:

1. A picture taken in Regent Street of model Vicki Hodge wearing a calf-length coat with an adjustable hem. It could be shortened by ripping off the hem. We had fun looking for someone who would do this. A passing city gent complete with a bowler hat was delighted to have a go and we had lots of laughs as he most efficiently ripped it off in one go. We attracted a mini crowd of amused onlookers.

2. Another time we featured a maxi coat and decided to hire a Borzoi hound and made him a maxi coat from a blanket. We photographed model Vicki Hodge striding across the road with the dog straining to take the lead and the fashion picture came to life.

3. Stick-on motifs became a popular '60s fashion gimmick. They were made of plastic and came with a skin glue allowing you to decorate your body with these motifs. Firm favourite: butterflies down the back.

4. The Beatles helped to promote fashion novelties and had their own Apple boutique in Carnaby Street. We photographed stockings with The Beatles heads printed on the legs and their faces and autographs on the stocking tops. London store C&A sold a cotton dress with four large images of the Fab Four printed across the front and it made a great fashion picture.

I was very happy to work for the wonderful *Daily Mirror* and to be accepted as the only female photographer on the staff. I was also delighted to work with Felicity and to accompany her to Russia where we photographed the latest mini-skirts in Moscow! Chance of a lifetime. ■

Active, outdoor fashion photography always attracted the interested onlooker, especially men. Model Vicki Hodge holds tight on to an impatient Borzoi hound in a matching maxi coat, photographed by Doreen Spooner

PENNY VINCENZI

Penny Vincenzi is one of the UK's best-loved and most popular authors. She began her journalistic career at the Mirror, later writing for the Times and the Daily Mail amongst many other newspapers before turning to fiction. Her sixteen best-selling novels have sold seven million copies worldwide, and she is acknowledged as the doyenne of the modern blockbuster.

No doubt about it, I would have killed to work for the *Daily Mirror* in the '60s. Rather more conventionally, I was interviewed first by Marjorie Proops, agony aunt *extraordinaire*, who wanted an assistant, and then a couple of years later by Felicity Green, then Associate Editor in charge of the women's and fashion pages – her department was known as the Fragrant Department on account of it being entirely female – and I was taken on in both cases in an act of faith.

It was an amazing place; a great, great newspaper, wonderful looking, truly investigative, superbly written and edited. While I was there, it hit the five million mark for the first time. I felt immensely proud and as if I had achieved it single-handed.

It was an amazing time to be at the *Mirror*; the Profumo scandal happened, man walked on the moon, Kennedy was shot. To this day, when something monumental happens in the world, I see it through the eyes of a newspaper, rather than my own. While I was with Proops I typed up interviews with such famous figures as Edith Sitwell, Cary Grant, and Mary Wilson. When I joined Felicity I went with her to cover Paris and followed her from fashion show to dazzling party to 2am photographic sessions. The world's greatest fashion photographers – John French, David Bailey, Terry O'Neill – worked for Felicity's brilliant, sexy, witty pages.

A girl called Barbara Hulanicki did ultra-stylish fashion drawings for us, and later she and Felicity created that famous matching gingham dress and headscarf – an exclusive for the *Mirror* – which really launched Barbara's mail-order fashion business, Biba.

A skinny, good-looking lad called Michael Grade worked on the sports desk and drove the girls mad, another called Auberon Waugh wrote features, a third called Mike Molloy did wonderfully witty cartoons, and a decade or two later he went on to edit the paper.

The whole place felt alive, electric, exciting; the *Daily Mirror* at this time was at the heart of everything that happened in whatever field. It set standards; it was a class act. It was also just the best fun. ■

"Even then we were worried about being London-centric and determined to include our readers all over the country"

EVE POLLARD

EVE POLLARD

Eve Pollard OBE, journalist: Fashion Editor, Honey, 1967; Fashion Editor, Mirror Magazine, 1968; joined Felicity Green's Women's Department, Daily Mirror, 1969; Woman's Editor, Observer Magazine, 1970; Woman's Editor, Sunday Mirror, 1971; Assistant Editor, Sunday People, 1981; Features Editor, TV-AM, 1983; Launch Editor-in-Chief, Elle USA, 1985; Editor, Sunday Magazine, 1986; Editor, You Magazine, 1986; Editor, Sunday Mirror, 1987; Editor, Sunday Express, 1991-5; broadcaster and author.

The *Daily Mirror* launched *Mirror Magazine* in 1968, the first and only newspaper colour supplement given away free every Wednesday. Months later it died, a victim of its own success. The *Mirror* was selling five million copies a day and the readership was judged to be about 15 million. There were too few companies who could afford to advertise at that time and so all but four of the staff were jettisoned!

I was rescued by Felicity Green. As fashion editor of the *Mirror Magazine* I had often made my way to her busy office in the main Mirror building. There she gave me all sorts of advice. How to work with men – my previous experience had been on women's magazines – how to get the best photographers for less, she passed on what she had discovered about *Mirror* readers' likes and dislikes gathered during her years on the paper. She was fun, helpful and knowledgeable. We always laughed a lot, she was chic, petite and neat with huge eyes. Felicity took me onto the *Daily Mirror* staff, though, in fact, there was no real job for me!

I went to work in the Women's Department. It was next to Felicity's office and was packed with all the female staff. There was her

deputy, the impeccable Jean Dobson, blonde razor-cut bob and flawless skin, plus her secretary, Sheila Basten, and the all-female feature writers. We sat close together with cupboards of clothes, big steel filing cabinets with huge files piled on top containing everything from fashion pictures to information on far-flung boutiques all over Britain. Even then we were worried about being London-centric and determined to include our readers all over the country.

This testosterone-free area made us a destination stop for the men working on the paper. At that time there were far fewer women in the newsroom so the male journos would often pop in asking for help with this and a suggestion on that. They came because Felicity was charming and encouraged them. If she was busy, and, by golly she was, they often came into our room for advice.

We "girls" worked in an atmosphere that was friendly and collegiate, but hardly glamorous. Mad Men it wasn't. The ceiling was gently tinged with ancient yellow nicotine stains. We sat at mis-matched dark wooden desks, all with old typewriters lashed to them by ugly chains. Too many had "walked". (You even had to put a deposit on your knife and fork when you had a meal in the staff canteen!) Old wire baskets stood on every desk containing copy, readers' letters, magazine tear-outs and Press invitations.

It was there I learned not to look up when someone came in. So many did, if I had, I would never have got any work done, there were so many comings and goings. Sub-editors used to come by with copy, captions to be checked, layouts and proofs to be approved. We had all the other newspapers, endless magazines, and the beginnings of PR "giftery" – books, perfume, and make-up.

It was heaven.

So, I set about, with Felicity's help, turning my non-job into something. At that time the newspaper's centre pages were the highlight of the day's photographic offerings. The photographs on this, known as "the spread", could come from very different departments in the paper. The Royal correspondent could have been given a set of approved Royal pictures or a show-biz writer could have persuaded a film producer to give us pictures of his latest film. The photos could be anything from the Crufts winner to a story about a skating duck.

I was friends with a handsome photographer called Terry O'Neill and we became determined, with Felicity's encouragement, to make that spread ours. Tel and I would talk about eight times a day. We cosied up to film PRs and pop stars. We weren't interested in the photos that everyone else had. We wanted exclusives.

We had the most glamorous pictures of film stars and warm family scenes long before *Hello!* magazine was invented. We had peepholes into the lifestyles of the rich and

"Felicity's fashion pages looked to me as if she had kidnapped the Vogue art editor"

SHIRLEY CONRAN

famous – all done with their approval. We did all this under the aegis of Felicity, who we could always turn to with our ideas. Her suggestions and encouragement meant that very gradually her influence spread over the paper. She understood earlier than anyone that it was usually the women who paid the newspaper bill, and if she was happy, she would stay loyal to the paper.

Felicity, forging her way ahead in Fleet Street, understood that even though we were the newspaper of Mrs Florrie Capp, the very essential partner of Andy, our female readers were better educated than any of their forbears and changing more rapidly than any part of society. The Pill, the opening of new jobs for women, their new-found ability to take on mortgages and run their own finances were making these readers curious about other lives. About giving their families better lives.

Felicity also understood that the young were taking over the world. So she sensibly championed young ones like me.

She taught us that there is no substitute for hard work, that second-rate was not good enough. She understood that some mad ideas were essential and inspired a legion of journalists that went on to bigger, better things because she had taught us.

Even now, I think it is very important to make Miss Green smile.

After about a year the *Observer* offered me a job as Woman's Editor of their colour supplement. Now it is more commonplace, but then very few journalists made the jump from tabloid to broadsheet, especially not a woman, who was in her twenties! Hugh Cudlipp, then our supreme boss, was delighted and gave me a party. I left, only to return to the group some years later – due to the advice and help from my heroine and mentor, Felicity Green.

PS One of the writers who lost her job on *Mirror Magazine* was Delia Smith! ■

SHIRLEY CONRAN

***Shirley Conran OBE, writer, designer and pioneering social entrepreneur, was Women's Editor of the Observer Magazine, 1964, Fashion Editor of the Observer, 1967, and Women's Editor of the Daily Mail, 1968. Her international, best-seller books include* Superwoman *and* Lace.**

Felicity Green was occasionally glimpsed passing through Fleet Street, a small, but daunting figure in the back of a glossy, chauffeured car, something that Evelyn Waugh might have imagined. Felicity's pages for the *Daily Mirror* were what we women journalists measured our own performance against: the words had the laconic clarity, simplicity and elegance of a Savile Row suit while Felicity's pages looked as if she had kidnapped the *Vogue* Art Editor.

When I first slunk on Fleet Street feeling – as many females did – that somehow I didn't deserve to be there, I never dared to imagine that powerful Felicity Green would one day be a much-valued friend: it was as unlikely as imagining that next Sunday HM The Queen planned to drop in to help you paint your kitchen.

Felicity's voice commands attention. Even when chatting, she knows when to use a 5 milligram word or a 2 kilo devastater. Because of her thoughtful expression plus the slow, deliberate voice, some people find Felicity intimidating. But, Felicity's aim in life is to be helpful, "It's not hard if you think about it."

When I founded The Work Life Balance Trust, I was occasionally obliged to write a – free – newspaper article to publicise it. Felicity edited my articles – free – for the next six years, until flexi-hours became legal. I loved to read her corrections; carefully edited in red ink, they looked as if someone had haemorrhaged over the pages. Why hadn't I seen that? Why hadn't I cut that? I was fascinated by her perfection.

Once – unwillingly – I was made fashion editor of the *Observer* and for my first assignment, my boss threw me in the deep end by sending me to Paris for the fashion collections. At the first show I scribbled notes on every outfit, but couldn't read my own writing afterwards. Despair! At the second show, I got lucky: I found myself seated next to Felicity Green. Hoho, I thought, I will see what the mighty Felicity writes about, and I will write about the same outfits. From time to time I cast a furtive eye at the notepad on Felicity's lap as model after model swished in front of us, but to my dismay Felicity wrote nothing until the last model passed us, after which I saw she had scribbled no more than: MID CALF – FRINGE – BLACK.

This was the lesson I needed. Forty years later, when I told Felicity about this, she said thoughtfully, "Mid calf, fringe, black... must have been Givenchy." ■

VIEW FROM THE TOP

The men at the top – and they were all men then – gave the Daily Mirror what it took to become the biggest selling newspaper in the world – with a little help from their friends, who now included women!

MIKE MOLLOY

Mike Molloy trained as an artist before beginning his career in journalism. He was Editor and Editor-in-Chief of the Daily Mirror, and has since become a successful author of adult and children's books. In 1985 he returned to painting, and has exhibited in France and London.

The Swinging '60s took longer than people realise to get going. It was 1965 before a young girl from Neasden called Lesley Hornby became better known as Twiggy; 1964 before Mary Quant began selling mini-skirts in the King's Road; and 1963 before Vidal Sassoon created his famously geometrically designed haircuts for women.

But in 1962 The Beatles had their first hit with 'Love Me Do' and I started working with Felicity Green on the *Daily Mirror*. At first Felicity wasn't very popular with the bastion of male executives on the paper. Until she'd arrived on the scene, the inhabitants of the fashion department had been strictly limited to their quarters, like concubines in a sultan's harem.

Felicity leapt over the wall and then crashed onto the news pages. She pointed out that women everywhere were storming off in a series of exciting new directions and the paper had better keep up with them. Apart from the sexual revolution and the growing demand for equality with men, a new generation of female shopkeepers and designers were changing the way women looked in new and wonderfully outrageous ways. Good God! Women and fashion were suddenly real news and London's King's Road in Chelsea was beginning to intrigue the whole world.

Felicity put fashion pictures worthy of *Vogue* in the paper, which were followed by millions of young women – and then the whole of the UK fashion industry. Men liked the pictures too because they were often terrifically sexy. I designed her pages, which was easy because she knew exactly what she wanted and Felicity and I agreed about design. Keep it plain, keep it simple and let the pictures do their work.

I'm glad we agreed so much because Felicity, although slim, and only a shade over five feet tall, had a resolve forged in stainless steel. Even when we agreed, she could still be stubborn and demanding about details. She's tiny, she's the only woman I've ever met who could actually look *up* her nose at me. Felicity has all the determination of a bulldog and the arrogance of a pekingese. She has great human intuition, huge awareness of what makes people tick. She is also a bloody good journalist. I once told her she was the first member of the opposite sex I'd wanted to hit since I'd exchanged blows with my elder sister. But the *Mirror* glowed brighter with the brilliance of her contribution. ■

TONY MILES

Tony Miles joined the Daily Mirror as a Feature Writer in 1954. He became Editor in 1971, Editorial Director from 1974-1984 and Chairman 1980-1983.

Every paper has its golden era. For the *Mirror* it began in the late '50s when Hugh Cudlipp grabbed the attention of the nation with his Shock Issues and political front pages, but the paper's golden age really burst into life throughout the '60s.

The Editor was Lee Howard, the shrewdest observer of the human condition ever to occupy that chair. The *Mirror* tuned in to what was happening in the street and in particular the tide of change that the young were bringing about after the drab austerity of post-war Britain.

The most accurate listening post was Felicity. She not only listened, she actively encouraged this new world before any other

"Felicity put fashion pictures worthy of Vogue in the paper, which were followed by millions of young women"

MIKE MOLLOY

national paper had caught on to the young revolution about to explode. She gave it a voice.

The *Mirror* was also tuning in to the new educated, aspirational public. The traditional bland gossip column populated by the same old show business names, was dropped and replaced by the Inside Page, an incisive background look at the people who were really running the country. In 1966 it won the What The Papers Say Columnist of the Year Award.

Mirrorscope, a pull-out covering politics, foreign affairs and the cultural world that would not have been out of place in a Sunday broadsheet, was launched.

In 1964, the *Mirror* announced a world record average daily sale of 5 million – a readership of 15 million equal to one in three of every adult in the country.

The 1960s was a good decade for news. It began with the First Man in Space in 1961, finishing with the first man on the Moon in 1969. Along the way came the Profumo Scandal, the Great Train Robbery, the Kennedy Assassination, the Vietnam War and two catchy General Elections, both won by Labour – with a little help from the *Mirror*.

These were exciting times and Felicity was changing the predominantly male attitudes in the office. All female staff were expected to wear skirts or dresses. Felicity turned up one day in a trouser suit. The Editor was shocked, but the dam had broken and the girls began following Felicity's example.

During the feminist bra-burning campaign, Felicity came in one day evidently braless. I don't know how many girls followed that trend. Happy days...

But the *Mirror's* golden age was facing a threat from an unlikely quarter. Rupert Murdoch bought the broadsheet *Sun* from the Mirror Group and relaunched it as a tabloid in direct competition. The end of the *Mirror's* golden era was looming. It was fun while it lasted. ■

ROY GREENSLADE

Roy Greenslade is Professor of Journalism, City University London, and writes for the Guardian and London Evening Standard. He was a subeditor on the Daily Mirror and Sunday Mirror in the 1970s, Assistant Editor of the Sun in the early 1980s and Managing Editor (news) at the Sunday Times 1986-89. He was Editor of the Daily Mirror 1990-91.

As a baby boomer, I came into my teenage years in the middle of the '60s social revolution. We had no real idea what we were doing or where we were going, but it was such fun simply to be alive and part of it.

In my first job on a local weekly paper, I wrote a column that featured local pop stars such as Brian Poole and the Tremeloes and Sandie Shaw. I dressed like a mod. I spent money I didn't have on records. We didn't know we were living through a changing world even though our parents told us we were. It was our reality. Oddly, however, Fleet Street was slow to catch on to the path-breaking changes of the time.

The *Daily Mirror* did have the advantage of Felicity Green and Christopher Ward to showcase new fashion and new youth-orientated features. They could not have done so without encouragement from the *Mirror's* editorial overlord, Hugh Cudlipp, who gave them their head despite his own lack of enthusiasm for society's rapid transformation.

Most of the national press did not wake up to the Swinging '60s until we entered the next decade. It was hard for the men who owned and edited newspapers to understand the benefits of sexual permissiveness and women's liberation.

They were persuaded only when they saw the commercial advantages as the so-called alternative society showed early signs of turning itself into mainstream society. Youth culture, the music, the clothes, the climate of seemingly uninhibited freedom, was complemented by growing affluence and, most significantly, an influence over society's values and direction. It was at that point, in 1969, that I arrived in Fleet Street at the *Sun*.

In early 1971, I achieved my long-held ambition to join the *Mirror* subs desk and I can still remember my first splash – the wedding of Mick Jagger and Bianca De Macias in St Tropez. Giving a rock star's nuptials such prominence was confirmation of the paper's engagement with the zeitgeist.

Seen in hindsight, it was the culmination of the *Mirror's* long battle to forge a less deferential, more meritocratic, society. The *Sun*, largely staffed by former *Mirror* journalists and owned by a man unhindered by old-fashioned English class values, Rupert Murdoch, understood that too. Fleet Street may have swung late. Once it did, however, its influence was mighty. ■

MIRROR MEMORIES ARE MADE OF THIS...

...the highs and the lows, the fun and the frustration, **the praise and the blame...** ...my journalistic history in the making.

I AM SPORTS-ALLERGIC and until 1966 I had never been to a football match and never wanted to. So when the *Mirror* sports editor grabbed me by the neck one Saturday afternoon and said, "Come on, we're going to a match," I said "No, I'm not, I'm too busy." "No, you're not," he said, exhibiting a bit of force. "Yes, I am and I hate football." "It's us playing Germany," he said. My coat was on and we were off! So when I mention I was actually at the '66 World Cup to a taxi driver I frequently don't have to pay the fare. Even now!

MIRROR MOMENTS? How about going round Silverstone with racing driver Stirling Moss? Wow! So I said yes please and off we went. Mr Moss said "We'll go round once and if it's okay put your thumb up and we'll go round again. If it's not, thumb down." Terror! He spun the wheel and I saw potential collisions at every corner. I thought I felt sick with fear. And then I didn't. I loved it and my thumb went up and I wondered why I couldn't walk when circuit number two was over. Must have been my shoes.

WHEN I BECAME DIRECTOR OF PROMOTIONS AND PUBLICITY I was entitled to my own car and could choose from a Rover or a Jaguar. No, thanks, I said. I'd like a Citroen Pallas. Cheaper and smarter. Nice shape. Black, please. **Did I want a blue or cream interior? Neither – I wanted dark chocolate brown.** This apparently was a Big problem, but such was my new status that I got what I wanted. Très chic – Citroen agreed – and then Marje Proops wanted one exactly the same. And she got one. What power we women suddenly had!

AS A DIRECTOR I COULD CHOOSE my own office décor. All the chaps had deep-buttoned leather chairs, ocean-going desks and an atmosphere of chief executive clubland prevailed. I hated it so off I went to Liberty and bought myself a bright red modern lacquer desk that was really a dressing table. I had dark brown corduroy velvet banquette seating installed along with lots of mirrored walls and large green rubber plants. The cost was extremely modest by comparison and my fellow male directors patronised me and told me I was wacky. I held all the union meetings in my office and there were no adverse comments from that source.

THE UNIONS PLAYED A LARGE PART IN MY LIFE and I spent hours arguing with the union bosses. These meetings were held in my new very trendy office. One day I got a strange call from the Chairman. "Reg (top union bully) likes your office," he said. "Oh good," I said. "So," continued the Chairman, "he wants you to design his new office." "I am a journalist," I reminded him, "not an interior decorator to a bloody union boss!" "You're both," said the Chairman. So that's how I found myself at the union HQ in Slough. I suggested to Reg's assistant I might have a look at the office. Correction: "It's not an office – it's a suite." Next question: "What's the budget?" Another correction: "Reg doesn't have a budget." So that's how I became an interior decorator and as I never heard another word, Reg must have liked it.

IT SEEMED THERE WERE UMPTEEN STRIKES in the late '60s and we were on strike yet again. Holes in the *Mirror* were filled in ingenious and unlikely ways. **My role was strictly secret.** For two weeks I wrote the horoscopes about which I knew nothing. But I made sure every sign was optimistic and full of exciting and unexpected events – particularly my own.

PART OF MY NEW ROLE INVOLVED making *Mirror* television commercials and booking prime-time slots. One expensive Friday night slot didn't appear. Monday morning, with justified fury I "sent for" the managing director of the television station. "Be in my office in one hour!" (I was such a big spender I could do this sort of thing.) He came. He was shown into my office. Filled with fury, I stood up to my full five feet one to meet him eye-to-eye. "Good grief!" he said, "Is that all there is?"

I ONCE WROTE A CRITICAL PIECE about Royal Designer Norman Hartnell, creator of HRH's fashion sense. Was Norman angry? No, but Nice Norman as he signed one of the heavily-jewelled simply gorgeous Christmas cards he sent me each year before he died addressed them as follows: **Miss Mendacity Mean, Sweet Spleen Green, Miss Velocity Spleen, Felicity Greenspleen, Dear Duplicity, Miss Ferocity Spleen.** And I loved you too, Norman.

THE MORNING AFTER HIS APPOINTMENT was announced, I went to congratulate Percy Roberts, the new managing director of MGN. Percy, always a shirt-and-trousers man was wearing a formal suit and tie! The tie, which he immediately pointed out, read: "I am a Male Chauvinist Pig". What a laugh.

PS WHEN I DID DESERT ISLAND DISCS back in 2011 as I left the studio presenter Kirsty Young asked: **"Felicity, when are you going to write your book?"** and I replied with some force: "Never, ever! Absolutely not." **And look what happened.**

ACKNOWLEDGEMENTS

In some cases this word is just a useful cliché when the author wants to say thank you without worrying too much about it. Well in my case this simply isn't true, I've been worrying about it ever since I got to page 5.

This was the book I said I'd never write and I don't know exactly what changed my mind, but once my mind was changed I could never have succeeded without the following two wonderful people.

Sinty Stemp is not only an original, but has revealed more highly differing talents than I have encountered in one person. I'll name just a few. Sinty can write. Her prose, as I have discovered is fluent and elegant and there are three of her books to prove this. Sinty is highly educated so she can keep me off the rocks of too much journalistic laxity. (She does this very gently) Sinty has a background in fashion and is completely knowledgeable about both historical and contemporary worlds of style. Other equally valuable contributions – Sinty has dealt with the publisher, the legal advisor and ensured the flow of vital copy to the Art Director in good time. She is thorough, trustworthy and an amazing amalgam of everything I could have wanted in a companion in this mammoth task. And yes it was mammoth. So thank you Sinty – I think you're wonderful and you're not allowed to contradict me xxx Felicity
PS Without Sinty I'd have given up on this book around page 102.

This book is based on forty bulging *Daily Mirror* press cuttings books that were begun without my even knowing. Sheila Basten, who was so much more than my secretary on the *Daily Mirror* from 1960 – 1973, decided that my priceless prose and picture pages had to be saved for the nation. I had no idea she was creating these scrapbooks that began in 1960 and finished in 1973. Without Sheila and her precious cuttings books this book could not have happened. So thank you Sheila from the bottom of my appreciative heart.
PS Sheila's books are destined to fill shelves at the Victoria and Albert Museum's Archive at Blythe House, Olympia, where I hope they will be a useful source for future fashion and style enthusiasts including students.

Honorary mentions must go to the following contributors. Terry O'Neill and Robin Morgan for encouraging me, even insisting that I write this book, and helping to fill it with stunning pictures and memories. My friendship with Barbara Hulanicki started in the '60s and was confirmed with the huge success of the famous pink gingham dress. We have been close friends ever since, professionally and personally, and I was delighted when she agreed to write the Foreword to this book, especially as she was busy working on her latest bumper Biba book. Vidal Sassoon, a long-time friend, wrote his piece for me before he died when he was extremely ill – I valued it then as I value it now – and it's all the more precious.

A big thank you to every one of these friends and former colleagues, all of whom are busy people and all of whom took the time and trouble to write contributions and/or hunt out and provide photographs:
Margaret Allen, Geoffrey Aquilina Ross, David Bailey, Jeff Banks, Suki Bishop, Shirley Conran, Lady Cudlipp, Orna Frommer-Dawson, Lauretta and Martin Dives, Stephen Fitz-Simon, Kent Gavin, Roy Greenslade, Moira Hodell, Barbara Hulanicki, Jenny Jeffery, Sam Keegan, Jill Kennington, Likrish Marchese, Deirdre McSharry, Tony Miles, Mike Molloy, Robin Morgan, Terry O'Neill, Eve Pollard, Mary Quant, Vidal Sassoon, Doreen Spooner, Darren Thomas, Ian Tuttle, Twiggy, Justin de Villeneuve, Penny Vincenzi, Katharine Whitehorn, Geoff Windram.
Thanks also to Grant Dommer and Charlotte Rae Miller of Sunny Snaps.

Thanks must also go to Mark Eastment at V&A Publishing for a combination of practical advice, friendship and endless good humour, all constant throughout the long gestation period of this book and also Alexia Kirk at the V&A Archive for her patience, waiting for my 40 cuttings books.

James Smith and Diana Steel and the entire team at ACC Editions for their hard work. And Sophie Haydock for her eagle-eyed subediting.

Art director Stephen Reid was a joy to work with for several different reasons. First his brilliant design talent, secondly because of his experience on *The Sunday Times Magazine* which meant I was able to work with him as journalist to journalist, and last, but not least, for his patience in dealing with my frequent changes of mind.

I am enormously grateful to Paul Vickers, Secretary and Group Legal Director at Trinity Mirror for allowing me to reproduce the *Daily Mirror,* pages and images in this book. Without their immense generosity this book could never have happened. And a special thank you must go to Roy Greenslade for his expert and practical advice on so many different fronts. Dear Roy you have been – and always are – invaluable.

I would like to thank all my colleagues on the *Daily Mirror* whose help and talent I so appreciated; if everyone is not mentioned I blame it on my memory and I hope they will forgive me.

And then of course there's Geoffrey Hill, my husband of thirty-nine years – without Geoffrey's tolerance, patience, unfailing good humour and love to support me all the way, my career simply couldn't have happened. So thank you darling Geoffrey.

PS And then of course there's our beloved poodle Polly, real name, Vulcan Champagne Blackbird, a breed renowned for their sweet expression and gentle behaviour. Polly, almost as tall as me, was my constant companion throughout my Fleet Street years – and, like me, she always loved having her hair done. I taught Polly to sing 'God Save the Queen'.

PHOTOGRAPHIC CREDITS

I would like to thank *Daily Mirror* Picture Editor Simon Clyne and all the talented *Mirror* photographers I worked with, particularly Doreen Spooner, but also Kent Gavin, Eric Harlow, Mike Maloney, Alisdair Macdonald, Freddie Reed, Bill Rowntree, Arthur Sidey and Peter Stone.

It was also a pleasure and a privilege to work closely with many of the leading photographers of the day, including: John Adriaan, Richard Avedon, Bailey, Gordon Carter, John Cole, Monty Coles, John Cowan, Terry Donovan, Duffy, John French, Hatami, Murray Irving, John Kelly, Chris Killip, Gunnar Larsen, Barry Lategan, Lewis Morley, Peter Mullett, Terry O'Neill, Regina Relang, Philip Stearns, Peter Tebbitt, Justin de Villeneuve.

Page 3, Frontispiece: FG and Roger Moore
Pages 4-5, Contents: FG
Page 9, Introduction: Why Style Works Better than Fashion: FG
Page 10, FG child, FG's mother's wedding pic
Page 13, Me and the Mirror: FG in Mirror T-shirt
Page 14, FG and Harold Wilson, FG and Barbara Castle
Page 15, FG and the Queen, FG and the Duke of Edinburgh
Page 17, Mirror People: FG and Marje Proops
Page 18, FG and Lee Howard and Rex North
Page 20, FG and husband Geoffrey Hill by David Olins
Page 21, Polly the Poodle
All Felicity's private collection.

Page 7, Foreword: FG and Barbara Hulanicki by Terry O'Neill
Page 11, Audrey Hepburn: Paramount/ The Kobal Collection/Fraker, Bud
Page 11, Phyllis Digby Morton by John French, courtesy Suki Bishop
Page 19, Hugh Cudlipp, courtesy Lady Cudlipp
Page 180, Doreen Spooner, courtesy Doreen Spooner
Page 181, Penny Vincenzi by Trevor Leighton, courtesy Penny Vincenzi
Page 182, Eve Pollard, courtesy Eve Pollard
Page 183, Shirley Conran by Joe McGorty, courtesy Shirley Conran
Page 184, Mike Molloy, courtesy Mike Malloy
Page 184, Tony Miles, courtesy Tony Miles
Page 185, Roy Greenslade, courtesy Roy Greenslade
Page 187, Mirror Memories are Made of This: FG by Terry O'Neill.

Imagemakers:
Page 48, John French, 1957, © Victoria and Albert Museum, London
Page 148, Justin de Villeneuve by John Adriaan
Page 152, Terry O'Neill, courtesy Terry O'Neill
Page 160, Barbara Hulanicki and Stephen Fitz-Simon by Doreen Spooner
Page 176, David Bailey by Terry O'Neill.

My thanks are also due to fashion illustrators Barbara Hulanicki, Marje Proops, Gerry Richards, Ruth Sheradski and to *Mirror* cartoonist Moira Hodell.

INDEX

All page numbers in **bold** refer to illustrations

Adam, (Maria) Letizia **78**
Adriaan, John 14, 48, 92, 169
photos **40/41, 76, 77, 92, 93, 113, 118, 131, 133, 148, 155, 158, 169, 172**
Alexander's restaurant (*see also:* Quant, Mary and Plunkett-Greene, Alexander) 136
Alligator – designs **113**
Amies, Hardy – designs **50/51**
Angela at London Town **97**
Apple boutique (*see also:* Beatles, The) 180
Aristoc **173**
Arnberg of Sweden **113**
Associated Fashion Designers **87**
Austen, Gerard (Carita) **66/67**
Austen, Primrose **96**
Avedon, Richard **98, 150;** 98, 150, 176
photos **98, 150**

Bagcraft **113**
Bailey, David **150, 176;** 14, 29, 48, 58, 104, 108, 149, 150, 152, 176, 177, 181
photos **150, 151, 177**
Baker, Carroll "Baby Doll" **85**
Balenciaga 69, 90
designs **75**
Balmain – designs **72/73**
Banks, Jeff **163, 165;** 164
Bardot, Brigitte **36;** 6, 36
Basten, Sheila 182
Bates, John 14, 103
designs (*see also:* Varon, Jean) **117**
Bazaar (*see also:* Quant, Mary) 65, 136
Beatles, The 18, 148, 164, 171, 176, 180, 184
Bernard (of Andre Bernard) **66/67**
Bernstein, Reginald – designs **102**
Berthelsen, Maud **116**
Best, George **167;** 166
Biba (*see also:* Hulanicki, Barbara) 6, 77, 78, 128, 147, 148, 160, 161, 180, 181
designs **79, 128-129, 146, 161, 162, 178, 179**
Birtwell, Celia 171
designs **171**
Blackman, Honor **102**
Blanchflower, Danny 40

Bohan, Marc **80;** 70, 125
designs (*see also:* Dior) **70/71, 82, 101, 122**
Boyd Harrison, Patti **143, 171;** 142, 171
Brown, Joe 47
Brown, William 47
Byrne, Kiki 14

C&A **130**; 180
Caine, Michael 152
Cardin, Pierre **80, 84;** 21, 175
designs **27, 32, 72/73, 83, 84, 94/95, 101, 144, 145, 174**
Caring, Louis – designs **61**
Carrot on Wheels (*see also:* Bailey, David) **125;** 176
Carter, Gordon – photos **61, 105, 120, 134, 135, 137, 138**
Castle, Barbara **15;** 14-15
Cavanagh – designs **50/51**
Chanel, Coco **38, 62;** 38, 62
Chanel, Maison – designs **39, 63, 72/73**
Checker, Chubby 29
Christie, Julie **112**
Clark, Ossie **171;** 14, 171
designs **171**
Clobber (*see also:* Banks, Jeff) 164
Coddington, Grace **44/45, 96;** 45, 48, 66, 90
Cohen, Alfred 90
Cole, John – photos **61**
Coles, Monty – photos **146**
Collins, John **44**
Conran, Shirley **183;** 183
Cooper, Lady Diana **36**
Corocraft **158**
Courrèges, André **74, 80, 84;** 69, 80, 92, 175
designs **72/73, 74, 82, 84, 95, 140, 145, 175**
Courtaulds **113**
Cowan, John **57;** 14, 55, 57, 58
photos **54/55, 56/57, 59**
Coward, Noël 148
Crahay, Jules François **80**
designs (*see also:* Lanvin) **72/73**
Crawford, Joan **36**
Cudlipp, Hugh **19;** 12, 16-20, 92, 183, 184, 185

Davies, Nigel *see:* De Villeneuve, Justin
Dawnay, Jean 48
Debenhams **113**

Deneuve, Catherine 176
De Villeneuve, Justin (Nigel Davies) **147, 170;** 66, 147, 148-149
photos **147, 149, 171**
Dior (*see also:* Bohan, Marc) 53, 62, 70, 80, 125
designs **27, 32, 46, 52, 53, 70/71, 72/73, 94, 100**
Donovan, Terence 14, 48, 152
Dorothy Perkins **130**
Duffy, Brian 14, 48, 152
photos **94-95**
Dunaway, Faye 152

Eales, Norman – photo **102**
Echo **156, 173**
Edinburgh, Duke of **15;** 15
Eggar, Samantha **42;** 42
Elizabeth I, Queen **15, 35;** 15, 34
Emcar **97**
Erté **147**
Etam **117, 130**
Evansky, Rose **66/67;** 66

Faithfull, Marianne 171
Farrow, Mia 66, 90
Farrow, Stephanie **161, 162**
Finola **56**
Fitz-Simon, Stephen **128, 160;** 6, 78, 160
Foale and Tuffin 14, 80
Frederica – designs **34, 61, 77**
Freedman, Carol – designs **87**
French (hair stylist) **66/67**
French, Barbara **85**
French, John **48, 49;** 14, 48, 49, 70, 96, 160, 176, 181
photos **11, 37, 47, 49, 50/51, 65, 72/73, 82, 83, 96, 99, 100-101**
Frost, David 47

Gair-Ray **45**
Gardner, Ava 148
Gavin, Kent – photos **114, 143**
Gernreich, Rudi **81;** 80, 92, 104
designs **81, 104, 159**
Gibb, Billy 148
Gilders, Frederick **107**
Ginger Group (*see also:* Quant, Mary) **65, 113;** 65
Givenchy **11**; 8, 69, 183
Goalen, Barbara 48
Goldsmith, Oliver – designs **118**
Goma, Michel **80**
designs (*see also:* Patou, Jean) **33, 52, 72/73, 82, 101, 123**

Grade, Michael 181
Grant, Cary 181
Green, Felicity **3, 4, 7, 9, 10, 13, 14, 15, 17, 18, 20, 21, 22-23, 187;** *and throughout*
Greenslade, Roy **185;** 185
Gres, Marie-Lise **79, 96**
Gunning, Anne 48

Hammond, Celia **96;** 48, 58
Harlow, Eric – photos **114**
Harlow, Jean **85**
Harrison, George 164
Harrison, Patti *see:* Boyd Harrison, Patti
Hartnell, Norman 186
designs **50/51**
Haslam, Nicky **29;** 29
Hatami – photos **63, 74, 75, 94-95**
Hayes, Elizabeth – designs **105**
Heim **52, 82, 100**
Heller, Randee – designs **158**
Hepburn, Audrey **11;** 6, 8-10
Hildebrand **87**
Hill, Geoffrey **20;** 20, 21
Hodell, Moira 22
cartoons 22-23
Hodge, Vicki **96, 181;** 180
Hopkinson, Sir Tom 169
Hornby, Lesley *see:* Twiggy
Howard, Lee **18;** 16, 18, 184
Hughes, Alan 103
Hulanicki, Barbara (Biba) **7, 79, 128, 160;** 6, 14, 77, 78, 80, 104, 128, 147, 148, 152, 160, 181
illustrations **77, 87, 104**
Humperdinck, Engelbert **166;** 166
Hustler, Tom **41**

I was Lord Kitchener's Valet 164
Incodinc **134**
Incorporated Society of London Fashion **51**; 51
Irving, Murray – photos **70**

Jaeger – designs **30, 159**
Young Jaeger – designs **77**
Jagger, Bianca (née De Macias) 171, 185
Jagger, Mick 164, 171, 185
Jane & Jane **60**
John of Knightsbridge **66/67**
Johnson, Amy **99**
Jones, Brian 164
Jones, Tom **167;** 166

INDEX

Kashmoor **139**
Kelly, John – photos **173**
Kennedy, Jackie **35;** 34
Kennington, Jill **54/55, 57, 59, 96;** 55, 57, 58, 59
Khanh, Emanuelle **68;** 69
designs and illustration **68/69**
Khanh, Quasar – designs **121**
Killip, Chris – photos **170**
King, Cecil 19
Kinks, The 148
Knight, Pat 176
Koger, Marijke **143**
Kwan, Nancy 66

Lagerfeld, Karl 38
Laing, John – designs **45**
Lake, Veronica **36**
Lanvin – designs **72/73, 83**
Laroche **52**
Larsen, Gunnar 126
photos **116, 121, 120/121, 126-127, 142, 144-145**
Lategan, Barry 132
Laver, James 47
Leeger, Josje **143**
Lennon, John 99, 164
Leonard (of Raphael and Leonard) **66/67;** 66, 132, 150
Lombard, Carole **36;** 36
London Fashion House Group **87**
Lord, Cyril 128
Lore **131**
Loy, Myrna 148
Lulu 18

Macmillan, Harold 164
Mallett, Tania **96;** 48, 176
Malloy, Mike **184**
Mann, Adrien – designs **158**
Mann, Edward – designs **99**
Manners, George **139**
Marks, John **87**
Marlborough Dresses **77, 87**
Marshall, Francis 11
McCartney, Paul 164
McDouglas of Paris **159**
McGowan, Cathy 103
McNee, Patrick **102;** 103
McSharry, Deidre 132
Michael (of L'Elonge) **66/67**
Michael **41**
designs **50/51**
Miles, Tony **184;** 184
Moffitt, Peggy **104;** 104
Molloy, Mike 181, 184
Mono **87**
Monroe, Marilyn 108
Moore, Bobby **167;** 152, 166
Moore, Roger **3;** 2
Morley, Lewis 14
Morton, Phyliss Digby ("PDM") **11;** 10, 11
Morton, Digby – designs (*see also:* Reldan) **87**
Moss, Stirling 186
Muggeridge, Malcolm **41**
Muir, Jean 14
Mullett, Peter – photos **117, 119**
Murdoch, Rupert 19, 185
Murray, Susan **96**

Natasha **29**
Neatawear **105**
Neufeld **158**
North, Rex **18;** 16, 18
Nutter, Tommy 149

O'Neill, Terry **152;** 14, 108, 152, 153, 156, 164, 166, 175, 181, 182
photos: **7, 103, 139, 153, 154, 156, 157, 163, 165, 166, 167, 174, 175, 176, 187**
Olofson **66/67**

Paterson, Ronald – designs **50/51**
Patou, Jean – designs (*see also:* Goma, Michael) **33, 52, 72/73, 82, 94, 101, 123, 144**
Paul, Sandra **96**
Peck, Gregory 8
Peter Pan **105**
Peters, André – designs **87**
Pickering, Edward 15
Pipart, Gerard **80**
Plunkett-Greene, Alexander **43, 113;** 43, 136
Pollard, Eve **182;** 182
Polly the Poodle **20;** 19, 20
Poole, Brian 185
Proops, Marje **17;** 16, 181, 186
illustration 46

Q Form Youthlines **113**
Quant, Mary (*see also:* Bazaar; Ginger Group) **43, 64, 91, 113, 135, 137, 155;** 14, 29, 43, 47, 48, 49, 65, 66, 69, 80, 90, 91, 99, 113, 136, 137, 148, 152, 154, 179, 180, 184
designs **28, 47, 49, 65, 135, 137, 155**
Quorum **171**

Rabanne, Paco **116;** 69
designs **116, 144**
Rand, Mary **157;** 152, 156
Raymond of London **92/93**
Real **94**
Reed, Ricki – designs **87**
Relang – photos **94-94**
Reldan – designs **87**
Rene **66/67**
Ricci, Nina – designs **26, 27, 32, 33, 52, 72/73, 94, 101, 140**
Richard Shops **130**
Richards, Gerry – illustrations **97**
Riche **66/67**
Rickards, Marilyn **153, 154**
Rigg, Diana **102, 103, 139;** 103
Roberts, Percy 186
Roy, Rhona – designs **87**
Russell, Mark – designs **87**

Sabrina **154**
Saint Laurent, Yves **63, 80;** 62, 70, 80, 141, 175
designs **52, 62, 72/73, 122, 123, 141, 144, 174**
Sandler, David (of Leon Sandler) **66/67**
Sassoon, Vidal **66/67, 91, 151;** 66, 90, 91, 99, 148, 150, 152, 184
Saxone **111**
Scarabocchio **25**
Shaw, Sandie **163, 165;** 164, 185
Shearer, Norma 8
Sheradski, Ruth 10
illustrations **62, 71**
Shrimpton, Jean "The Shrimp" **96, 106, 107, 108;** 29, 48, 58, 96, 104, 106, 108, 109, 149, 164, 176
Shubette **111**
Sidey, Arthur **115**
Simpson, Sally **78**
Sitwell, Edith 181
Small, Susan – designs **34**
Smith, Delia 183
Smith, Sam 47
Spiers, Alan **66/67**
Spooner, Doreen **180;** 126, 180
photos **87, 110, 128, 129, 160, 180/181**
Springett, Ron **45**
St John, Carole **126-127;** 126
Stamp, Terence 58, 108, 152, 164
Starr, Ringo **98;** 98
Stearns, Philip (Image Studios) – photos **85**
Stephens, John 164
Stephens, Paul – designs **158**
Stiebel,Victor – designs **50/51**
Stone, Paulene **96;** 6, 48, 160
Stones, The 148, 164, 171
Streisand, Barbra **112**
Swordtex **158**

Taylor, Elizabeth **35;** 34
Tebbitt, Peter – photos **89**
Thocolette **139**
Torres, Reuben 92
designs **163, 165**
Tree, Penelope **150;** 150
Tremeloes, The 185
Twiggy (Lesley Hornby) **131, 133, 147, 148/149, 170;** 14, 42, 66, 132, 133, 147, 148-149, 150, 171, 184
Twilfit **173**
Tyrrell, Ann (*see also:* Marks, John) – designs **87**

Ungaro, Emanuel 90
designs **100, 118, 140, 144**

Varon, Jean – designs **117**
Vaughan, Victoria **28**
Vendome **158**
Victor (of Dumas) **66/67**
Vincenzi, Penny **181;** 181

Wade, Virginia **156;** 152, 156
Walker, Billy **139**
Wallis Shops **45, 85, 118, 130;** 38
Ward, Christopher **144;** 21, 185
Watkins, Ros **37;** 36
Waugh, Auberon 181
Weiss **157, 173**
Welch, Raquel **174-175;** 92, 175
Whigham, Margaret **36**
White, Ed **99**
Wilkinson, June **154**
Wilson, Harold **15;** 11, 14, 15
Wilson, Mary 11, 14, 181

Zec, Donald **41**

SEX SENSE AND NONSENSE

FELICITY GREEN ON THE '60s FASHION SCENE

ISBN 978 1 85149 773 7

British Library Cataloguing-in-Publication Data
A catalogue record for this book is available from the British Library

Printed and bound in China for ACC Editions
an imprint of the Antique Collectors' Club Ltd, Woodbridge, Suffolk, UK